The Truth About Dirty Tricks

The Truth About Dirty Tricks

from Harold Wilson to Margaret Thatcher

by

Chapman Pincher

SIDGWICK & JACKSON
LONDON

First published in Great Britain in 1991 by Sidgwick & Jackson Limited

ISBN 0-283-06060 3

Typeset by Florencetype Ltd, Kewstoke, Avon

Printed in Great Britain by Billings of Worcester

for Sidgwick & Jackson Limited
Cavaye Place
London SW10 9PG

Contents

To 'Winnie', my word-processor who has played
a few dirty tricks on me.
May God preserve her and all her chips.

Introduction

Immediately following the death of Kim Philby in Moscow in 1988, a retired officer of MI6, the Secret Intelligence Service, urged his old colleagues to take advantage of the situation. He suggested that Philby should be posthumously awarded the CMG (Companion of the Order of St Michael and St George), an honour commonly bestowed on loyal intelligence officers. This, he suggested, should be followed by an authoritative obituary notice in the *Times* stating that, in the author's opinion, Philby was the bravest man he had ever encountered.

Following on Philby's ostentatious funeral, this move would cause consternation because, had it received the Royal imprimature, the KGB would have needed to consider the possibility that Philby had always been a British Secret Service plant. The KGB knew that the Queen had been a willing part of a deception operation on at least one previous occasion by agreeing to keep the self-confessed spy Anthony Blunt on the Palace staff to avoid a public security scandal. There could be no certainty, however, that this was a further involvement of Her Majesty in a counter-intelligence dirty trick.

The KGB might, therefore, be driven to waste time, backtracking on all the operations involving Philby and the advice which he had given them over many years, to check if it could have been deliberately tainted with British disinformation. The publicity for the award, which would surely have been international, would also take the edge off the anti-British propaganda which the KGB had achieved by exaggerating Philby's importance to them through his spectacular burial, which had been shown, worldwide, on television.

1

The plot foundered because the MI6 authorities realized that the Queen's advisers, while usually prepared to oblige the secret services, would have to reject the ploy as bringing the whole honours system into disrepute. I record it because it is a classic example of the disinformation dirty trick regularly practised against their adversaries by MI6, the KGB and other intelligence agencies.

Ever since Harold Wilson's resignation in 1976, which mystified so many people, Parliament and the media have devoted much time and space to dirty tricks, which are known, professionally, as deception operations or, in KGB parlance, 'active measures'. A dirty trick can be defined as an action carried out by an individual or group against another for the purpose of inflicting damage, usually surreptitiously and in a manner regarded as reprehensible in normal circumstances, the dirt being in the eye of the receiver. When it is successful the target country or individual may remain in ignorance of it or keep quiet about it so that, so far as recorded history is concerned, it never happened. Some dirty tricks may exert so great an impact on events as to be crucial components of the secret history of the world, which is never revealed. Obvious examples are the assassination of a world leader which looks like a natural death or an accident, character assassinations of politicians by planted information, true or concocted, the influencing of high-level policy decisions by a spy or false defector planted on a President or Prime Minister as an adviser, and the deception of an adversary government in the field of grand defence strategy.

There are also numerous SAS-type operations so skilfully contrived and deceptively concealed that they remain unheard of by the public. Recently the Count de Marenches, a former head of the French Secret Service, claimed that, during his eleven years of command, about forty military operations on the scale of the famous Israeli hostage rescue at Entebbe had been carried out with total success and in absolute secrecy. The French Secret Service has its own specially trained troops for such adventures, which have included the toppling of dictators like the 'Emperor' Bokassa of the Central African Republic and the preservation of others.

I have been assured that in recent times similar British operations have been quietly achieved, even when people have been killed in them, because only a couple of Ministers and the small Defence Intelligence teams involved knew about them. In peacetime the SAS and the Special Boat Squadron do rather more than just train and take part in occasional anti-terrorist operations. Such missions have to be kept quiet, if possible, because they usually involve crossing borders and infringing sovereign territory, which gives them an extreme degree of political sensitivity. They can sometimes be accomplished by the surreptitious use of ordinary transport such as commercial aircraft, trains and merchant ships, but may be entirely military. Whenever an operation is successful, the offended country usually keeps quiet about it to save loss of face.

In the counter-intelligence world designing dirty tricks to confound adversaries, both real and potential, is an art form, with expert practitioners commanding the highest professional respect. By common consent of the intelligence community, an ingenious deception is the most exciting and most satisfying venture when it is known to have worked.

With the apparent ending of the Cold War and the startling revolutions in the Soviet satellite states, it has been widely assumed that there will be little future for intelligence officers, spies, defectors and others involved in such clandestine activities. In fact, while some armaments are being cut, with the prospect of massive disarmament by the year 2000, no government in any country is talking about reducing spending on security and the gathering of intelligence. On the contrary, the Soviets are spending more than ever and so are the British and Americans. President Bush has secretly pledged to the British intelligence authorities and to NATO that, whatever cuts the USA makes in weapons and military manpower, there will be no diminution of the money and effort spent on aerial surveillance and intelligence on the ground. Iraq's sudden move against Kuwait in 1990 highlighted the continuing necessity for intelligence about the intentions of dictators and ruling cliques which can be gleaned only by the human penetration agent. So there is plenty of scope for the art of the dirty trick, which will continue to exert political impact on history. The time is, therefore, opportune for a wide-ranging account of dirty tricks in recent times. My involvement in some of them, sometimes inadvertent but often deliberate, along with my friendship with many of the players, qualifies me to attempt it.

While the secret world lives by dirty tricks they are common enough elsewhere – in politics, diplomacy, journalism, commerce and, with the upsurge of Islamic terrorism, even in religion. In fact probably the dirtiest trick known to me was revealed in the Vatican where I had been taken by a Polish friend who lived in Rome. Our host for the day was a Polish priest called Father Flavian, whose particular distinction was that he served as confessor to the Pope who, also being Polish, could confess his sins in his native language. After a tour of the Vatican gardens we were taken up to Father Flavian's cell – a small room, plainly furnished. Above the fireplace was a crucifix which the priest took down from the wall. The cross itself was black, apparently made of ebony, some eighteen inches long and eight inches wide. The carved Christ was of ivory, yellow with age. It was clearly no great work of art: a workaday cross to remind, to pray to and to be revered.

Father Flavian said that it was English and had been in regular use during the time when faithful Roman Catholics were being hunted down by the rabid Protestant authorities. He asked me to kneel and go through the motions of kissing the cross, as a gesture of faith which, though a lapsed Catholic, I was prepared to do. As I inclined my face towards the figure proffered by the priest, he smartly pulled the section above the Saviour's head away from the rest. It was now the handle of a long, viciously pointed and razor-edged dagger for which the lower part of the cross served as a scabbard. The blade looked well used. If, as I hope, Father Flavian remains in residence, no doubt the cross with its hideous secrets still rests above the mantelpiece as historic evidence of dirty tricks practised in the name of religion.

That was deception by old technology. New technology is dominating the current world of dirty tricks, which is what concerns us, and nowhere has their importance been more dramatically demonstrated than in the evidence provided by a recent French spy in the KGB, known by the codename Farewell.

Trained as an engineer in the Soviet Union, Farewell joined the KGB in the early 1960s and served in Paris as an officer charged with securing Western technological secrets and hardware for both military and commercial use. When he returned to Moscow in 1970 a French electronics businessman, with whom Farewell had been friendly and who had reason to visit the Soviet Union frequently, was approached by French Intelligence and asked to keep in touch with the KGB man in case he might decide to be 'helpful'. Farewell reported the contact to his KGB superiors and they agreed to let the relationship run in the patient hope that the Frenchman might help them.

The friendship bore no fruit for the French for several years; but finally Farewell hinted that he was prepared to be of genuine assistance, having come to hate the Communist regime and the KGB in particular. He was then given his English codename and contacted over the years in Moscow, obviously at considerable risk. He was run, at first, from an office which the French businessman had established in Moscow, and later by a military attaché in the French Embassy. Farewell handed over many hundreds of documents and photographs, showing for the first time the enormous size and scope of the Soviet deception operations to secure technological secrets from every advanced Western country, including Britain.

The British and American counter-intelligence services had been aware of the sustained effort being made by the KGB and its sister organization, the military GRU, to obtain technical secrets and equipment barred to them on security grounds, but were stunned by the extent of the Soviet success in securing them by fraud, bribery, forgery, blackmail and theft. The British authorities have remained quiet about it, but a CIA document released in 1985 revealed the extent of the West's losses – each year Moscow was receiving 'thousands of pieces of Western equipment and many tens of thousands of documents'. An average of more than five thousand Soviet military equipment and weapons programmes was benefitting, explaining how the Russians had been able to copy advanced American, British and French weapons, aircraft and submarines so quickly.

The CIA called the army of Soviet spies and their assistants 'techno-bandits'. They had practised bribery on a massive scale, and had smuggled out huge computers and defence equipment by setting up dummy firms and diverting goods intended for allies to the Soviet Union by roundabout routes. The techno-bandits had been so ingenious at covering their operations with deception, disinformation and other dirty tricks that the intelligence authorities had needed a chance defector, like Farewell, to inform them of their full scope. As the long-running saga of Soviet agents inside the British and American secret services had already shown, Western counter-intelligence had not been effective enough.

The spy was able to name specific KGB agents and the countries in which they were working, but his main contri-bution was a detailed plan of the enormous network which had been set up over the years by the Soviet Military Industrial Commission. Every major agency had been brought into it – the KGB, GRU, the Ministry of Foreign Trade, the State Committee for Science and Technology and even the Soviet Academy of Sciences, which had always had a technical espio-nage function. The network also embraced the intelligence agencies of the satellite countries – especially Poland, East Germany and Czechoslovakia. The techno-bandit successes saved the Kremlin billions of roubles and helped to make its military machine what it is. The information, which was passed to Britain and France's other close allies, enabled Western intelligence to counter the techno-bandits and crooked busi-nessmen to some extent, but the whole campaign has been markedly intensified since Mikhail Gorbachev came to power and the West has responded with counter-measures.

To understand the predicament of both sides it is necessary to appreciate the extraordinarily difficult position in which Gorbachev found himself on taking over the Soviet leadership. A dedicated Leninist at heart, he has been forced into profound political changes only by the desperate state of the Soviet economy caused by seventy years of Communism, which, wherever it has been tried, has proved to be a disastrous system for providing goods and services. He urgently needed to cut the crippling cost of the colossal military machine to provide money and manpower for civilian production. Yet he needed to maintain the Soviet Union as a superpower if it was to continue to exert worldwide influence. And the only reason that the Soviet Union is a superpower is because of its military strength. As an economic power it belongs to the Third World.

As a consequence, the years of Gorbachev's leadership have seen more Soviet penetration of Western defence and intelli-gence communities than any other time. Scores of Soviet agents have been expelled or arrested as a consequence. In May 1989 Britain expelled fourteen Soviet spies and could legitimately have expelled many more. Similar expulsions have occurred in most of the other technically advanced Western countries. Gorbachev is so urgently in need of Western technology, for commercial as well as defence purposes, that the KGB's several thousand 'technology collection officers', trained to acquire such secrets surreptitiously, have been encouraged to take risks which they would normally avoid. So more of them are being caught.

The requirement of technology to jump-start the stagnant Soviet economy is understandable but, in spite of the end of the Cold War, there has been an increase in Soviet attempts to recruit traitors to secure purely military secrets. There are two reasons for this. If the Soviet Union is to remain a superpower, any substantial reduction in the size of its forces requires the modernization of what is left. Cuts in the size of the military machine must, therefore, be compensated for by improved quality; and by stealing Western technology the Soviets can do this at greatly reduced cost. They also need continuing intelligence about Western military advances to see how far they need to modernize. And, as with the West, the smaller the military forces become, the greater the need for intelligence so that what remains can be used with maximum effect.

The West is doing what it can to stem this haemorrhage of technological secrets, and Britain's intelligence agencies have scored successes in unmasking diversions of super-computers and other equipments and countering the 'bandits' in other ways. In the battle both sides have deployed dirty tricks in abundance, and will continue to do so.

Farewell was executed in 1983, confessing to his treachery after committing a stupid murder. News of his death was followed by the expulsion of forty-seven Soviet spies from France. Many more were thrown out of other countries, including Britain. Inevitably the Kremlin protested, claiming that all the spying allegations were lies intended to damage relations with the peace-loving Socialist democracies.

The lie and counter-lie form the basis of all dirty tricks and the organizations perpetrating them can legitimately be called lie machines, although, of course, they also have other functions. Nobody doubts that lie machines are essential in war, when good deception operations, like the fooling of Hitler about the real D-Day invasion beaches, are hailed as brilliant. But many consider them unacceptable in peacetime. In the intelligence war, which all countries wage, there is no peace, so the lies and the dirty tricks based on them must continue as an essential means of survival.

Those who would contest this should ask themselves: Are dirty tricks permissible to prevent outrages on ordinary people like IRA car bombs or the Lockerbie airliner disaster? If the answer if affirmative, then it applies to the dirty tricks which have been perpetrated by intelligence services to prevent the subjection of free nations to Communist or any other totalitarian system. The unexpected exposure of the appalling conditions of life behind what was the Iron Curtain have shown that the anti-Communist propagandists, of whom I have been one, have not exaggerated the danger. Suddenly the free world has been able to see on television how a tiny minority of power-hungry, self-seeking fanatics, with nothing to recommend them intellectually or in any other way, has been able to enslave whole nations for decades. Intelligence and counter-intelligence, including dirty tricks, have played a crucial role in keeping Britain and other nations free of those soul-destroying shackles; and, while conditions remain so uncertain, their practice must continue. Further, the need for deception operations to counter adversaries is by no means restricted to the major powers. Middle East countries too are actively engaged in them, as the astonishing saga of the Iraqi supergun has demonstrated.

Inevitably there are some dirty tricks which are not acceptable to true democracies in peacetime, and I shall be describing some of them. There are many which are planned but never executed because officials or politicians decide that the end does not justify the means – a major consideration in all clandestine operations, especially when casualties are likely. Once a powerful intelligence agency accepts that the end justifies any means, as the KGB has done so cavalierly in the past, then atrocities are inevitable.

Several dirty tricks which have been the subject of much heated discussion never really existed at all, being fantasies born of the truth that the secrets world is like a wilderness of mirrors in which, to quote the legendary CIA dirty trickster,

James Angleton, 'the myriad of stratagems, deceptions, artifices and all the other devices of disinformation present an ever-fluid landscape where fact and illusion merge'. Since anything is possible, it is easy for people to delude themselves. Conditioned by spy fiction, as well as by fact, they are prepared to believe anything about intelligence services.

Having 'bought' more than one mythical dirty trick myself, centred on the alleged MI5 plot against Harold Wilson and his Labour Governments, I shall be modifying some statements I have mistakenly made in the past and making a few retractions. In this shadowy area where so much deliberate disinformation is in circuit, one learns a great deal with hindsight.

1

Death to the Godfather!

The most emphatic and sometimes most effective dirty trick that can be encompassed by a counter-intelligence agency is the assassination of a political leader, especially when he or she is head of state. This is not uncommon in the Third World, nor was it previously so within the Soviet Bloc, but most leaders of the greatest powers in the free world have shunned it as a usable weapon. For reasons which some people find hard to understand, even the possible assassination of a genocidal murderer like Hitler was frowned upon on principle – if only, perhaps, because it might attract similar retribution.

The communication which the British Prime Minister, Margaret Thatcher, received from President Reagan during the first week of April 1986 was, therefore, probably unique in modern times. It was nothing less than a request for essential assistance in an operation which had the assassination of Colonel Muammar Gaddafi, the Libyan political leader and effective head of state, as one of its major aims. Reagan's message created a difficult situation for her because earlier that year she had publicly expressed her opposition to any action against terrorists which infringed international law. In particular she had opposed any military strike against Libya, which was being openly canvassed in the USA in retaliation for atrocities attributed to terrorists sponsored by Gaddafi.

What Reagan was seeking, apart from political support for a military strike which would convey an unmistakable message to the whole Libyan leadership, was formal permission to use American FB111 precision bombers based at two British air-fields, along with British-based American in-flight refuelling tankers to support them. He had firmly decided that such a strike would be made, and the use of the British-based planes would make the operation not only easier but also more likely to succeed than if it were restricted to planes launched from aircraft carriers in the Mediterranean.

As Mrs Thatcher later told Parliament, Reagan assured her that the operation would be 'limited to clearly defined targets related to terrorism'. Whether he said or hinted that these included the acknowledged godfather of international terrorism himself is not known.

Whatever Reagan did or did not tell Mrs Thatcher, then or later, one of the raid's major missions was a meticulously planned attempt to eliminate Gaddafi, as impeccable sources, both British and American, have confirmed. The prime target was to be the Azaziya barracks in Tripoli, Gaddafi's military headquarters, which was believed to be the centre for terrorist planning but contained a compound that was also his family residence. As a nomad's son, Gaddafi had the habit of sleeping there in a Bedouin-style tent, and the time for the raid was chosen when intelligence reports indicated that he would be there.

Sir Geoffrey Howe, the Foreign Secretary, and George Younger, the Defence Secretary, were at Number 10 when Reagan's message came through, and were presumably told about the projected raid. Mrs Thatcher then consulted the Attorney General, Sir Michael Havers, who indicated that a self-defensive strike against terrorist targets might fall within international law. There was more communication with Washington. Eventually, she gave the US President formal permission for the British bases to be used so long as the targets were specific and all known to be linked with terrorism, from which, of course, Britain had suffered more than its share. Whether she had consciously realized, by then, that Gaddafi himself fulfilled that definition is unknown, but she had called for and studied the relevant MI6, GCHQ (the British interception organization based at Cheltenham) and Defence Intelligence reports. Further, some of her defence chiefs knew details of the projected raid and its prime purposes and Mrs Thatcher was specifically briefed about them.

It was obvious that the raid would cause Libyan casualties and was intended to do so. It was certain that these inevitable deaths would cause outrage in some quarters, not least in the United Nations. While it is most unlikely that the word 'assassination' was ever mentioned, it beggars belief that the President did not alert Mrs Thatcher to the additional political problems she would face if Gaddafi himself was killed. She must at least have realized that possibility – a probability as she had been given full details of the planning, as her defence chiefs did – and accepted it. This gave Reagan the further advantage that he would not be alone in facing world opinion. The precise time when Mrs Thatcher told Reagan that the British-based planes could be used is not known, but it must have been quickly because the detailed planning and training for the raid went ahead after the first communication.

More Cabinet Ministers were told of Britain's complicity on the evening of 14 April, a few hours before the raid, so the Prime Minister must have received an 'It's on tonight' message. While some ministers expressed reservations, Mrs Thatcher insisted that it would be unthinkable to withhold assistance from the US Government when requested. What had changed her mind, for previously she had opposed a military strike?

The likely answer has been provided by Casper Weinberger, the former US Defence Secretary, in his recent memoirs, which show that, short of military intervention, the US Government had been unstinting in its support of the British effort in the Falklands War, abandoning its neutrality in the process. On 1 May 1982 Weinberger had ordered the Pentagon to ensure that all requests for materials and assistance be granted with extreme urgency. Sidewinder missiles, which wreaked havoc on the Argentinian planes, were supplied. The USA extended its intelligence survey to include the Falklands and the resulting information was passed continuously to the British Task Force. Even before that, the CIA and the National Security Agency, the American equivalent of GCHQ, had been supplying intelligence about the Argentines under existing treaty arrangements. In whatever terms President Reagan may have worded his request to Mrs Thatcher, pay-day had arrived.

The CIA and its tough chief, William Casey, had been gunning for Gaddafi for months by devoting major resources to penetrate his entourage, and to bug his telephone calls and general conversations. Shared British and American intelligence had proved Gaddafi's logistical support of terrorist

attacks on American targets. A Libyan serving as a CIA penetration agent, with the codename Alba, had established that a
team of about a dozen terrorists was operating out of the
Libyan Embassy in East Berlin with the connivance of the East
German secret police.

A Libyan-backed plan to massacre Americans lining up for
visas outside an American embassy had only narrowly been
prevented. Attacks on an American barracks, a hospital and a
headquarters building in West Berlin had also been thwarted.
There was confirmed evidence that Gaddafi had declared his
intention of having Reagan killed. He was openly threatening
to attack US naval patrols in the open Mediterranean and
generally trying to assert himself by causing problems anywhere that offered, including the US mainland.

As President Havel of Czechoslovakia has recently confirmed, the Czech Communist organization Omnipol had been
supplying hundreds of tons of Semtex plastic explosive to
Libya and Gaddafi had been farming it out to terrorists. More
frighteningly, there were intelligence signs that he was planning to heighten terrorism to a new level – mass terrorist
attacks with chemical weapons, threatening whole communities. The CIA was in no doubt that a big new factory had been
built to manufacture nerve gases for chemical bombs.

As far back as 1984 a secret CIA assessment had concluded
that no course of action short of accomplishing Gadaffi's fall
would bring any enduring change in Libya's terrorist policies.
Since then no way of inducing an agent or dissident group
inside Libya to kill Gaddafi had been found, or was likely to
succeed even if it could be authorized. A military strike on
'terrorist targets' was the perfect cover and would have the
support of the American public, whatever happened.

Political assassination had been banned to the CIA by executive order originally signed by President Ford, and Reagan had
reaffirmed it in 1981. Military action aimed at 'terrorist targets'
would absolve both the CIA and the White House. There had
been leaks about the possible assassination of Gaddafi in
American newspapers; so, as a deception, statements were
issued suggesting that the President would never agree to a
personal attack on a head of state because foreign policy advisers and others would talk him out of it. In fact, the resolution to eliminate the Libyan leader was solid and Reagan had

volunteered to take the flak personally if it succeeded. All that was needed was a legitimate reason. Early in April it came.

The British and Americans had been intercepting messages from the Libyan intelligence HQ in Tripoli to the Libyan embassies abroad – the so-called 'People's Bureaus'. On 4 and 5 April messages to the Bureau in East Berlin indicated that a Libyan-inspired terrorist attack on an American target was about to occur. Within a few minutes of the last interception a bomb exploded in a discotheque in West Berlin used by American servicemen. One American soldier was killed, and there were about fifty others among more than two hundred injured. This was the final straw which provided the excuse to put an already well-planned attack into action. It also led to the contact with Mrs Thatcher.

If Reagan did not tell her that one purpose of the operation was to assassinate Gaddafi, those of her advisers in the know must soon have made the danger plain to her. The British Defence Ministry had not been involved in the early deliberations and decisions, which were entirely American, but officials there soon became aware of exactly what was going on at the American airfields in Britain, which are shared by the RAF. British Intelligence could hardly have failed to learn of the plan, soon after it had been formulated, and is more likely to have been briefed about it. Further, the intelligence intercepts on which the CIA had operated had been shared with GCHQ. I suspect that Whitehall's Joint Intelligence Committee knew exactly what was in the wind. If they did not, they were falling down on the job.

In short, anyone as perceptive as Mrs Thatcher must have been aware of the danger of assassination and she must have accepted it, along with the other Libyan casualties. It is not difficult to see why. She would not have been human had she not savoured the prospect of sweet satisfaction on two counts. The first was the murder of Policewoman Yvonne Fletcher, gunned down in April 1984 from the window of the Libyan 'Embassy' in St James's Square. The second was her own dreadful experience in the Brighton bombing later in the same year, and her certain knowledge that Gaddafi was the main supplier of the IRA's weapons and explosives.

On the evening before the raid Reagan telephoned the US commander of the British-based bomber force to wish the pilots luck, and assured him that whether it went well or not he would take full responsibility. Two routes for the British-based bombers, based at Upper Heyford and Lakenheath, had been planned. The shortest route was over France. The much longer one, if the French refused permission, involved flying west of France and Spain to Gibraltar and taking a dog-leg turn into the Mediterranean. The French did refuse, and the F111s faced a round trip of about six thousand miles which meant repeated in-flight refuelling by tankers from the Fairford and Mildenhall air stations.

The attack was fixed for the small hours of Monday, Libyan time, when intelligence had indicated that Gaddafi would be sleeping. According to the Pentagon, the F111s, backed up by Navy carrier bombers, a force of about thirty attack planes, struck with almost total surprise at 2 a.m. on Tuesday, 15 April 1986 in and around Tripoli, which was brilliantly lit, and in Benghazi. Every kind of electronic deception had been turned on by the Americans before the raid. Some of the F111s had to turn back because of the range problem, but several of them, fitted with 'smart' laser-guided 2000lb bombs, attacked the compound where Gaddafi was asleep in his tent. The plan was to obliterate the area and all in it, but most of the bombs either missed the main target or failed to explode. One dud fell close to Gaddafi's tent. Ancillary attacks on the Security Police building, the Naval Academy, Benina airfield and Benghazi were more successful. The raid lasted only a few minutes and about a hundred people were killed. Two of Gaddafi's sons were injured and a baby, said to be one of his adopted daughters, was killed, but the Libyan leader himself was untouched.

Reagan kept his word to the commander of the British-based bombers and announced the attack on television, courageously increasing the risk of a revenge assassination attempt on himself. He explained that the raid had been in self-defence for the loss of American lives in the discotheque bombing and declared that, if necessary, there would be more attacks. As planned, Reagan said that the raid had been against Gaddafi's 'terrorist and military assets' and that the US forces had succeeded in their mission. At that point nobody in Washington knew, with certainty, whether Gaddafi had survived or not; but because of the possibility that he had been killed top-secret information had to be sacrificed to justify the assassination.

This was the disclosure that intercepts had shown that Libyan intelligence had been informed in advance of the Berlin disco bombing, and must therefore have had some hand in it. This and other disclosures about intercepts must have ruined the sources of them for the future, but the publicity stakes were considered high enough to justify it. In fact, a month after the raid an Arab believed to be the CIA's agent Alba was shot dead in East Berlin. The East German police established that the single bullet which had been pumped into his head had come from the same pistol which had been used two years earlier to kill another dissident Libyan. So it would seem that Alba had been the victim of the extreme dirty trick of being considered expendable in the interest of an urgent political purpose – a danger which all double agents face. The CIA could not have been pleased with President Reagan and his advisers for the loss of such assets, especially as they were sacrificed unnecessarily because Gaddafi had not even been injured, though he had been shocked.

In Parliament Mrs Thatcher backed up Reagan's statement by giving details of seventeen Libyan-backed terrorist incidents in Britain and Europe in the 1980s. But in spite of such support, and general American feeling that the attack had been thoroughly deserved, Reagan and Casey were deeply disappointed by the results of the raid, which had been a technological failure. The 'smart' bombs had been anything but. What Mrs Thatcher's general feelings were is not known, though she deplored the cavalier way that intelligence sources had been endangered, her principle being to remain tight-lipped on such matters, whatever the personal political cost.

Had Gaddafi been assassinated, what the deception machines call 'plausible denials' of any such intention had been prepared for issue in both Washington and London. Reagan was brilliant at playing the 'daft lad' when it suited, as he displayed later when questioned about the Iran-Contra affair, but was a different and determined man off stage. Nor, after the Falklands War, can there be any doubt about Mrs Thatcher's resolution. It had been anticipated that the 'wets' in Parliament would have condemned an assassination, as some condemned the raid. Some of her Cabinet colleagues complained that the first they had heard about the raid had been on the radio, but nobody resigned.

She responded robustly, telling the Commons on 16 April that the Americans had not only been right to bomb Libyan targets but had a duty to do so as an act of self-defence against the scourge of terrorism, an act which had also been in the British interest. Eventually Congress offered her the highest praise and thanks for her co-operation.

Terrorists apart, few people outside the Arab world, and not all that many in it, would have grieved had Gaddafi been eliminated, whatever verbal protests might have been made. General reaction to the attempted use of assassination to resolve a political problem was strangely muted, as though that aspect of the raid had not been widely appreciated.

The raid had a profound psychological effect on Gaddafi and quietened him down for several months as he wondered what might be coming next. In showing the Libyans what they could expect if terrorism continued, it achieved some temporary success. It also had a salutary influence on Syria, which closed down its terrorist training areas in the Bekaa Valley, fearing strikes – though they have reopened since.

I have been assured that, if Gaddafi had been killed, there was no intention to follow up the raid with any further attacks. In fact, intelligence sources had indicated that Gaddafi's likely successor would probably continue with similar policies. Instead, the so far indestructible Gaddafi himself has done so.

Hoping to profit from Gaddafi's experience, the Iraqi dictator Saddam Hussein arranged to have British and American hostages close by his homes and headquarters to deter any air attacks designed to kill him during the Persian Gulf crisis in 1990. I have little doubt that both the CIA and MI6 were involved in encouraging his Iraqi enemies to dispose of him, but such are the diplomatic niceties that assassination by American or British intruders remained banned by both Governments so long as there was no shooting war.

2

Terrorism – the Truth Emerges

While Gaddafi is the terrorist godfather who immediately springs to mind, revelations from the freed countries of eastern Europe have shown him to be but one member of a massive conspiracy nurtured and sponsored by Communists for their cold-blooded political motives. It is difficult for people reared in a true democracy to credit that a group of intelligent men with great responsibilities for a major country could sit round a table and decide to finance activities which were bound to lead to atrocities like the Lockerbie airliner disaster. Yet the breakdown of the Soviet Bloc, with the escape of former satellites such as East Germany, Hungary and Czechoslovakia, is gradually producing devastating proof of its former terrorist activities for all to see. And formerly secret documents show that the decisions were indeed taken by the political leaders of those countries, sitting in solemn session.

The ruling cliques decided to sponsor terrorism in the West for the specific purpose of destabilizing free democracies and so encouraging the chaos on which Communism might thrive. For most people the ingredients of terrorism constitute the dirtiest tricks of all, because totally innocent people are so often involved in their horrific consequences, but Leninists have always accepted that any means to 'smash' capitalism are justified, violence being an essential element. Even totally mindless murderers, like those of the West German Baader-Meinhof gang and the Italian Red Brigade, were deemed worthy of sponsorship.

Further, there can now be no doubt that the conspiracy was formally approved and masterminded from Moscow, which always maintained strict control of the satellite secret services which were responsible for the direct assistance to terrorists. Western intelligence authorities have long been convinced that the KGB and its military counterpart, the GRU, have trained and sponsored terrorists, but undeniable proof was not previously available.

The first irrefutable evidence of Soviet Bloc sponsorship of terrorism has come from East Germany with the disbanding of the former Stasi, (Staatssicherheitsdienst) the secret police who kept Erich Honecker and his cronies in dictatorial power. In June 1990 a cell of six Red Army Faction terrorists living in East Germany was exposed; the Stasi with the Communist Government's blessing, had given them false papers, a safe haven and other support. They were West Germans wanted in their own country for many atrocities for which they now face charges. Their East German base had enabled them to continue to strike across the border and then return to safety, where they were almost honoured for their bestial endeavours. More have been arrested, and further details of Communist implication in international terrorism is likely to come to light when they are all tried.

Other West Germans who had 'retired' from active terrorism had been given permanent sanctuary for their past services. The regime also trained and equipped new terrorists. Its chief training camp was at Finsterwalde, near Dresden, where men and women from several countries were taught pistol and rifle marksmanship under all manner of conditions including shooting from moving cars.

The Stasi files show that East Germany assisted the terrorists as a deliberate policy of destabilizing the West; in June 1990 the Interior Minister of the new East German Government, Peter-Michael Diestel, described this policy and its consequences as 'one of the most shameful chapters in East German history'. In the following month he disclosed that, with the personal blessing of the previous leadership, even the notorious Carlos, wanted for many murders and other violent crimes in the West, had been given asylum in East Berlin for several years. It was Carlos – a Venezuelan Communist whose name was Ilich Ramirez Sanchez – who shot my old friend Teddy Sieff, of the Marks and Spencer family, at his home in London. Miraculously, Teddy survived the bullet which Carlos pumped into his mouth.

Terrorists from several Palestinian factions, responsible for car-bombings, airline hi-jacks and other atrocities, were fervently assisted by the Stasi. The killer Abu Daud, wanted in the West for many crimes including the bloody attack on the Israeli team at the Olympic Games in Munich in 1972, also received Honecker's personal support.

The former head of the Stasi, Erich Mielke, was recently arrested on suspicion of aiding terrorists, among other charges, but may escape prosecution on the grounds of old age. Terrorists still active in West Germany responded to such moves by trying, but failing, to assassinate the chief anti-terrorist official, Hans Neusel.

Stasi documents are providing firm evidence of the international ties long suspected to exist between various terrorist groups, which met and exchanged expertise at the training schools. Herr Diestel has claimed to have evidence that the Stasi had contacts with the IRA. The secret police files have also produced proof that they had detailed knowledge of the terrorist group in the East Berlin Libyan Embassy which blew up the West German discotheque, the event which triggered off the American air attack on Gaddafi's headquarters in Tripoli.

In March 1990 President Havel of Czechoslovakia, while on a visit to London, disclosed that the previous Communist Government had sold 1000 tons of Semtex explosive to Libya deliberately to further terrorism for ideological reasons. Semtex, a Czech development in the plastic explosives field, has made the terrorists' work much easier. Being very stable, it is safe to handle; being odourless, it is difficult to detect; and, being powerful, only a few ounces are needed for a bomb. Havel revealed that it had been sold cheaply by the state organization making it 'on political orders which came from above', meaning the former Communist Czech leadership which, presumably, felt suitably rewarded when an airliner was destroyed with all its passengers. Czech government scientists had even been involved in terrorist 'research' establishing, for example, just how much Semtex was needed to incapacitate an aircraft in flight and where it could be placed for greatest effect.

After the Lockerbie disaster, when an American airliner was blown out of the sky by Semtex hidden in a cassette recorder, resulting in the loss of some 270 people in the air and on the ground, the Czech Government lied by saying it had stopped exporting Semtex in 1982. In fact it had continued supplying terrorists by roundabout routes such as East Germany. The Czech Government even sent a delegation 'to assist' the Lockerbie investigators, but really to spy on the progress they were making.

The IRA, Palestinian groups, the Basque separatist organization ETA and the various Red Army Factions have benefitted from Gaddafi's generosity with Semtex, while hundreds of the victims and their families have suffered. Many more are likely to suffer, even though further supplies are being denied. The IRA, in particular, has sufficient stocks to prime several thousand bombs, so the Communist Czechs' responsibility for death and destruction is likely to reach far into the years ahead.

The Czechs have also been deeply involved in selling machine pistols and other weapons to so-called freedom fighters and instructing them in their use. A major training camp for terrorists has been identified at Dolni Brezany, about ten miles outside Prague. Many Palestinian terrorists were trained there in hand-to-hand combat, assassination, and methods of infiltration into Western societies and escape from them.

The new Hungarian Government has admitted that its Communist predecessor gave sanctuary to terrorists wanted by Western police forces, including the notorious Carlos and Ulrike Meinhof, joint leader of the murderous Baader-Meinhof gang, and assisted them in further acts of violence. In the late 1970s Carlos holed up for at least a year in Hungary, which served as something of a rest and recreation centre for terrorists. The new government has started a criminal inquiry into the culpability of its predecessor in assisting Carlos.

The Romanian defector Ion Pacepa has documented much evidence of Ceausescu's association with leading terrorists and his support for them. Ceausescu sponsored a particularly close relationship with Yasser Arafat and set up a training camp mainly for Palestinians north of Bucharest. Those who witnessed the behaviour of the Romanian Securitate at the time of the revolution there can have no doubts about its capability to be involved in violence anywhere which suited it.

Little has yet emerged from Bulgaria but there is no doubt that it was another safe haven for terrorists, with several training camps, and they may still be welcome there. With the former Communists still in power under another name there is little possibility of any admissions of past misdemeanours. Efforts to induce the Bulgarian intelligence service even to admit responsibility for the assassination of a Bulgarian defector, Georgi Markov, in London in 1987 have been fruitless at the time of writing, though his widow has tried hard. There can be no doubt that he was killed by a professional organization, and the Bulgarian intelligence service was the only one with an obvious motive.

Markov, a dissident journalist, was murdered by a highly sophisticated poisoning technique. A pinhead-sized metal pellet had been implanted in his right thigh, probably by a dart disguised as an umbrella, though this has never been proved. The pellet contained an extremely toxic substance called ricin, prepared from castor oil seeds. Similar pellets were recovered from two other Bulgarian dissidents who survived, one in Paris, the other in the USA. There was little doubt that the attacks had been ordered by the Bulgarian leadership because the victims had been very critical of it; Markov, in particular, made use of the BBC overseas service for that purpose. All three attacks – and there may have been more – were the work of an assassination organization with access to advanced techniques, ricin being virtually undetectable once it is distributed in the body. The implication of the Bulgarian and Soviet intelligence services in the shooting of the Pope will be considered in Chapter 3.

In the past, the Kremlin has been able to deny complicity in terrorism because it deliberately distanced itself from most of the activities by farming them out to the satellites, but events, witnesses and documents are now demonstrating that the actions were fostered and overseen from Moscow. Further, high-level defectors have provided evidence showing that important decisions concerning terrorism had to be taken by the Soviet Defence Council, a select group of the Politburo chaired by the Secretary General of the Communist Party. All attempts to assassinate important foreign figures had to be sanctioned by the Council.

While the function of the KGB was mainly to oversee and finance the activities of its satellites, it had its own terrorist training camps within the Soviet Union, as did the GRU. They also supplied senior teaching staff to the satellites. Many Arab terrorists, especially from Iraq and Syria which have long been major customers for Soviet arms, were trained inside the Soviet Union. Palestinians trained by the Soviets set up camps in Lebanon to train others.

The extent of the Iraqi training in terrorism was emphasized in the early stages of the blockade of Iraq, following the seizure of Kuwait, when Saddam Hussein, the Iraqi dictator, called for an upsurge of terrorism against all those nations taking part. Western authorities had little doubt that he had the trained terrorists and the infrastructure to mount it. This use of terrorism was not new in war. It had been the foundation concept of Britain's Special Operations Executive (SOE) when Churchill ordered it to 'set Europe ablaze' in World War II.

British Intelligence has hard evidence that IRA terrorists have been trained by Soviet instructors in Europe. The Irish police have confirmed that the Palestine Liberation Organization has been involved in training the IRA and the Irish National Liberation Army in the Middle East. Agca, the Turk who attempted to kill the Pope, was trained in a pro-Communist Palestinian camp in Lebanon.

In Moscow itself, the so-called Patrice Lumumba Friendship University for foreigners served not only as a meeting place where senior terrorists from different organizations could forge international links, but as a centre of advanced study. One distinguished alumnus, who attended there in 1968, is Carlos, who majored in murder.

The KGB has consistently assisted terrorists by means of its propaganda machinery, usually with a political spin-off for itself. When Italian Red Brigade terrorists shot the five bodyguards who were protecting Aldo Moro, a prominent Christian Democratic politician, in March 1978, the KGB immediately claimed that the CIA had been responsible for the outrage. They persisted in this obvious myth when the kidnapped Moro was eventually murdered. Later the KGB mounted a campaign to blame the CIA for the attempted assassination of the Pope.

An advanced training school for terrorists in the Ukraine has only recently been shut down, and it would seem that the Soviet leadership may be ending its expensive logistic support and sponsorship completely. As a result the Soviet Union, which was virtually immune to terrorism because of its support for it, may become a target. The KGB already fears Palestinian reaction to the mass emigration of Soviet Jews to Israel, perhaps in the form of terrorist bombing against its Embassies and other missions abroad and attacks on Soviet planes carrying the emigrants. The North Koreans have already called Gorbachev a traitor, and the Palestinians may do so if Soviet support is entirely withdrawn as part of the Kremlin's campaign to present a kinder face to the West. KGB anxiety also centres on Islamic radicals in the strongly Muslim states, where recent uprisings had strong religious overtones. There could be terrorist incidents in support, launched from Iran.

In readiness, the KGB now has a special counter-terrorist division which is getting plenty of practice as the number of plane hi-jacks inside the Soviet Union increases, though these are mainly perpetuated by people trying to escape to the West. The KGB has a decided advantage over Western countries in the degree of ruthlessness it is permitted and prepared to use in countering terrorism. When the fanatical pro-Iranian Hizbollah terrorists extended their kidnapping campaign in the Lebanon by seizing four Soviet diplomats and killing one of them, the KGB responded in the only way the barbaric murderers would be likely to understand. They grabbed a close relative of one of the Hizbollah leaders, shot him and returned his body, with his testicles in his mouth, along with a message that this was only the start if the diplomats were not released. They were, and none have been kidnapped since. While deploring such savagery, many Western agencies envied its efficacy.

By contrast, the British Army in Northern Ireland is allowed to hold a captured terrorist or suspect for only half an hour before having to hand him over to the police. Previously it was allowed two hours, which provided the opportunity to apply pressure to secure information, but most terrorists find it easy to withstand it when they know that it will end in half an hour.

In July 1990 the British Foreign Secretary, Douglas Hurd, signed an agreement with Czechoslovakia to co-operate in countering terrorism. Having abandoned Communism, Czechoslovakia is an obvious fanatics' target for the car bombs, plane bombs and assassinations which its former government fostered. Such an agreement with the Soviet Union, which seems likely, would be an even more intriguing consequence of the ending of the Cold War in view of the part played by that country in promoting terrorism in the recent past and, through the killers it has trained, into the future. No official condemnation of Moscow's former sponsorship of terrorism is likely, especially by the British, to avoid embarrassing Gorbachev who was party to it in the earlier stages of his career. The accent will be on international co-operation, which is essential if terrorism is to be effectively countered, and many terrorist assaults throughout the world are already being prevented by interchange of intelligence. The number which have been secretly aborted, not only by good intelligence but by deception and rugged counter-action, runs into many hundreds worldwide and are rarely the subject of publicity. Much depends on the recruitment of informers in many countries, and both MI5 and MI6 are deeply involved in that area while GCHQ tries to intercept terrorist communications, passing on any successes to MI5 for action.

Almost any dirty trick or deception is regarded as justified in countering terrorists, especially when they are holding hostages. The recently attempted coup in Trinidad was ended when the gang of gunmen were offered amnesty with safe passage and then found themselves treated as common criminals. Nobody blamed the elected Government's ruling that promises secured under duress could be ignored, but it is surprising how often they have been honoured in other countries in the past.

Like terrorism itself, most counter-measures are becoming increasingly high-tech. It was advances in communications technology, for instance, which facilitated the mid-air interception by American fighter planes of the airliner carrying the four PLO men who had hi-jacked the Italian cruise ship *Achille Lauro* in the Mediterranean in October 1985. The plane was forced to land in Italy and the hi-jackers were arrested.

The international linkage of anti-terrorist computer systems is yielding dividends. West Germany pioneered the mass application of computers to countering terrorism with a huge system codenamed Komissar, into which every detail of known and suspected terrorists is fed, including voice prints. Britain has followed suit, and the co-operation deals which the government has signed with nearly thirty countries include computer linkage. Those countries which decline to co-operate brand themselves as sponsors.

The Soviet Union, Czechoslovakia and Poland are even joining Interpol, the international policing organization, which already has 150 members. This should lead to further information about terrorist organizations, the past movements of terrorists and their possible whereabouts today.

The international battle has assumed new urgency with the threat of mass terrorism, as sponsoring nations such as Libya and Iraq secure chemical weapons and, possibly, nuclear bombs. The power of blackmail alone if terrorists possessed nuclear weapons, or could even convincingly claim to do so, would be enormous.

The agreement which Britain has signed with Czechoslovakia and many other countries to co-operate in countering terrorism also extends to drug-trafficking. No proof has yet emerged from the former Communist countries to confirm statements by certain defectors that the Soviet Bloc has been using drugs as a political weapon. But there is no doubt that the Cuban intelligence service, for instance, has been running drugs into the USA not only to raise funds for its other activities but as a deliberate policy to damage the fabric of American society. US troops in Vietnam were successfully targeted by drug-pushers believed to have been serviced and financed by Moscow. There is also some evidence that NATO troops in Europe have been deliberately subjected to the temptation in an attempt to undermine their morale. It is possible that documents and witnesses from former Soviet Bloc countries will confirm the belief of some intelligence specialists that there has been a widespread and sustained operation, targeted particularly on the USA, though the CIA is unconvinced. Such 'narco-terrorism' does not seem to have been a problem in Britain, but MI5 is aware of its potential and has some responsibility for countering it.

One aspect of terrorism which the Soviet leadership is unlikely to relinquish is the training of its Spetsnaz forces and the recruitment of traitors to assist them in the event of war. Spetsnaz troops – special service units which belong to the GRU – can legitimately be considered as terrorists because two of their functions, for which they are rigorously trained, are to assassinate political and military leaders in target countries and to cause chaos there by sabotage. The chief informant on the Spetsnaz threat has been an important defector from the GRU, Vladimir Rezun, who now writes under the name of Suvorov. His disclosures of the extent to which Britain has been targeted for Spetsnaz action, in the event of war, led to changes in British Army training which now, in major home defence exercises, takes account of the threat. Rezun has revealed the extraordinary degree to which the Spetsnaz troops are trained in deception, using violence to achieve their objectives.

The Soviets also recruit local freelance saboteurs, usually pro-Communist fanatics, to assist their Spetsnaz intruders. They function as 'sleepers', apparently perfectly respectable people who have instructions about what to do if called upon in an emergency, being assigned to assist with the 'reduction' of certain prime targets in their areas. They have radio receiver-transmitters, usually buried in the ground, which they dig up once a year to test if they are working. This may sound far-fetched, but in 1980 a farmer ploughing near Llangollen in North Wales dug up a sealed metal box containing a Russian-made transmitter clearly intended for use by a local subversion unit, probably centred on Liverpool. Inquiries showed that it had been buried by Russians staying at a nearby hotel in the guise of trade delegates. Such transmitters are used only rarely, and while GCHQ occasionally picks up the coded messages played to the sleepers via Soviet radio stations they are difficult to detect and pinpoint. Other devices have since been discovered, along with further evidence of sleepers targeted on various military headquarters and other key points.

With the collapse of Communism as a viable political system, local recruits to serve as sleepers may become progressively difficult to find, but Defence Intelligence is in no doubt that the 'infrastructure' built up so laboriously in Britain over so many years is still in being and will be maintained, if possible, by the GRU as an insurance policy.

In advance of any war, it is MI5 which is responsible for countering the Spetsnaz threat, a situation which has led to conflict with the Defence Intelligence Service, which contends that operations against such specialist troops should be in military hands. In conjunction with the police, MI5 is responsible for countering terrorism as a whole and can call on military forces such as the SAS. Such occasions are kept secret whenever possible but sometimes cannot be concealed, as happened in March 1988 when SAS men in civilian clothes gunned down three members of an IRA active service unit in Gibraltar.

The degree to which SAS men are trained to kill terrorists was described to me by a former Home Office Minister following a visit he made to SAS headquarters in Hereford. The commanding officer sat at a table in a small room with four realistic dummies representing terrorists holding him hostage. SAS men, who had no idea exactly where the commander would be sitting, burst into the room and, using live ammunition, shot all four dummies through the head in seconds without harming the 'hostage'. It would seem, however, that the SAS has little opportunity to put this expertise to effective use, and whenever it does so there is an orchestrated outcry on the victims' behalf.

Terrorism has intruded insidiously into the lives of all civilized peoples, who have quickly come to accept body and luggage searches at airports as part of the travelling routine. At times of high risk, searches of handbags and briefcases at the entrances of hotels and restaurants occasion no surprise. The car bomb, the parcel bomb, the hold-all bomb command little newspaper space unless the results have been particularly horrific or involve some well-known person. The permanently increased security at public and government buildings has ceased to cause comment, but not all such precautions derive directly from the terrorist threat. For several years, the Ministry of Defence main building in Whitehall has been protected by security turnstiles into which each staff member has to feed his plastic pass to be let through. This looks like an anti-terrorist installation, but it really resulted from a rape case. What happened was that five feminists, who were furious when a soldier was acquitted on a rape charge, ran into the building past the guards in an attempt to kidnap the then Defence Minister, Fred (now Lord) Mulley. It was after that episode that the gates were fitted.

Such targets would not seem to be 'soft' enough for the IRA, which is currently concentrating on bandsmen's barracks, the Stock Exchange, private houses and public figures who have denied themselves special protection. One of the last who springs to mind was Earl Mountbatten. Shortly before he was assassinated by a bomb in a small boat containing children and other members of his family, I dined with him in a private house where his safety came up for discussion. As any sane person might have said, his reaction to our suggestion that he needed a bodyguard in his eightieth year was: 'Who in his right mind would bother to blow up an old sod like me?'

3

Star Targets

Whether by the hands of deluded fanatics, hired hit-men or professional secret agents, the dirty trick of political assassination has been employed down the centuries and never more so than in recent times. While many such attempts are ultimately pointless, often affecting the ordinary and the innocent, others are successfully targeted on political figures whose swift removal can change the fate of whole nations. In seeking the perpetrators, the question that must always be asked is: Who stands to benefit?

Such a killing occurred during the afternoon of 17 August 1988, when Britain and the West lost its staunchest anti-Communist ally in southern Asia with the assassination of Mohammad Zia ul-Haq, President and dictator of Pakistan. The C130 Hercules transport plane, in which he was travelling from a military air base to Islamabad, crashed in the desert a few minutes after take-off and became a ball of fire. There were no survivors among the thirty-one on board. The crash killed Zia, five of his generals, the US Ambassador, Arnold Raphel, and an American general, Herbert Wassom, who was head of the US military aid mission. Fearing that the killing of Zia, who was also the forces' Commander-in-Chief, might be the opening move of a coup or invasion, the Army took up defensive positions in the capital.

The plane had not exploded in the air as it would had a terrorist bomb been aboard. Examination of the wreckage proved that it had been intact when it had hit the ground. Nor had it been shot down by a missile. There had not been any engine or electrical failure, nor any signs of trouble with the control systems. Pilot error seemed most unlikely, as the machine had made a perfect take-off and the weather was clear and fine. Benazir Bhutto, whose father, the former President had been hanged by Zia, called it an 'act of God', but a board of inquiry concluded that the only possible cause was sabotage or some other criminal act.

Further examination discovered traces of an explosive, and it has been suggested that they were the remains of a small charge used to open a canister of poison gas. Regrettably, no full post mortem examinations of the bodies were performed to see if any of the crew and passengers had been poisoned. This seemed possible because, although it was certain that the radio had been working, there had been no Mayday signal or any other verbal message, suggesting that the crew had been unable to speak during the several seconds when the plane had been seen see-sawing through the air before crashing. There had been plenty of opportunity for someone to place a canister or some other device aboard the plane while it was being serviced at the military airfield.

Such a poor effort seems to have been made to discover the truth that it may never be known. But who stood to gain from Zia's death? It could have been someone acting on behalf of the political faction which eventually put Mrs Bhutto in command. It could have been an agent of the Afghan Government, because Pakistan had been serving as the supply centre for American weapons for the Mujahideen guerillas. Or it could have been an agent of the Soviet Union, which was fighting the guerillas and suffering so many casualties that its troops had eventually to be withdrawn from Afghanistan.

Soviet authorities had warned American and Pakistani officials that some action was to be taken against Zia. The Foreign Minister, Eduard Shevardnadze, had stated that 'Zia's support for the Mujahideen would not go unpunished'. Only ten days before the assassination, Shevardnadze's deputy, Yuliy Voronstov, warned the American Ambassador in Moscow that the Soviets were going to teach Zia a lesson. The KGB and the GRU military intelligence, which had a major interest on behalf of the Red Army troops in Afghanistan, had already shown that they meant business by staging or sponsoring more than a hundred terrorist attacks inside Pakistan.

British and American intelligence officers with whom I have discussed the assassination are inclined to attribute it to an agent acting on behalf of the Soviet GRU. They pointed out that, if that were the case, then the Kremlin leadership, including Gorbachev, must have agreed to it. There is no doubt, from the evidence of high-level defectors, that any deliberate attempt to assassinate the political leader of another country has to be considered and agreed to by the Kremlin's Defence Council, of which the party leader was then chairman.

The alacrity with which the whole incident was swept aside and ignored, not only in Pakistan but in Britain and America, which had lost an ambassador in the assassination, is a further indication that the Soviets were the chief suspects. The easing of East-West tension was well under way, with Gorbachev's popularity in the West an essential part of it. Any finger publicly pointed at him would be 'counter-productive' in the eyes of the US State Department and the British Foreign Office. As an ally Zia was, literally, 'burned', and recrimination could serve no diplomatic purpose. Even if proof of the Kremlin's culpability should ever be forthcoming, it would be suppressed; and, whatever changes may occur inside the Soviet Union, there will never be any admission there of the assassination of a head of state. If Zia was killed by a political act, whoever was responsible accomplished the perfect ultimate dirty trick.

From inside informers and other sources, Western intelligence agencies have been certain for many years that the sponsorship of assassination and general terrorism has been an important component in the relentless efforts of the Soviet Bloc to undermine the West. In its overall control over terrorism as a political weapon, the KGB tended to farm out specific operations to its satellite surrogates so that if any went wrong they could not be traced directly to Moscow. Its preferred agency for murder was the Bulgarian intelligence service (Durzhavna Sigurnost), and it remains strongly suspect as being the controller of the attempted assassination of Pope John Paul II, the Pole Karol Wojtyla.

On 13 May 1981 a Turkish hit-man called Mehmet Ali Agca, then aged twenty-three, shot the Pope twice in St Peter's Square, obviously intending to kill him. There were two gunmen in the Square. One was photographed holding a gun, but escaped; Agca, however, was captured after a nun held on tenaciously to his jacket, and he is now serving life imprisonment. The fact that the other escaped indicated that it was likely that both thought they could so so. Agca was to state later that his accomplice was supposed to detonate panic bombs to create a diversion, but failed to do so.

After being silent for a year Agca, who had a degree from Ankara University and was a qualified teacher, claimed that the KGB, acting through the Bulgarian intelligence service, had trained him and financed the operation. In return his Turkish terrorist outfit, called the Grey Wolves, were to be given £750,000. Lech Walesa, the Polish Solidarity leader, was said to be an alternative target during a previous visit to Rome, and Agca had allegedly been in Rome at that time.

Evidence from Turkish trial records indicated that Agca had first been recruited by Bulgarians to assassinate a Turkish newspaper editor in 1979. When Agca had been arrested for that crime, Bulgarian agents managed to spring him from prison and he fled to the Bulgarian capital, Sofia, where he spent the summer of 1980.

In Rome Agca allegedly associated with three Bulgarians, all believed to be officers of the Bulgarian Secret Service working under cover – Sergei Antonov, deputy chief of the Bulgarian State Airline office, Todor Ayvazov, a cashier at the Bulgarian Embassy, and Colonel Zhelyo Vassilev, an assistant military attaché. Agca claimed that they were all involved in planning the operation, and GCHQ and other intelligence services noted a substantial increase in Bulgarian coded traffic after the shooting.

The Italian Defence Minister, Lelio Lagorio, told the Italian Parliament that the shooting was an act of war against Poland by the Bulgarians, committed on Vatican soil. The Kremlin responded with the standard upside-down ploy and, through the news agency TASS, dismissed the charge as absurd, blaming the CIA as being really responsible. The CIA's alleged purpose had been to stir up anti-Soviet feeling to induce West Germany to accept the deployment of new American nuclear missiles. A KGB officer posing as a Soviet journalist was sent to Italy to investigate and duly wrote to order, establishing the innocence of the Bulgarians and supporting the guilt of the CIA. On the other hand the Kremlin, then headed by Leonid Brezhnev, had a strategic motive that was genuinely urgent.

The Pope was serving as a major inspiration to the Polish people, who remained strong in their Catholic faith, to liberate themselves. He was giving his fullest support to Solidarity, the trade union movement which was threatening hard-line Communist control and stimulating the general collapse of the fear on which the Communists relied. The Soviets needed to crush Solidarity, and the death of the Pope would be a step in that direction. His Holiness openly opposed the 'Brezhnev doctrine', which most Western politicians had abjectly accepted, that the Soviet Empire was permanent. Preceding Gorbachev, he promoted a vision of a united Europe stretching from the Atlantic to the Urals.

The Soviet military chiefs were appalled at the possible defection of Poland because loss of that territory would greatly reduce their option for a surprise attack on western Europe, which was the centre point of their offensive strategy. Poland constituted a third of the protective zone round the eastern border of the Soviet Union and was essential for supply lines for East Germany, which might follow Poland out of the Soviet orbit. In Soviet eyes, therefore, the Pope was a valid target for removal.

After prolonged investigation the Italians arrested the Bulgarian Sergei Antonov, and eventually tried him for conspiring to kill the Pope, along with six other men, four of them *in absentia*. Vassilev and Ayvazov were safe in Sofia and refused to attend the trial. Meanwhile the fifteen-year-old daughter of a Vatican employee was kidnapped, and the abductors demanded Agca's release in exchange for hers.

Agca's story was implausible in some respects and he changed it several times. In March 1986 the Bulgarians were cleared of conspiring with Agca for lack of evidence, which does not count as a full acquittal. Antonov, the only one in custody, was freed after more than two years in jail, one year of house arrest and ten months in court. A Turk who had been extradited from Switzerland was jailed for three years for smuggling the pistol used by Agca into Italy.

Who, apart from a deluded madman, which Agca may have been, had a major motive for killing the Pope? Only the Soviet Union. Though Agca was a Muslim there was hardly a religious motive, because one Pope is quickly replaced by another. The Soviet Union was the only entity likely to benefit from the removal of this particular Pope. When convicting Agca, the Italian court decided that he was not a lone ideologue or criminal but 'the fruit of a complex plot orchestrated by hidden minds interested in destabilization'.

The CIA and MI6 have taken the official view that the Soviets were probably not involved. They argue that the KGB would have selected someone more professional than Agca for the contract, though in fact, he had killed two people before and very nearly killed the Pope, pumping two bullets into him. The chief of Rome's anti-terrorist police squad described him as 'cold, lucid and well-trained to shoot'. Individual British and American intelligence officers with whom I have discussed the case suspect that the Soviet leadership did authorize the shooting, indicating that the official line has been taken to avoid political embarrassment to Gorbachev, who was not responsible.

In March 1990 Victor Ivanovich Sheymov, a former KGB officer who had defected to the USA in 1980, claimed to have seen a cable showing that the Soviets had indeed planned to assassinate the Pope when Yuri Andropov was head of the KGB. Sheymov had worked in the KGB directorate which handled intercepts and other communications intelligence, but it was odd that he had waited so long to provide that information

More convincingly the Count de Marenches, while chief of the French Secret Service (SDECE), has revealed that he had advance warning from an intelligence source that there would be an attempt on the life of the Pope. He sent emissaries to the Vatican to warn His Holiness of an assassination plot in January 1980, but the Pope responded by saying that his life was in the hands of the Lord. Judge Martello, who led the Italian inquiry, visited de Marenches in Paris, but the former intelligence chief would not reveal his sources and was unable to give any indication about Bulgaria's involvement.

What is certain is that, if Bulgarian Intelligence *was* involved, it would not have acted without the initiative of the KGB or possibly the GRU and the authority of the Soviet Defence Council.

The Pope's survival from his injuries was a factor in maintaining the spirit of the Polish people, which has led to their virtual independence of Soviet domination. The satellite empire has collapsed and the Warsaw Pact exists in little more than name.

Recently Gorbachev had an audience with the Pope as evidence of his 'good European' stance. In the half hour which the two spent entirely alone without interpreters I wonder if he apologised for any Soviet complicity in the Agca affair, as Soviet apologies have recently been made for various mass murders. The Pope would, at least, have had to go through the motions of forgiveness.

No doubt surrounds the immediate perpetrators of the bomb which almost wiped out most of the British Cabinet in 1984. It was the acknowledged work of the IRA, but the advance planning and the nature of the weapon showed a degree of sophistication suggesting possible outside professional assistance.

In what was a most effective deception operation, a bomb containing between 20 and 30lb of explosive and fitted with a long-endurance microchip timing device and long-life batteries had been hidden behind a partition in a bathroom in Room 629 of the Grand Hotel in Brighton. The assassin, a thirty-four-year-old Irishman called Patrick Magee, had taken the room during the previous month using a false name and address. The hotel had been chosen as the residential centre for the annual Conservative Party conference, and the room had been well selected to cause maximum damage in an area where it was expected that the Prime Minister and members of her Cabinet would be sleeping.

The weapon exploded at 2.54 a.m. on Friday, 12 October when Mrs Thatcher could reasonably have been expected to be in her bed. It sliced four floors out of the centre of the building and a bathroom which the Prime Minister had visited two minutes earlier was wrecked. The five dead included the Tory MP Sir Anthony Berry and the wife of the Chief Whip, John Wakeham, who was himself seriously injured. Norman Tebbitt, then Secretary of State for Trade and Industry, was badly hurt and his wife permanently paralysed. A public notice by the IRA removed any doubt that Mrs Thatcher had been the star target by stating, 'This time you were lucky. But you have to be lucky all the time. We only have to be lucky once.' She had already made her comment – 'We carry on.' While behaving with admirable calm and courage, she was deeply shocked, as was the nation.

The prolonged security, intelligence and police inquiries

which eventually led to Magee's imprisonment for thirty-five years came to no definite conclusion about the possibility that the IRA had specific outside assistance with the operation, and the file remains open in that regard. That those who had supplied the components for the bomb had been accessories was without question. The weapons and explosives supplied by Gaddafi and other pro-terrorist sources include some of the latest military-style fuses and timing devices, so that the IRA has become progressively more sophisticated in its own right. This, of course, applies to other terrorist outfits, and it is only comparable technical advances in detection that will defeat them. It is a sad commentary on what should be the most civilized era of the human story that terrorism has become a permanent hazard which most of us have accepted, like earthquakes and gales.

4

Gay Deceiver

As a major part of its duties the Secret Intelligence Service, MI6, is required to practise dirty tricks, and this is one of the prime reasons why it has never been established by statute and officially does not exist. MI6 is run by the Foreign Office, and no Foreign Secretary or Prime Minister has any wish to be required to answer for any backlash from its dirty tricks in Parliament. So long as it does not officially exist they can usually decline to respond, relying on the convention that, in the interest of national security, secret matters are never discussed if they can possibly be avoided. When Anthony Eden was Prime Minister in 1956 he had been nastily embroiled in the MI6 dirty trick when a frogman, Commander Lionel Crabb, had died in Portsmouth harbour while trying to inspect the hulls of Soviet warships which had brought visiting Russian leaders. Yet in spite of the furore he still managed to avoid admitting that MI6 was run by the Foreign Office.

The charade has continued. When Sir Robert Armstrong, the Cabinet Secretary, was questioned about MI6 during the *Spycatcher* court case in Australia he declined to admit its existence. The former CIA chief, Admiral Stansfield Turner, told me that when he was writing his book *Secrecy and Democracy* he was forbidden, at MI6's request, to mention it. When Dr David Owen was Foreign Secretary and James Callaghan was Prime Minister both were keen to 'legitimize' MI6, but its then chief, Sir Maurice Oldfield, successfully advised against it, being afraid of parliamentary questions. In 1987, however, an admission that MI6 not only exists but is run by the Foreign Office was tacitly made by David Owen in connection with an unfortunate personal deception which had been practised by

Oldfield on his own service. As a further consequence, more light was shed on Oldfield's nature and behaviour.

In that year, in a book called *Traitors*, I had revealed that Oldfield, a lifelong bachelor, had been involved in homosexual activities which had been detected by Scotland Yard, leading to his suspension from secret work. His behaviour, which would have barred him from service in MI6, had not come to light until after he had retired as Chief in 1978. Courageously, in the autumn of 1979 he had come out of retirement at Mrs Thatcher's request to take on the onerous job of security supremo in Northern Ireland – officially Co-ordinator of Intelligence – a post which plunged him back into the secrets world. Oldfield informed me that he took the post only because he admired the Prime Minister so much that he could not refuse. They had been friends for several years after I had introduced them when Mrs Thatcher was Leader of the Opposition. Oldfield told me that it seemed so likely that she would become Prime Minister that it was a great pity that she was not being briefed on intelligence affairs and that he was prepared to do that. As he could not approach her directly, he asked me to do so on his behalf. I saw Mrs Thatcher, who said that she was keen to meet him provided that the Labour Prime Minister, James Callaghan, approved. Callaghan asked David Owen, then Foreign Secretary, for his agreement, which was readily given. Recently I discovered just why Oldfield, a master of deception if ever there was one, took this initiative. He had heard that she was receiving intelligence briefings from a free-lance group and did not approve of it, wishing to keep all intelligence affairs under his control. As with most actions in the secrets world, his approach to me had not been quite what it seemed.

Around the same time he learned that I was in regular touch with one of his former colleagues and sent a note, by courier, saying, 'I would prefer that you did not go on seeing Harry Chapman Pincher.' The retired officer happened to know that I was seeing Oldfield, so he simply returned the note with the inscription, 'Maurice, fuck off!'

After his posting to Ulster, Oldfield, who was frequently in London, retained his bachelor flat in Marsham Court, Westminster; he required protection there because he was a prime target for the IRA, which had previously attempted to assassinate him in 1975 with a bomb in a hold-all hung on the railings below the flat. Protection officers supplied by Scotland Yard became suspicious of the type of men who visited the flat – waiters and young men who seemed to have no connection with the intelligence world. Some of them were traced and proved to be homosexuals of the type known as 'rough trade'. Oldfield frequently complained that he was never left alone and demanded occasions when he could be entirely free.

A close watch was kept and, concluding that Oldfield might be a security risk, a report was submitted to the Head of Special Branch which, in turn, alerted Sir David McNee, the Metropolitan Police Commissioner. McNee was so perturbed that he went to see the Home Secretary, William Whitelaw (now Lord). Sir Robert Armstrong, the Cabinet Secretary, was informed and he told the Prime Minister, who was shocked and distressed. MI5 was also alerted and took some investigative action. Oldfield was then recalled from Ulster to London, ill health being the excuse for his absence, and he was formally interviewed by MI5. His positive vetting clearance was temporarily withdrawn, meaning that he was no longer allowed access to top secret information, a dreadful predicament for a man who had been the trusted head of a most secret service.

Confronted by the evidence, Oldfield confessed his homosexuality and admitted that he had consistently lied through several positive vettings. When asked routinely, and probably apologetically, by some official, 'Are you a homosexual? Have you ever indulged in homosexual practices?' he had denied the suggestions and signed the positive vetting (PV) form.

The fact that he had faked his positive vetting made him a security risk because he was automatically a target for blackmail, and not necessarily by the KGB. He had become Chief of the Secret Intelligence Service by deception and though most people who knew him, including myself, are confident that he would have been immune to blackmail, nobody can be certain how anyone else will react when threatened with such scandalous exposure.

Investigation of Oldfield's homosexual contacts and other inquiries produced no evidence that Oldfield had been compromised in any way. There was no suggestion that Soviet counter-intelligence was aware of his habits. The standing Security Commission, which was already engaged in a rigorous review of security following publication of my book *Their Trade is Treachery*, was asked by the Prime Minister to investigate the Oldfield case; it adduced further evidence, from several extremely sensitive counter-intelligence operations, that he had not been suborned.

Nevertheless there is no escaping the fact that for many years the master of deception had been deceiving his political masters and that, had his deviant behaviour been discovered while he was Chief of MI6, he would have been required to resign. By faking his PV form he kept others out of the post, which was something of a dirty trick on his senior colleagues. It also meant that Mrs Thatcher had been responsible, unwittingly, for sending a security risk to Ulster in an extremely sensitive position. If the Scotland Yard report had leaked while Oldfield was in post, the IRA and Sinn Fein would have made the most of it.

Anglo-American relations had also been prejudiced because Oldfield had served in Washington as liaison officer with the CIA, with the remit of repairing the damage caused there by the Maclean-Burgess-Philby affair. The CIA chiefs were profoundly disturbed by the Oldfield disclosure, because it was regarded as yet another example of the sloppiness of British security. There also happened to be a special difficulty with the Americans at the time because of another problem which remains secret.

As Oldfield was within three months of completing his task in Ulster it was decided that he should be allowed to return if he wished. He was then seen personally by the Attorney General, then Sir Michael Havers (now Lord). Havers asked him to give an undertaking that he would not misbehave himself and, though the requirement was presented in precise man-to-man terms, Oldfield gave his promise without reserve. During the rest of his brief time in the post he may have been under some degree of MI5 surveillance – an extraordinary situation for the security supremo. Surveillance was probably in Oldfield's interests, because a former Scotland Yard official serving in Ulster during Oldfield's last three months there noticed that he was drinking so heavily that he and others thought that he was beyond doing the job.

Oldfield died in March 1981, but his duplicity was not publicly revealed until 1987. I had first heard of Oldfield's homosexuality problem from Fleet Street sources in 1982, after his death. I immediately reported all I knew to Sir Arthur Franks, a friend of Oldfield's who had succeeded him as MI6 Chief and had recently retired. I could not confirm the information and took no further interest until 1985 when I learned the details from senior authorities who had no axe to grind on MI5's behalf.

Two years later I was engaged in writing *Traitors*, a book about the motivations for treachery, and when dealing with the subject of homosexuality I felt that it would be professionally dishonest to suppress the Oldfield case just because he had been a friend. If I did, I could be accused of covering up for friends while exposing others. Further, I knew that my prime sources, who considered that Oldfield had achieved his position by fraud, were speaking openly about it to others. My disclosure was regarded by some as a dirty trick against Oldfield, his relatives and the reputation of MI6. It is a tenable point of view, but the only way for an investigative writer to resolve the issue is to ask himself two questions. The first is: If I was writing a biography of the man, would it be honest to suppress information which deals with the most crucial event in his life? The second is: Is the appointment of a practising homosexual to the highest secret service position, and then to further secret work, of public concern? The answers to both seem obvious to me. It was a further example of weakness in choosing senior officers for the secret services and of what a man who reaches the top can get away with. Once there he becomes above suspicion, and if he is suspected it is stifled. I know of no investigative writer who would have suppressed the information.

Oldfield's friends disbelieved my statements and some of them publicly denied them. However, the Prime Minister shot them down by confirming in Parliament that, in March 1980, Oldfield had admitted that from time to time he had engaged in homosexual activities, and that as a result his positive vetting had been withdrawn because his behaviour had made him a security risk. She added that a lengthy and thorough investigation had produced no evidence to suggest that he had ever compromised security.

Various people were interviewed about the Prime Minister's statement. One of them, Dr David Owen, whose appearance on television confirmed the association between the Foreign

Office and MI6, looked and sounded particularly shattered by the news. He called it a devastating blow to the credibility of the security services and said, 'I am dismayed and dejected that Maurice Oldfield could have lied about his private life and put himself at risk in a way that he would never have tolerated in others'. Soon afterwards I was able to ask him why he had been affected so strongly. His explanation will shatter Oldfield's friends who have not yet heard of it and, perhaps those other supporters who felt that his deception should have remained suppressed.

When Owen was Foreign Secretary, between 1977 and 1979, he was approached by one of the Foreign Office security chiefs who told him that two men in sensitive positions had been found to be practising homosexuals. They were both effective in their jobs and did not seem to pose any threat, but they had concealed their personal problem when questioned while they were being positively vetted. The security man was in favour of taking a liberal view and leaving them in the jobs if the Foreign Secretary agreed. Owen concurred in principle but said he would need to take advice from Sir Maurice Oldfield, whom he saw frequently, liked and admired. Oldfield's advice, which was followed, was that the men definitely did pose a security risk and could not be allowed to remain. Understandably, when Owen learned that Oldfield had been in exactly the same position he was disgusted by the hypocrisy.

It is now known that at least one homosexual MI6 officer, who must have also faked his positive vetting form, continued to serve in sensitive positions until his retirement. Homosexuals can usually recognize each other, and it may be that Oldfield could take no action against him for fear that the man was aware of his Chief's position.

Astonished and dismayed by Mrs Thatcher's confirmation of the circumstances, Oldfield's close friends began to claim that he had been the victim of a dirty trick by MI5, which allegedly was conducting a black propaganda campaign against him. They were led by George Young, a former Deputy Chief of MI6 who had retired in 1961, and Anthony Cavendish, who had served in MI6 for only five years as a young man. Cavendish, who was known in MI6 as Anthony Castle, has frequently been put forward as an authority on that service and almost a spokesman for it. In fact he was dismissed, following adverse reports, in 1953, though he remained in close contact with Oldfield. He changed his name to Cavendish by deed poll in the following year.

Cavendish has said that an MI5 source, who had been identified, had deliberately leaked the information to me as part of an MI5 plot to blacken the reputation of MI6 and Oldfield in particular. That was rubbish. I received the information from Scotland Yard and had it confirmed by a Government Minister, neither of whom had any reason or inclination to promote MI5's interests. Cavendish claims that Oldfield confided in him about his early homosexuality and also believed that MI5 was plotting to make it public. That may well have been Oldfield's story when doing his best with his friends to explain away the withdrawal of his positive vetting clearance, but there was no truth in it.

In a review of Peter Wright's book *Spycatcher* in 1987, Cavendish claimed that the appearance of my book *Traitors* in the same year was timed to 'take the heat of the Wright case', the implication being that my disclosure about Oldfield's homosexuality was leaked to me on behalf of MI5 by Lord Rothschild. Total fantasy! The timing of the publication of *Traitors* was entirely a matter for the publishers, who had arranged its serialization with a newspaper. Rothschild had been a friend of Oldfield, and I felt that he disapproved of my action in exposing the case when I eventually discussed it with him for the first time in 1988. While rivalry between the two services still exists and probably always will, the suggestion that MI5 would ever try to sabotage MI6's work in a terrorist situation is ridiculous. Understandably MI5, which regarded Ulster as its responsibility, could not have relished the intrusion of a former chief of MI6 as security supremo, but his main brief was to co-ordinate the work of the Army and RUC, as he told me himself. It had certainly not been Mrs Thatcher's intention to upset MI5 in any way, because she had first offered the post to a former ambassador who declined it.

Oldfield's apologists also alleged that the claims about his homosexuality originated in Northern Ireland and that, under that pressure, he volunteered to the security authorities that he had lied on his positive vetting form about his long-past homosexual behaviour. As Oldfield was a lifelong bachelor, rumours may well have circulated in Northern Ireland, but he volunteered nothing until his confrontation with the security authorities. That event was not the result of any smear campaign by MI5 or the IRA but resulted only from the report submitted to the Home Secretary, in line of duty, by the Metropolitan Police Commissioner, Sir David McNee, and based on Oldfield's behaviour in 1979 and 1980.

It is possible that Oldfield told Cavendish and others that he had taken the initiative and voluntarily confessed that he had been homosexual but only when young. In that case it would have been another deception operation on his friends, fearing, as he probably did, that his disgrace might be revealed one day.

Oldfield may well have been subjected to a smear campaign originated by the IRA, which had made two previous attempts to assassinate him. A newspaper story that Oldfield had propositioned a man in the lavatory of a pub in Ulster while drunk had no foundation in fact and may have been an IRA plant. A suggestion that it was a smear by MI5 makes no sense, because Oldfield's duplicity had already been made public and confirmed by the Prime Minister.

It has even been suggested that the alleged MI5 smear campaign made him ill and eventually killed him. In fact he died of cancer of the stomach, which had been misdiagnosed. If there was a stress factor, the stress of his secret experience with the security authorities and Ministers who had admired and trusted him would have been more traumatic than the stress of any smear campaign in Ulster.

As with Peter Wright, the Oldfield revelations provided insight into the type of people who come to inhabit the secrets world. Being required to practise deception in their professional work seems to make it easier for them to deceive in other respects.

Although Oldfield's work demanded secrecy, he enjoyed publicity. When he was first appointed Chief of MI6 in 1973 Anthony Cavendish telephoned me at the *Daily Express* to suggest a way of publicizing the fact without revealing his name, which was then covered by a D-Notice – an arrangement under which the media agree to withhold certain sensitive information. I realized at the time that this could eventually lead to the exposure of his name and that photographs would then be published, as duly occurred. It was most unlikely that

Cavendish would have made his suggestion without Oldfield's agreement or, more likely, his initiative. Yet when his identity was revealed Oldfield went through the motions of deploring it, and later claimed that it probably contributed to the IRA attempt on his life in 1975.

Evidence of other odd behaviour accrued after the ensuing publicity about him. It transpired that, during his service as Ulster supremo, when he was often in England, he had a secret hideaway in a council house in Slough. It belonged to a waiter who lived there with his wife and, according to her, was not a homosexual. Oldfield had met him when he had worked in a London restaurant and they did the football pools together. He was in the habit of going to the council house at weekends, without any security guard, to savour some home cooking and to sleep on a folding bed.

It is difficult to understand why such a highly intelligent and cultured man, who had so much to lose, could behave so irresponsibly and indiscreetly, but many others have done so. With a man as lonely as Oldfield his homosexuality was always a dangerous compulsion, but it was probably bouts of heavy drinking which drove him to take the risks which were eventually observed. In all areas of the sexual world, alcohol is the enemy of judgement.

When Oldfield was in hospital in London I went to see him, and it has been maliciously reported that I insinuated myself in order to question him on his death bed. The fact is that I was telephoned at Sir Maurice's request by a mutual friend, Nicholas Elliott, a former MI6 officer, who said that Sir Maurice would like to see me. He looked much better than I expected, and wanted to talk. The only reason I left him after about twenty minutes was that a CIA man had arrived, one of a continuous stream of visitors that day.

Elliott, who at that stage knew nothing about Oldfield's security predicament, had seen the Prime Minister on another matter and mentioned that Oldfield was dying. Upset, and wishing to show her forgiveness, she visited him next morning. She had behaved similarly some years previously when I had served as a messenger informing her that Lord Avon, the former Sir Anthony Eden, who had never met her, wished to do so without much delay because he, too, was dying from cancer. She visited him at his country house the following day.

A campaign of disinformation by her opponents has saddled Mrs Thatcher with an uncaring image. Actions should speak louder than images, but such is the impact of sustained disinformation that they frequently do not.

5

Own Goals

The media are usually thought of as the printed and spoken word as stated by reporters and their sources in newspapers, magazines, books, radio and television, but there is another major medium for the transference of information to the general public. Parliament has long been a medium in its own right through *Hansard* and now, through the radio and television relaying of its proceedings, is a more direct source of public knowledge. Further, it is no exception in that it is commonly abused to provide disinformation.

The chief offenders are politicians of the reigning opposition, whichever party it might be, who almost as a matter of accepted procedure make statements and air issues which are patently false in the hope of scoring a political point. This does not count as lying to the House but, as subsequent chapters will show, it is an effective means of lying to the public.

It is standard practice in the British Parliament that 'shadow' Ministers of Opposition parties avoid being privately briefed by the Government on the truth of important issues. The true facts, if provided officially, would inhibit their ability to harass their adversaries with mis-statements, usually presented in the form of parliamentary questions which they often know to be nonsensical. Some Opposition MPs become adept at priming the media, especially on radio and television, with wild allegations calling for public inquiries on all manner of issues. When challenged, they usually claim that all they want is to 'widen the debate', and though their efforts are rarely heard of again they achieve substantial publicity, working on the principle that some mud is bound to stick.

The use of such gambits, which are perhaps too commonplace to qualify as dirty tricks, is always intensified when a political party has been in opposition for many years and is showing signs of being desperate for office. It can then degenerate into paranoia, so that some of the worst offenders come to believe that the Government is incapable of telling them the truth – or, at least, they strive hard to give the electorate that impression.

This is not to say that politicians in office are not economical with the truth, sometimes bending it when it suits, and on several important issues the response of the Thatcher administration to such a charge has failed to satisfy its critics. Among the most memorable of these was the sinking of the Argentine cruiser *General Belgrano* during the Falklands War in circumstances which led the Government to cover up certain aspects, giving the impression that there was something heinous to hide.

The cruiser was torpedoed on Sunday, 2 May 1982 by the British atomic-powered submarine *Conqueror*, which was one of several, each guarding a different sector of the Exclusion Zone. The date was politically significant because the Government, with US assistance, was still involved in trying to set up negotiations to induce the Argentinians to withdraw from the Falklands and, on that very day, President Belaunde of Peru tabled a peace plan. The sinking of the cruiser with the loss of 368 Argentinian lives also sank any hope of a negotiated peace.

Initially it was stated that the captain of the *Conqueror*, on seeing the warship in his sights, perceived an immediate threat and sank it without consultation. In fact he reported to his Task Force Commander, Rear-Admiral J. F. Woodward, who then consulted the Navy chiefs by radio. The Government had set up a 200-mile Exclusion Zone around the Falklands and had warned all ships to keep out of it, pointing out that if they entered they did so at their peril. The *Belgrano* was some thirty-five miles outside the zone but Woodward, who was best placed to judge the tactical circumstances, was anxious to seize the opportunity to eliminate a major piece on the nautical chessboard. It was already his duty to attack enemy warships. What he needed was a change in the laid-down Rules of Engagement so that the *Belgrano* could be attacked outside the Exclusion Zone.

From the start of the whole operation the Navy chiefs had seen the *Belgrano* as a formidable threat, especially as they suspected that it might have been armed with French Exocet missiles which were eventually to prove highly effective. What they feared was a joint attack by the cruiser and Argentina's single aircraft carrier, *The Twenty-fifth of May*, which, according to intelligence reports, was at sea, preparing for action. Alternatively, the cruiser and the carrier, with destroyer escorts, could form two separate groups which might severely test the British Task Force's limited strength. The two main British troop carriers, the liners *Canberra* and *QE2*, were highly vulnerable and the loss of either would cripple the enterprise. The loss of either of the two aircraft carriers, *Hermes* or *Invincible*, would undoubtedly spell the end of the expedition, which would be forced to return in defeat and ignominy.

Without the support of the *Belgrano* the Argentinians would be unlikely ever to risk their carrier in action. So sinking the cruiser would not only eliminate that major warship but also effectively keep the carrier in port for the rest of the war. There is, therefore, no doubt whatever that the prime purpose of sinking the cruiser was military. No Task Force commander carrying such responsibility and in his right mind could have resisted such an opportunity. When the Task Force had set sail from Britain, the Sea Lords had given it no more than a 60 per cent chance of success. Getting rid of the *Belgrano* substantially increased its potential for survival.

On receiving Woodward's request the Navy chiefs immediately informed those members of the War Cabinet who were at Chequers – the Prime Minister; her deputy, William Whitelaw; the Defence Secretary, John Nott; and Cecil Parkinson the Paymaster General. Also present were the First Sea Lord, Admiral Sir Henry Leach, and the Chief of the Defence Staff, Admiral of the Fleet Sir Terence Lewin. The Foreign Secretary, Francis Pym, the missing member of the War Cabinet, was abroad.

When the message arrived the *Belgrano*, escorted by two destroyers, was outside the Exclusion Zone and moving away from it. The admirals pointed out that no warship in such a position would maintain the same course for more than a few minutes, so as to reduce the danger of submarine attack. So the cruiser could quickly turn about or could be on its way to rendezvous with the carrier, which was at sea with its destroyer escort. They therefore pressed hard for a decision to sink the *Belgrano* and so remove the carrier threat at the same time. The loss of the much-prized warship would also deal a savage blow to Argentinian morale while raising morale among the British forces.

It was obvious that if the *Belgrano* was spared and eventually played a part in defeating the expedition they would all stand accused of putting thousands of British lives at risk and failing in their duty. A defeat would also spell the end of the Thatcher Government. It seems that the War Cabinet was aware of the Peruvian President's peace proposal, but that was just another idea which might come to nothing, while the cruiser was a stark fact which had to be faced and immediately.

With general agreement the Prime Minister took the decision for the attack on the warship. The *Conqueror* fired two torpedoes and sank it. The destroyers were not attacked and, after moving away rather shamefully, were able to return and pick up survivors. Both Admiral Lewin and Admiral Leach have assured me that the *Belgrano* was sunk only because the opportunity offered itself and to have missed it could have put the entire operation at risk. As they had forecast, the Argentine carrier had immediately returned to harbour on hearing of the loss of the cruiser and took no part in the war.

All this could have been made clear to Parliament immediately after the event. Instead, details of the decision were covered up, continually laying Mrs Thatcher open to the charge that the sinking of the *Belgrano* had been a cynical dirty trick to kill the peace initiative because she was determined to have a military victory that would ensure her political survival. Some Labour MPs such as Tam Dalyell accused her of foisting a gross deception on Parliament, their anger being intensified when the *Conqueror* returned proudly flying the skull and crossbones to celebrate its kill.

While the war continued, any deceptions about the *Belgrano* operation were justifiable on operational grounds and would have been standard practice. The politicians were also concerned about world opinion, especially in the United Nations. The first deception was a statement to Parliament by the Defence Secretary, John Nott, who said that the cruiser had been closing in on the Task Force when, in fact, it had been moving in the opposite direction. It is possible that when the War Cabinet took its decision it knew only that the vessel was outside the Exclusion Zone and not that it was moving away, but Mrs Thatcher repeated the statement publicly a year later. So it may have been the kind of disinformation which has always been regarded as acceptable in hot war.

Why were the deceptions continued after the war had been won? As a rule, military deceptions are never formally admitted until official history comes to be written. In the case of the *Belgrano* there was an additional factor which borders on the sacred – intelligence sources were at risk and, because of their nature, they had to be protected.

The planners of the Falklands Expedition were astonished to find that MI6 was deficient in active agents in Argentina – one of the reasons why the Argentinians had been able to spring such a surprise when invading the islands, and why the British admirals did not know whether the *Belgrano* was carrying Exocet missiles or not. What they wanted was agents who could observe what was going on in the Argentinian ports but there were none, apparently as a result of previous financial savings in MI6. At one stage Cecil Parkinson was put in charge of psychological warfare operations for the expedition, but could do nothing because agents to promote the necessary disinformation on the mainland were simply not available.

American Defence Intelligence and the CIA had monitored the movements of Argentine warships in their own interests from the moment that the Falklands had been invaded. British Intelligence had received this information under the existing exchange agreements. Then, on 1 May, the USA Defence Secretary, Caspar Weinberger, with President Reagan's agreement, had ordered the Pentagon to give the British full and immediate military intelligence support. As he has put on record, the USA extended its satellite intelligence survey to include the Falklands and the resulting intelligence was shared, giving the Task Force further advance knowledge of Argentinian naval movements.

The Americans even provided radio receivers to permit communications with intelligence sources. Who and where these sources were has never been revealed, but they could have been Americans or South Americans working for the CIA. Some British military personnel were also landed secretly on the South American mainland by helicopter and by boat.

Mrs Thatcher, whose general attitude to intelligence is that nothing should ever be said about sources, especially human sources on the ground, was in a particularly sensitive position. Unlike any previous Prime Minister since Churchill, she had insisted on being shown the 'raw' intelligence reports instead of being content with summaries and 'considered views'. It has always been a golden rule of the intelligence world that it is extremely dangerous for anyone with such secret knowledge to be subjected to public questioning, and she was in that situation.

She had already shown herself to be prepared to be a vehicle for misleading information in the interests of the security services. In 1981 she had read an MI5 brief in Parliament about the Hollis case, which was so misleading that it disgusted those officers who knew the truth. There were precedents for her action. Harold Macmillan had consciously misled Parliament over the Burgess, Maclean and Philby affairs, while Eden had been miserly economical with the truth concerning the incident in which Commander Crabb had been drowned in an MI6 intelligence operation. In her handling of the Belgrano affair Mrs Thatcher stuck to tradition, preferring to risk personal censure than to prejudice sources of any kind or any other aspect of secret intelligence operations.

The issue might have died away, as other sticks to beat the Government offered themselves to the Opposition, but in 1984 Clive Ponting, a senior civil servant in the Defence Ministry, broke ranks. Surreptitiously and anonymously, he provided Labour MPs with official documents revealing some details of the Belgrano sinking and the efforts made to misinform Parliament about it. Eventually he was identified as the source and was prosecuted under the Official Secrets Act. He pleaded public duty and to the surprise of many people was acquitted. His case gave Labour politicians and their supporters ammunition for their campaign to brand the Prime Minister not only as ruthless but dishonest.

The attitude of some of the public and some parliamentarians who regarded the sinking of the Belgrano as a dirty trick was conditioned by the fact that the war was eight thousand miles away. Had they been at personal risk they would have taken a less charitable view of the Argentinian sailors. I never met anyone in World War II who did not cheer when a German warship was sunk, and the greater the casualties the better. For the sake of an opportunity to attack Mrs Thatcher, some MPs took a view which suggested that they would rather have the lives of British sailors risked than have the enemy's cruiser sunk when opportunity arose.

Like the next major 'scandal' which followed it, the Westland Affair, the *Belgrano* Affair had been a relatively minor issue which could have been quickly resolved to most people's satisfaction by the full truth but was inflated by the propensity of all governments to disinform when they consider it necessary 'in the national interest'. In retrospect it looks like a deliberate own goal rather than a professional foul, and I am told that Mrs Thatcher has no regrets about the handling of it.

Although basically of little consequence, the Westland Affair came near to enforcing the Prime Minister's resignation, which may have been prevented only because her chief opponent, Neil Kinnock, failed to use the weapon which had been put into his hands. In the saga, which dragged on for months, deception, disinformation, threats, leaks and even 'moles', including one well known to me, were involved in the action. Ministers are expected to 'fight their corners', but this was a political punch-up as one dirty trick after another was deployed by Ministers determined to get their way over their own colleagues.

It began in the middle of 1985 with a visit from Admiral Sir John Treacher, an executive of the Westland helicopter company based in Yeovil, to the offices of British Aerospace in London. Treacher explained that the company was in serious financial trouble, and asked British Aerospace directors, led by a former naval colleague, Admiral Sir Ray Lygo, to take a 25 per cent stake in it. Knowing that Westland shareholders had lost nearly £100 million in the year ending September 1985, they declined.

The company, which provided helicopters for the forces, then approached Michael Heseltine, the Secretary of State for Defence, for assistance. His solution was a European consortium, which would pump money into Westland by purchasing 25 per cent of its shares. At the personal request of Heseltine to Sir Ray Lygo, British Aerospace agreed to join the consortium in return for concessions on other matters. The British General Electric Company, the French firm Aerospatiale, MBB of West Germany and the Italian Augusta company also agreed to participate with the consortium, which would put £73 million into Westland.

Meanwhile Sir John Cuckney, a businessman of wide experience who had been brought into Westland as chairman, had sought a full takeover by British Aerospace. When all he got there was tea and sympathy he came to prefer a deal with the big American helicopter manufacturer, Sikorsky, then part of a company called United Technologies, which was linked with the Italian Fiat company. (Later, when the Westland Affair was at its height, Treacher, an old shooting friend, told me, with some amusement, that Cuckney had been officially informed that he would figure in Peter Wright's *Spycatcher* as the man who had first indoctrinated him into the dirty tricks business in MI5).

The American solution was also much preferred by the Department of Trade and Industry, which had an economic responsibility for the survival of firms in financial difficulty. Leon Brittan, who had been demoted from Home Secretary in somewhat mysterious circumstances, was in charge of the Department and took up the cudgels on Westland's behalf in the belief that its board probably knew best and should be free to choose on behalf of its shareholders. This inevitably meant a personal collision course with Heseltine.

The Prime Minister's views in the early stages of the affair seem to be in doubt. Some witnesses say that she began by favouring the European solution but suddenly switched to supporting the American deal. The possibility that this was the result of pressure or a request from someone in Washington was rumoured, but there was no evidence for it. The odds are that, being opposed to government intervention in such cases, she also believed that the Westland board should be free to make the choice it preferred.

She had chaired several meetings involving various Ministers to try to resolve the issue but Heseltine, the Minister most responsible, an interventionist, a pro-European and an ambitious politician, was determined to have his case heard and discussed by the full Cabinet. He believed that he was being consistently thwarted in this by the Prime Minister and those acting on her behalf to an extent which was unconstitutional. He therefore ensured that the debate should become public through media briefings by Defence Ministry officials, and secured a considerable measure of support. Nevertheless, he failed to secure a discussion in the full Cabinet of what was clearly a legitimate and important issue.

The matter appeared to be settled when Brittan told the Commons that Westland was free to do what it wished but, shortly before Christmas 1985, Heseltine seemed to be scenting victory even though he knew that his continuing battle was politically risky, especially with the Prime Minister against him. Although careful not to say much about her in public, he was expressing his general frustration by telling friends and business acquaintances that 'it was all very difficult' and 'very strange'. There were those who thought that he was flexing his muscles provocatively, and might have more than Westland in mind.

On Boxing Day, when the newspapers were hungry for copy, the Defence Ministry leaked a warning that the American deal would jeopardize thousands of jobs in the British avionics – air electronics – industry, the suggestion being that Sikorsky would want only American avionics in any aircraft it built in Britain. Rumours were also put about that the American deal would convert Westland into just a 'metal-bashing' operation, with all the major parts for helicopters being manufactured in the United States and shipped to Yeovil for assembly. It was known that Sikorsky had a big contract to supply its Black Hawk helicopters to Saudi Arabia. It was suggested that Congress might veto the deal because of the Israeli implications, in which case the helicopters could be assembled by Westland and sold on by them. Sikorsky was also described as being 'desperate' to buy itself into the European market. It was alleged that European Governments would find it difficult to order from Westland if it became an American company. The leaks also promoted a Libyan scare, stressing that a Libyan bank held 9 per cent of Fiat, so that if the American deal went through Gaddafi would have some influence.

The Department of Trade and Industry was equally industrious in feeding the media and exerting influence in other ways on behalf of the American deal. The Downing Street support for that solution was put across through the daily briefings of the lobby correspondents.

Cuckney and the rest of the Westland board were infuriated by Heseltine's continuing interference but, like any company largely dependent on defence contracts, they were worried that the Defence Ministry might take revenge by not ordering its products if it did not accept the European solution. Over the years I have repeatedly heard 'We can't afford to offend the Ministry' as the excuse for some commercial action which seemed cowardly. The Prime Minister did something to relieve their fears by promising Cuckney, in writing, that the Government would do all it could to fight any discrimination against the company's products.

So, though much preferring the American deal and knowing that their right to make the choice was backed by the Prime Minister, the Westland directors agreed to pass on the European consortium offer to its shareholders, who had received information only about the Sikorsky (United Technologies)-Fiat deal. The board was, in fact, threatened with possible legal action if it did not do so. That move helped to give the European consortium a further lease of life.

Meanwhile Lygo, the chief executive of British Aerospace, who had originally been opposed to any purchase of Westland shares, was invited, alone, to the Department of Trade and Industry on a pretext. Not realizing that he was going to meet Brittan, he found himself taken to the Secretary of State's room. Brittan had several of his senior staff with him and they harangued Lygo about the folly of the European deal. Lygo gave no ground, and claims that on the way out he was told by Brittan, 'You must withdraw.' Understandably, he took this as meaning that British Aerospace must withdraw from the consortium. When Heseltine heard this he was understandably angry.

As a further kiss-of-life to his European solution, Heseltine had been negotiating by letter with the consortium's bankers, Lloyds Merchant Bank. One of the letters which he had written underlined and exaggerated the loss of European orders which Westland faced if it went ahead with the American option. He published it, obviously knowing that it would infuriate the Prime Minister, which it did.

If she had already been pondering the possibility that Heseltine might have to leave the Government, as seems likely, this new challenge could only have hardened it. She responded by getting Brittan to seek the view of the Solicitor General, Sir Patrick Mayhew, about the validity of the contents of the letter.

Mayhew then wrote to Brittan, giving his official legal view that Heseltine had overstated the danger and that he should be required to correct the damaging inaccuracies in Westland's interests.

Communications from law officers are always regarded as highly confidential as regards the general public, and the normal process would have been for a copy of Mayhew's letter to be sent privately to Heseltine to give him the chance to put things right. A copy was sent, but before Heseltine could act, had he been inclined to do so, Brittan had instructed his chief information officer, Colette Bowe, to seek the agreement of the press department at Number 10 Downing Street for Mayhew's letter to be leaked to the media. Believing that agreement had been obtained, Miss Bowe issued selected extracts of the letter that were highly critical of Heseltine to the Press Association, which wired them out to all the media.

It was immediately obvious that Heseltine, Brittan and the Prime Minister were in politically mortal combat, because it was reasonably assumed that Mrs Thatcher must have agreed to the leak. Some of the newspapers supporting her pulled no punches in branding Heseltine as a liar. The Solicitor General was angry that his letter to another Minister had been leaked without his permission. This strengthened the belief that there was open warfare in the Government, and the Labour Opposition leaped joyously into the fray.

Heseltine did not resign at that stage; but three days later, during a Cabinet meeting, the Prime Minister told him that in future he would have to clear any statements he made about Westland with the Cabinet Office, meaning her representative. This was too much for Heseltine, who walked out of the Cabinet Room and out of the Government.

A brief complication had arisen through the intervention of my old friend Alan Bristow, the ebullient founder of Bristow Helicopters, who bought a large number of Westland shares in his own right in the hope of taking it over. At one stage it looked as though he might succeed, but he was defeated by what he regards as a commercial dirty trick as the American deal was eventually clinched.

In a minor side skirmish, Brittan denied having told Sir Ray Lygo that he 'must withdraw' from the European consortium. Lygo insisted that he had done so, but was willing to compromise by admitting that Brittan had not said 'British Aerospace must withdraw' – only that he, Lygo, must withdraw, which did not make much sense but got Brittan off the hook. I have known Lygo well as an honest man for twenty years, and he had no reason to lie. The Downing Street press machine told reporters that Lygo had 'retracted' when he had done no such thing.

Under pressure from Tory backbenchers Brittan accepted ministerial responsibility for the action of his officials and also resigned, apparently against Mrs Thatcher's wishes. Mrs Thatcher did not feel she needed to resign, because she claimed she had not known in advance about the intention to leak the information. The Labour Opposition clearly did not believe her. A full inquiry into the exact circumstances of the leak was demanded by the media as well as Labour. Everyone involved seemed to have a different interpretation. Brittan said that while he wanted the letter to 'go into the public domain' as quickly as possible, it was Number 10 which had taken the final decision that it should. The chief information officer at Number 10, Bernard Ingham, who had been telephoned by Miss Bowe, insisted that he had not been prepared to leak the letter but had not disapproved of Miss Bowe doing so.

The bull question was whether or not Mrs Thatcher had been personally approached by Ingham, or anyone else, about the proposal to leak Mayhew's letter. Clearly, if she had been party to such an unorthodox action against one of her Cabinet colleagues she was in serious trouble. She repeatedly denied having been involved, though she admitted having been in favour of getting the correction of Heseltine's inaccuracies 'into the public domain' as soon as possible. Westland had been due to hold a press conference on the afternoon of the day of the leak, and it was argued that the inaccuracies had to be corrected in time for that.

Ingham agreed that Mrs Thatcher had not been informed, which was credible because some civil servants come to believe that they know their political chief's mind so well that they can safely act on their behalf, without bothering them with detail. Nevertheless, many people found it hard to credit that she had not been consulted about it, and the Labour Opposition chose to believe that she had been.

Sir Robert Armstrong, the Cabinet Secretary, staged an inquiry into the origins of the leak and came up with the solution that there had been a 'difference of understanding' between the two press departments. This too, though derided by Labour, was not impossible. I had several such experiences during my years in Fleet Street. One of them resulted in the loss of naval contracts with Spain worth many millions of pounds, entirely owing to an incredible error by an information officer in the Defence Ministry.

Later, Sir Robert appeared before a Parliamentary Committee investigating the Westland Affair to represent the Number 10 Downing Street staff. The Committee wanted to interview the press officials involved, especially as there should have been some hard evidence in the log-books which all press officers are required to keep. Instead, Armstrong insisted on interviewing the officials and gave the Committee his summary of what had occurred. He claimed that there had been a genuine mis-understanding between officials at the two departments, and that no blame attached either to the Prime Minister or to her Press Secretary, Bernard Ingham. The Tory majority on the Committee cleared Mrs Thatcher, while Labour accused Sir Robert of being responsible for a cover-up. It was a superb performance by Armstrong and good practice for his future appearance in the Australian courts where he would not be so successful – partly, perhaps, because his Westland experience had made him over-confident of his ability to ride cross-examination.

When Mrs Thatcher set off for the emergency debate on the affair called by Labour on 27 January 1986 she knew that there was a possibility that she might have to resign. Labour was loaded with ammunition, and this was their undoing. All Kinnock had to do was ask one question: 'Exactly when did you know about the plan to leak the Mayhew letter?' Instead, he rambled off into a thicket of words in which the main issue was lost. Mrs Thatcher was able to say that she knew about the leak 'some hours after it occurred'.

There are many, some of them who were very close to the action, who will always believe that she did know and came within an ace of being exposed and censured for misleading Parliament. Seasoned Whitehall watchers see the crucial clue as the fact that Bernard Ingham was not fired. They believe that if had taken the action on such a potentially explosive matter without consulting the Prime Minister, whom he saw several times a day, his dismissal would have been automatic.

The whole affair is a classic example of the difficulty of finding out where the truth really lies in Whitehall, where there is so much secrecy, disinformation and inter-departmental intrigue. Under standing convention, Labour leaders will not be permitted to examine any Cabinet Office documents concerning the Westland Affair if they achieve office. If the truth is revealed in AD 2016, when any relevant papers may become available for public scrutiny, it will be academic. The Thirty-years Rule was devised to prevent embarrassment to the individuals involved in the issues concerned, and one does not have to be conspiratorial to suspect that when the politicians formulated it they had themselves largely in mind.

Without question, Mrs Thatcher is an exceptionally clever and agile politician, so why did she become entangled in such a dangerous web? Like all effective Prime Ministers she has to be a good butcher, and there are more ways of getting rid of unwanted Cabinet Ministers than by long knives. So a final question presents itself: Was the leak a deliberately planned means of inducing Heseltine to resign of his own accord? Or, in professional intelligence terms, was it a 'dangle' which Heseltine took – a tempting opportunity deliberately offered for an ulterior motive? The facts all fit a positive answer, and they make little sense any other way. For any dangle to succeed, the nature of the quarry needs careful study. In Heseltine's case Mrs Thatcher's cavalier order, in front of all his Cabinet colleagues, that he must clear all future Westland statements with her staff, seemed calculated to make him resign.

Further, if it was a dangle, it seems possible that, having seen how effective it was, she repeated it to rid herself of Nigel Lawson, the Chancellor of the Exchequer, when he too became too difficult in 1989. For several months before Lawson went, senior City bankers of my acquaintance who regarded Lawson's recent policies as disastrous believed that the Prime Minister was aware of the urgent need to replace him but was so boxed in by political circumstances that she would be saddled with him until the next General Election. As Heseltine had done before him, Lawson then presented her with his own death warrant. He indicated that unless she repudiated the

influence of her private adviser, Sir Alan Walters, in unequivocal terms, he would have to resign. She had the opportunity to
do so in Parliament, but pointedly declined it. So Lawson
went.

The timing seemed to be significant. He could not have been
dislodged before the Tory Party conference, where a display of
ministerial unanimity was essential. The interval after that was
decent but minimal. Mrs Thatcher had secured a new
Chancellor more suited to her views and freer to make policy
changes. The City showed its satisfaction with a substantial rise
in share values.

There are those who believe that it was Lawson who cleverly
engineered his resignation, which Mrs Thatcher ritually
deplored, in order to return to more remunerative business. An
even more conspiratorial explanation for Heseltine's departure
has been suggested – that he trailed his coat as he did because
he wanted an excuse to fight for the leadership of the Tory
Party outside the Government, which he has done so expertly
that perhaps a majority of people see him as the Prime
Minister's successor whenever she goes. In that event, it would
be Mrs Thatcher who took the dangle.

It also remains possible, of course, that both events were the
result of cock-up rather than conspiracy and that the extraordinary behaviour in Whitehall and Westminster, which the
Westland and Lawson affairs unusually exposed to public
view, is not all that uncommon. For example, months after the
Government ordered a complete embargo on the supply of oil
to South Africa, an astute admiral discovered that the South
African Navy was continuing to draw oil, as it had been entitled to do, from British naval storage tanks in South Africa.
Nobody had told the Defence Ministry department which dealt
with the supplies to end them. Labour was in office at the time
and there was great concern about the reaction of its pro-black
backbenchers should they hear about it. It had been purely an
administrative cock-up but had the facts leaked, which they did
not, it would no doubt have been construed by some as a
conspiracy by the Admiralty to defeat the oil embargo in support of its South African friends.

Alleged deceptions like the Belgrano and Westland affairs
spawned a state of mind in the Labour Opposition leading to
wilder and wilder suspicions, with calls for so many inquiries

that if they had been heeded they would have tied up half of the nation's best minds for months on end. The suspicion surrounding secret research of any kind, for example, has grown so great that when any scientist involved in it has gone missing the media have immediately assumed that he might have defected or been kidnapped or murdered, and MPs have responded with demands for answers. Though the odd defection, such as that of the atomic scientist Bruno Pontecorvo, has occurred in Britain, the cause of a disappearance or sudden death has almost always turned out to be prosaic – financial problems, domestic strife or suicide. Nevertheless, an apparent spate of deaths among defence scientists in recent years has caused some MPs and some newspapers to scent a plot – murder, usually by the KGB, the CIA or, more popularly with Labour MPs, by MI5.

Over the years I have investigated many of these allegedly mysterious deaths and am convinced that none of them was the result of action by any intelligence or security agency. Many of the 'scientists' were not really involved in research but were technicians concerned with computer work that was not highly secret. Nor was the work they were doing related to any particular project, such as 'Star Wars', as has been suggested.

Though the number of cases, some thirty in the last ten years, may seem high, it is no greater than would be expected in an industry employing so many thousands of scientists, technicians and ancillary staff. Some of the methods used by those who committed suicide were peculiar, but no more so than comparable cases in the general population. The lack of any obvious motive is not uncommon among people whose minds are seriously disturbed. Even the theory that secret work subjects people to excessive stress does not stand examination.

Inevitably, when the media begin to investigate the work that was being done by dead or missing persons who were engaged in highly secret projects, the authorities clamp down on the issue of information; this always leads to charges of 'cover-up'. Because several of the people who died had been employed by the huge GEC/Marconi complex, Lord Weinstock asked a former Deputy Assistant Commissioner of Scotland Yard to make an independent investigation of the circumstances. He concluded that there was no evidence of 'deliberate outside influence'.

Perhaps the most extraordinary expression of the 'paranoia' surrounding all secret work concerned the death of Mrs Hilda Murrell, a seventy-eight-year-old rose grower living near Shrewsbury who was also an anti-nuclear peace campaigner. She had been killed by intruders at her home in March 1984.

I received an urgent call from the Labour MP Tam Dalyell to meet him at the Waldorf Hotel in London. Here he told me that he was sure MI5 had murdered Mrs Murrell to silence her because she knew something damaging to the Government. He thought it was information about the sinking of the *Belgrano*, because she had a nephew who had worked in naval intelligence. He suspected that MI5 agents had been searching her home for incriminating documents which could prove that Mrs Thatcher had lied to Parliament when Mrs Murrell returned and had to be silenced. Documents had, allegedly, been taken from her home.

Dalyell had no evidence in support and was hoping that I could supply some. I told him that when surreptitious entries are made by MI5 documents are not stolen but photographed and replaced. Further, such an operation is so professionally staked out that Mrs Murrell could not have caught them by returning unexpectedly. I could not convince him that, in any event, it was inconceivable that MI5 would resort to murder in such circumstances. He argued that, as the stakes – the Prime Minister's survival – were so high, MI5 might have employed an outside hit-man.

An independent policy inquiry carried out by Peter Smith, a former Assistant Chief Constable of Northumbria, rejected the allegations against MI5 or any other government organization, but Dalyell remained suspicious and hopeful of securing proof of Mrs Thatcher's mendacity. His belief, which seemed genuine, was based on little more than gut feeling and a readiness to believe that the Prime Minister and MI5 were capable of the dirtiest tricks.

He is far from being alone in being subject to fantasies concerning the integrity of the Prime Minister and her Government. But such delusions have been by no means peculiar to politicians of the Thatcher era. The long reign of Harold Wilson was conditioned by them.

" The trouble about life is that the people you *would* like kidnapped, never are ! "

6

His Own Executioner

In 1988 when the BBC *Panorama* reporter John Ware was researching the alleged plot by MI5 to destabilize Harold Wilson and the Labour Government, he telephoned me to say, 'Wherever I start it always comes back to you.' He was right, because I had been the originator of it. 'Alone I done it' sounds pretentious and may savour of delusion, but the *documented* facts which are freely available and will be quoted in this book, prove – and I freely confess it – that I, and not Peter Wright or any other MI5 spook, was essentially responsible for Wilson's fears about being overthrown by MI5. It was not a conspiracy, because that has to involve more than one person and, as always, I was a lone operator. Nobody from MI5 was involved in my 'machinations', and the truth is perhaps even more incredible than if the plot had been organized by dissident MI5 spooks, as Peter Wright, Colin Wallace and others have incorrectly claimed.

The MI5 plot story, which has occupied so much media space and parliamentary time, did not begin its rounds until the early summer of 1974, following a specific event which I will describe later, but the susceptibility of Harold Wilson to believe in it was present in his nature when he first took office ten years previously. His behaviour during that decade was so bizarre and entailed so many dirty tricks that it must be given close examination to understand his consequent actions, which were even more extraordinary. I am the last survivor of those involved in almost all the events concerned. I knew the bit-players as well as those taking the lead parts, many of them intimately. Having been responsible for the charge against

MI5, which has had such far-reaching repercussions, the least I can do is to show where the origins of the plot myth really lie.

They derived from the nature of a Prime Minister who from 1964 onwards effectively deluded himself, with assistance from a coterie of credulous aides and from an arch dirty-trickster who was to become known as 'Harold's Rasputin'. While paranoid is an outdated medical term, some of Wilson's closest friends and colleagues, who admire him for other qualities, use it freely to describe his behaviour.

The late George Caunt, who had been part of Wilson's 'kitchen cabinet', the pack of advisers and assistants who surrounded him, gave me a contemporary memorandum stating, among other things:

> Since I first knew Sir Harold Wilson in 1956 he has been foiling and surviving all kinds of plots from all quarters. He seemed to develop a persecution mania and lived in a fantasy world of innumerable plots aimed at destroying him. Of course, some plots did exist but most came from the imaginations of Wilson and his intimates.
>
> After becoming Prime Minister in 1964 he was haunted by plots inside the Cabinet, inside the Civil Service, inside the Parliamentary Labour Party, inside the BBC and inside the Press.

Joe Haines, Wilson's highly efficient Press Secretary and speech writer, both in Government and in Opposition, from 1969 to 1976, attributed the Prime Minister's belief in conspiracies to his chronic insecurity. For reasons which will become apparent, I suspect that there may have been a deep-seated basic cause, of which this sense of insecurity was just a symptom – Wilson may already have been a sick man, smitten with a slow but inexorably progressive illness. This concept explains so much that otherwise seems inexplicable in the nature and behaviour of a man who was endowed with enviable mental capacity.

Like many men with a sense of destiny, Wilson was unduly sensitive to criticism and susceptible to praise. He had therefore courted the press assiduously while in Opposition and, once inside Number 10, he regularly called in journalists for drinks. The 'honeymoon' with the media which most Prime Ministers expect was nevertheless short with many newspapers, and he did not get one from me at all.

I and others of the political right were never prepared to give him any respite from the attacks we had mounted in the hope of keeping him out of office. As a biologist, I became convinced early in life that socialism, while logically attractive on paper, cannot possibly succeed in practice, because it is contrary to human nature. Man is a social, pack species, but packs are not egalitarian. On the contrary, there is always an order of dominance on which the survival of the pack depends. Socialism stifles initiative and competition, suiting only the power-hungry, the envious, the idle and those who believe that 'society' owes them a living for which they need to make no return. For such reasons it has failed wherever it has been practised and that includes the Soviet Union and the various satellite 'socialist paradises'.

My personal fears of the effects of socialism in Britain had been exacerbated by Wilson's promises to the electorate in the defence field, such as the abandonment of the Polaris deterrent, which I did my best to expose as dangerous. With hindsight they were probably exaggerated, because while Wilson had 'talked left' to inherit the mantle of Aneurin Bevan and keep the far Left in line, he behaved 'right' once in office. Instead of scrapping Polaris, for instance, he was to spend more than £1000 million on improving its warhead – but one could only take notice of what he said he intended to do.

It is much easier for a campaigning journalist to operate when the party he opposes is in power and, as a specialist on defence, I was not short of targets to attack, with all the cuts which the Wilson regime was intent on imposing. As the Chiefs of Staff and many senior civil servants deplored the cuts, such as the abandonment of the TSR2 bomber, the attempt to scrap the Concorde and the threat to the Polaris missile deterrent, I was never short of ammunition either. I suppose that I did no more than get into print as quickly as possible whatever happened to come my way, but my cuttings books show a barrage sustained over more than twelve years, even when Labour was in Opposition. In those days the *Daily Express*, for which I functioned as defence correspondent, had a huge circulation and a wide and influential readership spread across all levels of society.

On no occasion did I receive any anti-Labour information directly from MI5 for during those years I had no regular sources there, though I was quite happy for people to think that I had. I did have sources in MI6 who were suspicious about some of Wilson's Ministers and associates and later became deeply involved in the Wilson plot story, but almost all my information came from the Whitehall ministries, especially the Ministry of Defence, and from politicians and industrialists.

Shortly after Labour achieved power, John Drew, a Defence Ministry friend who had been involved in deception operations, decided to retire early and suggested that we might write a novel together. His motive, apart from making some extra money, was to produce a book with the real flavour of Whitehall which, he said, had never been achieved. My idea for a scenario was to have a Defence Minister who was a Soviet agent of influence, and we needed to make a list of what such a man could achieve without making his position obvious. We produced about one-third of the novel in six months, but had to abandon it for libel reasons because the Labour Government was doing everything that we predicted. It has been suggested that this book was a 'propaganda venture', another plot presumably connected with MI5. It was conceived by Drew and me alone over lunch in the hope of making us both some cash.

Labour's review of defence spending quickly confirmed my worst fears. Following a secret deal with the US government, which Wilson made to secure financial assistance, huge orders were being placed for American aircraft to replace British planes, which were scrapped. In a Cabinet Room interview with Wilson he had assured me that he was an 'East of Suez man', but it soon became clear that his Government was hell-bent on pulling out of all the relevant bases. Early in 1966 naval defence cuts were so severe that the First Sea Lord, Sir David Luce, and the Navy Minister, Christopher Mayhew, resigned in protest. The whole Navy Board were so demoralized that they were prepared to resign *en bloc* but Luce talked them out of it.

While I was only one of several journalists attacking Wilson relentlessly, my sustained and virulent assault in the *Daily Express* particularly angered him, as he frequently proclaimed. But what shattered him was the unexpected enmity of the *Daily Mirror*, which had been the Labour Party's solid supporter, with its mass appeal and influence. Cecil King, the chairman of the *Mirror* group, took an immediate dislike to Wilson and began to criticize him. It turned into an obsessional crusade and by June 1966, shortly after Labour's second election victory, King was thinking in terms of an all-out attack. He castigated half the Cabinet, not just Wilson, as holding jobs beyond their capabilities. Whenever he met Cabinet Ministers, as he often did, he tried to undermine their leader.

By mid-1967 King was convinced that under Wilson's leadership the Labour Government was disintegrating in financial collapse. By 1968 the Labour leader was being subjected to an unprecedented 'Wilson must go' campaign of vilification by the media in general, and it was a tribute to his resilience that he was able to bounce back.

Wilson should have ignored the newspaper critics, but constitutionally he could not. He was so obsessional that he would always have the early editions of the morning newspapers the previous night and would often ring up his solitictors after midnight, urging legal action. He managed to issue a few writs, but generally was talked out of doing so by wiser counsel. He was petulant about individual journalists, keeping copious cuttings of their efforts over which the kitchen cabinet had to pore for hours trying to discover the sources of their contents; various Ministers 'plotting against him' were the usual suspects. He would tell colleagues jubilantly, 'I've got them this time!'

In December 1966 George Brown, the deputy leader, put forward the names of young back-benchers who should be given a chance in a coming reshuffle of the Government. Wilson declined, saying that they had all been involved in the 'July plot' which they had not. While Wilson had been in Moscow in July 1966, Brown had tried to bring him down in the hope of replacing him by inducing several senior colleagues to resign with him but failed to muster any support. Wilson even had journalists followed and kept records of whom they had seen. Concerning this obsession with his journalist critics, Barbara Castle wrote in her diaries, 'I sometimes think he's going mildly off his rocker.'

If 20 million people – the combined *Mirror* and *Daily Express* readership alone in those days – are being told, day after day, that you are a menace and a failure when you are working hard and doing your best it must be painful, however thick your political skin. From 1964 to 1974, when he was re-elected,

Wilson was convinced that it was the media – proprietors, editors and writers – who were conspiring to destroy him. He was absolutely right.

Additionally, of course, the Tory Opposition was joining in the fray. On 15 January 1967 Richard Crossman recorded in his diary, 'All the papers this morning had full stories from Conservative headquarters about the decision to destroy the image of Harold Wilson and to crucify him as a promise-breaker and a crook.' Some of his own colleagues had begun to doubt his sincerity. A week earlier Barbara Castle had written in her diary, 'One by one Harold is abandoning his earlier idealisms. Were they only gimmicks?'

Of the many threats to his leadership which were in Wilson's mind at that time the one that would later become his most potent obsession – the spectre of MI5 – had not yet intruded itself. Among the attacking journalists I was probably the only one associated in any way with MI5, and that only vaguely, because MI5 was widely, but wrongly, suspected of being the source of my disclosure of the exchange of two spies, Greville Wynne and Gordon Lonsdale, which had caused something of a sensation in 1964.

I had been informed of what was happening when Wynne, a British businessman who had been jailed in the Soviet Union, was in the process of being exchanged for Lonsdale, a professional Soviet spymaster who was imprisoned in Britain for running a network of agents. The details in my front-page report looked like a leak from a security source and Wilson was well aware of it, as it fell to him to present a Reporter of the Year award to me because of it. The information had really come to me as a result of a high-level decision by the Foreign Office, which wanted to announce the event before the Kremlin could issue its own version.

Over the following months, and years, MI5 was to insinuate itself into Wilson's thinking for various reasons, initially associated with his 'Rasputin', whose ambivalent role in Wilson's career must now be considered.

7

Harold's Rasputin

The voluminous private papers of George Wigg, Labour MP and later peer, deposited with the library of the London School of Economics according to the terms of his will, become available for scrutiny in 1993, ten years after his death. With unconcealed pleasure, Wigg predicted to me that they will cause considerable commotion, particularly on the part of certain politicians if they still happen to be alive then. In shedding new light on some secret history the papers will, I believe, disclose something about the occasional dirty tricks which he believed were played on him as well as about the multitude he played on others. As Wigg would have liked it, they will enable this natural dirty trickster to settle a few old scores from the grave.

It was inevitable that Wigg, the former soldier and then MP for Dudley, would get some sort of office when Labour won the general election in 1964. He had been instrumental in securing Harold Wilson's leadership of the party on the death of Hugh Gaitskell, when it looked like going to George Brown. He had also been responsible for organizing the Profumo Affair, a Tory scandal believed to have assisted crucially in securing Wilson his victory by four seats. Appointed to the sinecure post of Paymaster General at the age of sixty-three, he was to influence Wilson in so many areas, to the fury and frustration of full-blown Cabinet Ministers, that Barbara Castle called him 'Harold's Rasputin'. While they found private meetings with Wilson difficult to fix, Wigg's office adjoined Number 10 and he could slip in at will through a connecting door.

Wilson realized that his own party would be vulnerable to Tories looking for any juicy scandal with which to attack him and his Ministers. By nature a conspiratorial character, Wigg had convinced Wilson that the Tories and the newspapers supporting them would be actively gunning for him to exact revenge. So Wilson gave him his sinecure office so that he could serve as his Spymaster General and watchdog-in-chief to give early warning of any Tory plots or Labour scandals, which had to be scotched or concealed. If, in the process, any further scandals involving Tories came to light, they could be exploited.

The two were made for each other because Wilson also had an almost schoolboy conspiratorial streak. Sir Max Aitken told me of the extraordinary cloak-and-dagger arrangements which Wilson devised for a meeting at Number 10 to discuss his possible role in settling the Rhodesian problem. The Rhodesian leader, Ian Smith, had served with Sir Max in the RAF and, in some desperation, Wilson thought he might listen to reason if it came from an old comrade-in-arms. On a rainy evening Sir Max was asked to wait in a doorway near Trafalgar Square where he would be picked up by car and taken into Number 10 secretly through the garden door. He did so and, having agreed to fly to Rhodesia provided he could take Lord Goodman with him, was ushered out of the front door. I had a similar experience when visiting Wilson in the Cabinet Room, being smuggled in through Wigg's special entrance in another building and then leaving by the front door, after being spotted by my old friend Solly Zuckerman, who was waiting in an anteroom and was curious to know why I was there. Cecil King has recorded how, after visiting his office for lunch, Wilson liked to be taken back in his host's Rolls Royce but always put on glasses and had the car stopped short of the House of Commons.

Revelling in the job, Wigg was to probe the peccadilloes of other Ministers, reporting them all to Wilson though he never mentioned the steady mistress he had enjoyed for years. His pursuit of the popular Labour Minister Fred Peart (later Lord), concerning something in his private life of no political significance, so angered some leading Tories that they took Wigg aside and induced him to desist under threat of exposure in the House.

Wigg already had a private intelligence network and was extremely effective in gathering damaging information against those who had offended him or might do so. As he told me, it was the fact that he believed that Profumo had slighted him in Parliament over an Army issue which spurred him on to expedite the War Minister's downfall. 'I have a long memory, mate, and don't you ever forget it' was how he expressed his vindictiveness, which I was to experience later. His dingy basement flat in Pimlico, which I visited many times, was stacked with dossiers, diary notes and newspaper cuttings. His working axiom concerning confidential information was 'Give some to get some', and I operated on that principle with him, as did one or two other journalists. He employed researchers and even had one spy inside the Tory Party in the shape of Henry Kerby, the MP for Arundel and district.

Captain Henry 'Bob' Kerby, a huge man with a bald, cannon-ball head and indiarubber features, had a mutual interest with Wilson in the timber trade with the USSR, the Prime Minister having served, when out of office, as a consultant to Montague Meyer, a timber importing firm. Kerby's father had been a British diplomat in Russia, his mother was a White Russian and he spoke Russian fluently. He was always welcome at the Soviet Embassy and in Moscow, where he was given what he called 'the red carpet treatment'. At the same time he did odd services for MI5 such as taking pocket devices into the Soviet Embassy in London to facilitate bugging operations. Nevertheless, it is most unlikely that he was trying to serve as an MI5 spy on the Labour Party. Wigg would, assuredly, have made inquiries about him inside MI5 on that score before trusting him, though he must have appreciated that he was a man prepared to play both sides.

Kerby and I knew each other well enough to meet regularly and visit each others' homes. I was aware that he despised most of his Tory colleagues and particularly his leaders, calling Eden 'that pansy' and Macmillan 'Monarch of the Glen' but, at that time I knew nothing about his association with Wilson, which must be ranked as one of the dirtiest tricks in party political history.

A wad of about fifty letters, headed 'Dear Guv' and signed 'Henry', which he had written to Wilson, was passed to me by Lady Falkender, Wilson's influential political secretary, when we were considering writing a book together. They were all highly critical of the Tory Party and contained information which could be used against it. After a trip to Rhodesia he put in a longer report to Wilson than he did to his own side. In 1969 he offered to pass on 'all the Conservative election secrets'.

Enjoying the largest Tory majority, Kerby told me that all he needed to do was to secure the necessary OBEs and other honours for local dignitaries and party officials. He felt slighted by his own party because he had never been honoured himself, his parliamentary activity being limited to tabling hundreds of questions which produced little information and putting down motions that would never be debated. Nevertheless, his popularity was such that when I recently described his activities in a speech I made in Arundel, the centre of his old constituency, many people just refused to believe it. Kerby hoped to be rewarded for his services to Wilson with a knighthood or even a life peerage; he never received either, though Wigg probably jollied him along with encouraging noises.

Wigg had aroused the curiosity of MI5 when he was a backbencher because his parliamentary questions about the Army showed precise knowledge of the whereabouts of units. MI5 was shortly to have its curiosity more than satisfied. When Wigg and Wilson had read the official report on the Profumo Affair by Lord Denning they had been staggered by the way the Director General of MI5, Sir Roger Hollis, had kept Harold Macmillan in ignorance about the security aspects. Determined that nothing similar should happen to him, Wilson summoned Hollis, introduced him to Wigg and told him that he would be serving as his personal liaison agent with him.

He also took the opportunity, in Wigg's presence, of telling Hollis that he must seek his personal approval before carrying out any investigations involving any Member of Parliament – of either the Commons or the Lords. This meant that MI5 was forbidden to conduct any form of surveillance on a suspect MP or peer without the Prime Minister's express permission. The ban included telephone tapping, bugging, the opening of private letters and the examination of bank accounts. Wilson also warned Hollis that he regarded the evidence of defectors as unreliable and that he would be unlikely to accept it as a basis for MI5 investigations of Members of Parliament.

Wilson followed up his decision by issuing it as a written directive to MI5 and, presumably, to MI6, which also carries out domestic surveillance on occasion. A Privy Councillors' report on security had previously recommended that MPs and peers should be treated like any other citizens. Understandably there were some MI5 officers, like Peter Wright, who suspected that one reason for this move was Wilson's determination that his own telephones should not be tapped or to ensure that any taps already installed would be quickly removed.

I was seeing a great deal of Wigg at that period of our long love-hate relationship, and he confided in me that he was captivated by the prospect of finding out what went on in the secrets world and of making use of it. Wilson's aim had been to put his personal spy inside MI5, which he instinctively distrusted because, though 'Socialist' states from the Nazis to the Communists have been the most fervent in the use of secret police to control the 'masses', individual Socialists have a deep distrust of anything savouring of secret police. What Wilson had not appreciated was that, in the process, he was putting an MI5 spy right inside number 10, for Wigg was quickly captured by the MI5 machine. The atmosphere of secrecy and conspiracy was made for him, and he came to love MI5 even more than he had loved the Army. He often criticized Army security to me but never MI5, any censure of it being dismissed as 'Bollicks, mate, bollicks!'

As Wigg's relationship with Wilson and his entourage deteriorated, his loyalty to MI5 intensified. He was anxious to make a good impression there and, understandably, MI5 made maximum use of him both as a source and as an agent of influence. The Director General of MI5 possessed the right of direct access to the Prime Minister but exercised it only in emergencies. Through Wigg's personal liaison the MI5 management had regular access. Peter Wright was to tell me that while any 'prodnose' was usually unwelcome at MI5 headquarters, Wigg was such a prime source of inside information that he was made welcome. The effects of this situation on the Prime Minister have never been fully appreciated.

Operating directly with the senior MI5 management – he was not dealing with Wright or any other low-level officer likely to be dissident – Wigg brought back occasional information of use to Wilson but he regularly informed on Number 10 and all its inhabitants to MI5. While he was there MI5 did not need to bug it to know what was going on. It would be unfair to Wigg to suggest that he informed simply for the sake of it. He told me of several situations which he deplored, realizing that they were dangerous to Wilson, and which he reported in the hope of having them rectified. The first on which he took action concerned some of the people who had such unlimited access to Downing Street that he described the place to me as 'like a bloody railway station'.

For a Prime Minister, Wilson was behaving in an extraordinary manner in this respect. His close friend Joseph Kagan, a former Lithuanian, was in the habit of meeting strangers on trains and, to impress them, taking them straight from Kings Cross station into Number 10. One of Wilson's lawyers who needed a quick signature called at Number 10, leaving a young American friend in his car outside. Wilson, who was sitting alone in the Cabinet Room, insisted that the American be brought in and regaled him with his method of preventing plots against him by ensuring that there were always two Ministers struggling to displace him, one being far more dangerous.

In his position as a privileged confidant Wigg had expressed his concern to Wilson about this influx of peculiar people, but without result. He found the MI5 management, with the responsibility for the protection of classified information, to be willing listeners because they already had deep suspicions about several of the bizarre friends the Prime Minister had collected over the years.

The climate of suspicion within MI5 concerning Communism and Soviet subversion came as no surprise to Wigg. He had served inside the War Office as Parliamentary Private Secretary to Emanuel Shinwell and knew the extent of the Communist conspiracy to which Clement Attlee's Government had responded with a purge of all Communists and Communist supporters in sensitive departments and in industry. From then on, the attention paid by MI5 to Communists and those with Communist relations was in pursuit of Government policy and with the Government's blessing.

The group which Wigg wanted barred from regular access to Number 10 included a number of former refugees from central and eastern Europe, some of whom made regular journeys behind the Iron Curtain. Top of MI5's list was Rudy Sternberg, a Jewish refugee from Austria, who arrived in 1937. He had started a small plastics business and expanded it into a successful petrochemicals group. Concentrating on business relations with eastern Europe, he secured a huge contract for the import of potash from East Germany which lasted more than twenty years; he was also involved with Romania and the Soviet Union. Sternberg was in the habit of boasting about his Soviet and satellite contacts. MI5 assumed that he must have some special influence in Moscow, and it was its business to investigate why this might be.

Causing comparable concern in MI5 was Beattie, Lady Plummer, the wife of Sir Leslie Plummer, a Jewish Labour MP and a former colleague of mine at the *Daily Express* who had also been involved in eastern trade. When he died in 1963, Beattie (nee Lapsker), who was of eastern European origin, carried on his work. She was with Wilson in his Liverpool constituency when he won the election in 1964 and was then a regular visitor to Number 10 and to Chequers, especially after Wilson had made her a peeress in 1965. Her country house, Berwick Hall, in Essex became a left-wing political salon and Wilson was often there. Because of her frequent trips behind the Iron Curtain and her contacts with East German Communists, MI5 was understandably concerned about such a Communist agent of sympathy being in close touch with the Prime Minister. When she died in 1971 it was Wilson who wrote her obituary notice in the *Times*. Lady Falkender suggested to me, darkly, that Beattie Plummer's activities would merit close study.

The refugee who was to cause MI5 most alarm was Kagan, whose original name was Kaganas. He had arrived in 1946 from Lithuania, then part of the Soviet Union, after various vicissitudes there. It was a route which the KGB used to infiltrate spies. His father was already in Britain and Kagan had attended Leeds University before the war, studying textiles. He designed a waterproof fabric called Gannex, which had wool on one side and nylon on the other and made up into attractive coats. In the mid-1950s he met Wilson, who publicized his coats by wearing them. Kagan, who was also Jewish, told me that he had succeeded in getting some Jews out of Russia to Israel at a time when it was difficult to do so. Again MI5 wondered if there had been 'services rendered' and, if so, what these might have been.

Wilson's friendship with Kagan, Sternberg and others seemed to have developed when he had been the young

President of the Board of Trade in the Attlee Government. Later, along with other businessmen, they had supported his private political office financially while he was in opposition.

As the MI5 management explained to Wigg, they would have been derelict in their duty had they not taken an interest in such members of the Wilson *galère*, and Wigg encouraged them to do so. It was a time when the KGB was being very aggressive, and most officials with access to secrets were not permitted to travel in eastern Europe. Sternberg was subjected to full investigation by MI5 regarding his business links with eastern Europe, and Kagan later became the subject of intense interest. All the actions were taken with the MI5 management's agreement, and were not the result of 'cowboy' operations by any right-wing clique.

Wigg was in agreement because he could see such people doing nothing but damage to Wilson whom he believed had the potential to be a really great Prime Minister. 'I just can't understand it,' he told me. 'He's making nooses for himself.' In the absence of any other rational explanation, Wigg suspected they must have some sort of hold over him. He explained to Wilson that MI5 did not think that his friends would be searching drawers for documents or that he would deliberately leak to them. What they knew was that, with so much gossip among the kitchen cabinet, it would be impossible for a regular visitor not to learn something there that could be of use to the Soviet Bloc intelligence system. Both Sternberg and Lady Plummer were suspected of passing on useful information.

Wilson took no notice. Instead he took offence. He suspected that MI5 was being anti-Semitic and Peter Wright was to tell me that it was the reason why Wilson referred to the MI5 officers who investigated suspects as 'fascists'. His friends had been used to visiting his homes, and expected to be able to drop in on Number 10 in the same way. He had no intention of changing his habits because he had become Prime Minister. (He even sent out for fish and chips, which is not as off-beat as it sounds because, to this day, the nation provides no cook for its Prime Minister's personal flat in Number 10. When there is no official entertainment, the Prime Minister's wife is expected to do the cooking. Mrs Thatcher does it herself.)

Wilson requested MI5 to clear his suspect friends for regular access. MI5 were reluctant, and in some cases they declined. So

Wilson eventually showed his contempt for the suspicions by awarding almost all of the suspects with knighthoods, peerages or both. Sternberg was knighted by Wilson in 1970 and made a life peer as Lord Plurenden in 1975. He remained interested in developing trade with the Eastern Bloc, especially Romania, and was to claim credit for helping to organize the visit of Ceausescu to stay with the Queen in 1978, though he died before it took place. Kagan was knighted in 1970 and made a life peer in 1976.

In addition, Wilson cocked a snook at MI5 in 1966 by announcing to Parliament details of the secret directive he had issued making all MPs, including peers, exempt from all the usual security checks. Wilson had not consulted the leader of the Tory Opposition, Edward Heath, before taking this step, probably knowing that he would object to it, as many Tories did and still do. The immunity has remained, however, because no Government has had the political courage to remove it.

Wigg had begun by liking Wilson's political secretary, Marcia Williams (later Lady Falkender), whom he had met long before her entry into Downing Street. Shortly after he became Paymaster General he assured me that he and others were on the lookout for a good libel action which would set her up for life. But he soon began to deplore her intrusion and that of other members of the kitchen cabinet into Wilson's confidence, which he did not wish to share with anyone. He frequently expressed to me his astonishment at the Prime Minister's tame responses to her blazing tantrums, screaming accusations and demands, which were the talk of Whitehall, and became contemptuous of their relationship. He simply could not understand how or why a Prime Minister would tolerate it.

He explained his final fall-out with Marcia as due to her insistence on remaining in earshot when he wished to discuss secret matters with the Prime Minister, a matter which, no doubt, he had been advised about by MI5 when he had described the incredible relationship there. Once he was in close contact with MI5 he believed that any information impinging on security was for Wilson's ears only. He told me that the last straw for him was an occasion when, after Wilson had asked Marcia to leave, she had thrust her handbag under Wigg's nose and said, 'Secrets! I've enough secrets in here to bring the government down.' He said that Wilson had simply shrugged.

In 1967, having fallen in love with the political journalist Walter Terry, who was already married, Marcia decided to have two children by him quickly because she was thirty-five and she expected him to divorce his wife. Her pregnancies were concealed in a way certain to generate unwarranted speculation that the father might be the Prime Minister. Wigg was appalled, especially in view of his brief to nip Labour scandals in the bud.

When Fleet Street got wind of Marcia's predicament from other members of the kitchen cabinet there was a search for the birth registrations, which would enable newspapers to refer to Marcia's private life without fear of libel damages. Nobody could find them because she had registered the first child under the name of Williams-Terry and the other as Williams-Field, when she should have given her maiden name as Field – a mild, though actionable, deception operation. They were eventually discovered by Wigg's researcher, George Caunt, who distributed copies on Wigg's instructions, though Wigg showed them to me himself at a restaurant lunch table. They were not pushed around by MI5, as some authors have suggested. While Wigg was furious in pursuit of Ministers who leaked, he regularly leaked to me and others when it suited his private purpose.

He had already supplied copies of the birth certificates to MI5, mainly as proof that the children were not Wilson's, a fable which was widespread. MI5 was not interested in Marcia's sex life but was rightly concerned about the cover-up, the possible implication being that someone might be in a blackmailable position, which proved not to be the case. In 1965, when the KGB had destroyed the career of the Tory MP Anthony Courtney, which will be described in Chapter 24, Wigg had wondered, 'Who are they really cracking the whip at?' suggesting that the move was really a pointed warning to somebody else of greater importance. At one point Wigg briefly thought it might be Wilson or some other Minister, but then decided that it was probably the Labour MP Tom Driberg.

There can be no doubt that Wigg received information from MI5 about Ministers who were suspect and reported it to Wilson. He could also have been vindictive about some of his Ministerial colleagues whom he did not like, such as Anthony Wedgwood Benn. All he had to do to get a run-down on a politician or an official was to say that he needed the information for the Prime Minister. After Lord George-Brown, whom Wigg disliked, had retired from active politics he told me how Wilson had called him in more than once while he was in the Cabinet to complain of our friendship, knowing that Brown had been a source of leaks, and had told him that full details of our various lunches and meetings were available. This seemed to be fair evidence that some Ministers were under surveillance and that Wilson knew about it, though the information may have reached him from sources who had seen us together or Wigg could have supplied it from his own intelligence network. Wigg often warned Ministers whom he suspected of leaking or being otherwise disloyal to Wilson, by saying, menacingly, 'You know that I have good sources. . . .'

In 1967 Wigg was involved in a most unfortunate security episode which remained completely secret until Peter Wright revealed it to me in 1980. Wilson wished to make the MP for Acton, Bernard Floud, a junior Minister; however, Wilson had been told through Wigg that MI5 had serious suspicions against Floud because he was a crypto-Communist who was known to have recruited others to his secret Communist sympathies and possibly to the KGB. Wilson gave MI5 permission to interview the MP, in the hope that his activities would prove to have been restricted to youthful follies. During interrogration Floud admitted his former Communism, but denied being a Soviet agent. MI5 officers believed that he was still in touch with Soviet Intelligence but said that, if he confessed and could convince them that he was no longer active, they would not object to his appointment. Instead, after a further unproductive session he committed suicide. Floud had been deeply depressed following the death of his wife and, understandably, Wilson thought that MI5 had pressed him too hard on too little evidence. His relatives, and no doubt Floud himself at the time, regarded MI5's behaviour as dirty, but the organization was going through the proper motions originally required by a Labour Government and Wilson agreed to them. Wright appeared to have no regrets about Floud's death when he described the case to me.

A politically much more dangerous situation was presented by the name of Niall MacDermot, the Financial Secretary to the Treasury, who had every prospect of becoming Solicitor

General. A lawyer, who had served in MI5 during the war in counter-intelligence concerned with the D-Day landings, he had won a seat for Labour in 1957 and was quickly spotted as a political high-flier. He had been appointed a Minister in 1965 after becoming a QC two years earlier. In that same year he told Wilson that he had decided to divorce his wife to marry a woman who was half-Russian. The Prime Minister had raised no objections.

The lady, Ludmila Benvenuto, whose father was a Soviet citizen, had arrived in Rome in 1938 as a refugee from the Soviet Union with her mother, who had retained her Italian passport. After three years there they both applied for Soviet citizenship so that they could return to Russia, but the war made that impossible. By that time an official in the Soviet Embassy in Rome called Gorshkov had contacted her, and later she went to work for him. He was in fact a KGB officer.

MacDermot had eventually met her in England, where she was learning the language after securing a United Nations post in Geneva. Though they had fallen in love he remained married for another twelve years, during which Ludmila made several visits to Russia. They were married in Geneva in 1966. A year later, after Wilson had discussed his case with Wigg, MacDermot was called in by Wilson to be told that MI5 had raised a possible security problem. The KGB has always been interested in Treasury secrets as they afford so much political insight, and MacDermot was also on a Cabinet defence committee giving him access to top-secret matters. He was told that the problem lay in the possible danger that his wife might be suborned by the KGB and that he might then come under pressure. MI5 was taking such a serious view that Wilson removed him from the Treasury pending an investigation, the excuse of a reshuffle being made to switch him to a position in the Ministry of Housing and Local Government, where he would have no access to secrets.

MacDermot and his wife were asked if they would undergo questioning by MI5, and they agreed. Ludmila was questioned intensively for several days by Patrick Stewart, a tough interrogator who operated from a wheelchair. It was her past connection with Gorshkov which had been the key objection, though she insisted that she had no knowledge of his intelligence activities.

Eventually, in 1968, Wilson was required to tell MacDermot that MI5 was not satisfied with his wife's answers – they believed that she had lied – and that, while he could remain in the Government, he would not be allowed access to sensitive information. This meant that there could be no important promotion and certainly no service as Solicitor General or Attorney General, as he had hoped. Bitterly disappointed, and believing he was being penalized without proper cause, he resigned from the Government 'on personal grounds' and from Parliament in 1970.

The episode, which could have caused grave embarrassment to both Wilson and Wigg, was effectively stifled until after Wilson's resignation in 1976. MacDermot and his wife regard MI5's 'hounding' of them as a dirty trick and dismiss any suggestion that the KGB had put her under pressure as wholly absurd. But, again, MI5 was simply carrying out the duties originally imposed on it by a previous Labour Government.

Wilson must have agreed with the findings and George Brown, then Foreign Secretary, certainly did so. He told me that after being asked to find MacDermot some prestigious non-governmental post to cover up his departure he had firmly declined to do so after taking advice from MI6, which told him that the information on which MI5 had acted had first come from a previously reliable foreign source. MacDermot secured a position as Head of the International Commission of Jurists in Geneva, where he still lives with his wife. In 1987 he went public on the fact that he had been forced out of politics by MI5 because of suspicions about his wife, which, he insisted, were unjustified.

Whatever the truth, the MI5 action was standard procedure carried out with the agreement and participation of the Director General and Wilson's own security overlord to enable the Prime Minister to be warned of a potential danger. It was no part of any plot against Wilson or the Labour Government, as has been suggested.

Wigg must also have been informed of suspicions concerning the left-wing Labour MP Stephen Swingler, with whom he had once shared a flat, though the issue did not come to a head until a few months after he had left the security scene. Swingler, a Minister of State in the Transport Ministry, was under suspicion by MI5 because of east European contacts during the war and later. Barbara Castle, then Transport Minister, wanted him in the Cabinet, but Wilson said that he was ineligible because, according to MI5, he had compromised himself by his 'dabbling' in eastern Europe. He was, however, allowed to remain as Minister of State and died suddenly in 1969 from viral pneumonia.

Wigg was also given a list of Labour MPs who were known to MI5 as secret Communists and passed it to Wilson for information. Following surreptitious entries which gave them access to the Communist Party's secret list of membership, MI5 claimed to know of more than forty Labour MPs who were Soviet agents of influence – able, through their position and contacts, to promote Russian interests.

Christopher Mayhew (now Lord), the former Navy Minister who had resigned on a matter of principle, eventually attacked Wilson in print for making Wigg his private inquiry agent. He revealed that Wigg was so disliked within the government that the Defence Ministers, led by Denis Healey, the Defence Secretary, met to see how they could defend themselves. They decided to bar Wigg from access to certain secret information.

Wigg's papers may reveal a number of episodes in which his connection with MI5 impacted on political history. One which became known at the time was the strike launched in 1966 by the National Union of Seamen, ostensibly in pursuit of a genuine grievance but which would have brought the nation's trade to a halt to the advantage of the Communist Party.

All too often for the national interest, MI5 makes little practical use of much of the information it acquires for fear of being accused of meddling in politics. Later, it could have exposed the similar activities of the Communist agitator Jack Dash, who duped the dockers into destroying the Port of London and their jobs with it, another conspiracy against the workers in the Soviet interest, but may have been scared of compromising its sources. Because of its connection with Wigg, however, MI5 was able to operate against the seamen's strike without running that risk. Wigg gave Wilson undeniable proof from MI5 telephone bugs and penetration agents that the strike was politically motivated and orchestrated by a few Communists, including Bert Ramelson, the Communist Party's 'industrial organizer', meaning disorganizer. Their prime purpose had been to wreck the Government's Prices and Incomes Policy and then the nation's economy – a deception operation of the kind recommended by Lenin and all his successors as necessary to the noble end of world revolution.

Wilson told Parliament that the moderates on the Seamen's Union executive were being terrorized by a gang of professional Communists who planned their tactics 'with outside help', suggesting the Soviet Union. When he threatened the ringleaders with exposure they capitulated within twenty-four hours, believing that the extent of the Soviet involvement would also be exposed. Wigg told me that the evidence which could have been produced would have been sensational, but there was little possibility that it would ever be made public because of MI5 and Foreign Office sensitivities.

Inevitably, as Wilson had foreseen, the breaking of the strike and its exposure as a Communist dirty trick against the seamen, as well as the nation, earned him the enmity of all the Communist-dominated unions. In his diary, Richard Crossman recorded, 'We have had during this week the destruction of the Wilson myth in the public eye. It's amazing how his luck ran up to a certain point – the day he listed the nine Communists in the seamen's union and pulled off the end of the strike the next morning. That was the apex of his luck. Since then catastrophe after catastrophe.'

At no time was Wigg able to warn Wilson about any MI5 plot to unseat him because of suspicion that he was a secret Communist. In 1965 there had been a considerable flurry of interest when the CIA counter-intelligence chief, James Angleton, told the MI5 representative in Washington that the CIA had evidence from a KGB defector, still in place, that Wilson was assisting the Soviets. He insisted that, to protect the contact who was in a sensitive position, MI5 should take no action without consulting the CIA. Sir Roger Hollis, who was still MI5's Director General, consulted the Cabinet Secretary, Sir Burke Trend; they decided to take no action and not to inform the Prime Minister or Wigg. An opportunity was taken to ask Wilson if the KGB had ever tried to compromise him on his many visits to Moscow, and he said categorically that they had not. Angelton's information was filed under the codename Oatsheaf.

A year or so later Angleton, whose suspicions of Philby had proved accurate, discussed his information with the CIA chief

Richard Helms, who instructed him to say nothing further. In spite of the Oatsheaf claim there were no serious MI5 suspicions against Wilson and he was not put under surveillance, though his private activities may have occasionally been observed while some of his friends were being watched. A zealous MI5 officer (not Peter Wright) who sought permission to carry out surveillance on Wilson was denied. Nobody else tried.

MI5 had no evidence whatever that either Wilson or Marcia Williams was pro-Communist in any way, in spite of the numerous visits they had made in the past to the Soviet Union. When he was Chief of MI6 Sir Maurice Oldfield, who had access to all the previous intelligence reports from Moscow, assured me that he had seen no evidence that Wilson and Marcia had ever been compromised there. Other MI6 officers whom I questioned at that time scoffed at the idea that Wilson could be a Soviet agent or even an agent of influence. George Kennedy Young, the far right-wing former Deputy Chief of MI6, who hated Wilson and all he stood for, told me, in his direct Scottish way, 'It's a load of crap.'

If any serious evidence supporting Oatsheaf had arisen, MI5 would have needed to question Wilson about it. Had they done so, the odds are that he would have expressed his fear of an MI5 plot against him to close friends. He never aired that suspicion to anyone whom I have encountered until 1974.

Among the 2 million or more files then in MI5's Registry, and now on computer, there was a routine one on Wilson, said to have the cryptonym Henry Worthington – it was common MI5 practice to use the correct initials when hiding a real name. Much has been made of this, but I have been assured that the file was thin – not nearly as fat as mine!

8

A Pitiless Innuendo

One of George Wigg's last manipulations of his unique relationship with MI5 was his part in a complex operation which
is, surely, a classic example of the use of the dirty trick for
character assassination. In 1978 Lord Weidenfeld, a mutual
friend of Harold Wilson and myself, invited me to his Chelsea
flat for a hatchet-burying meeting with the former Premier.
Lord Wilson, as he had become, was most affable and then
staggered me with an admission which confirmed what I had
come to suspect – that a distinguished public servant who had
happened to cross him had been set up and destroyed by what
was nothing less than a cunning deception operation on
Parliament, the public and, incidentally, the secret services. In
1990 I was privileged to see documents about this case which
show the extent to which the Whitehall machinery can be
pressed into action in support of such a disgraceful operation.

When Wilson had published his book *The Labour Government
1964–1970* he had said that one of his 'costliest mistakes in near
six years of office' was the so-called D-Notice Affair, which
diminished his standing throughout the country. It was also
the dirtiest trick deliberately played by him, using all his prime
ministerial power and privilege.

The general story of the D-Notice Affair has been dealt with
in previous books, but the precise motive behind it has not
been fully exposed. On 21 February 1967 a front-page report in
the *Daily Express* under my name revealed that copies of all
private overseas cables handed in at post offices or cable companies were being collected every morning for examination by
the security authorities. I was later to learn that this had been
going on secretly for many years, but MPs and the public were
unaware of it and the report caused a furore. The Foreign

Office was particularly horrified because the security authority concerned was GCHQ, and at that time its interception function was highly secret. GCHQ was especially interested in foreign diplomats and intelligence agents, who sometimes used the ordinary cable network when quick communication was essential. I was told this by a man who had worked in cable offices as a telegraphist and felt aggrieved about the practice. He came into my office from the street, so the information did not come to me from M15 or any other official source.

A senior post office contact confirmed the man's story and, as was my usual practice in those days, I went through the motions of clearing it for publication with the Secretary of the D-Notice Committee, Colonel L. G. Lohan, a close personal friend known to all who dealt with him as 'Sammy'. The D- (for Defence-) Notice Committee, consisting of representatives of Government Departments and the media, laid down voluntary guidelines so that the media would not inadvertently betray important official secrets. It had been set up as an acceptable successor to wartime censorship by the first post-war Labour Government. Over lunch Lohan and I agreed that the cable-vetting story which I proposed to print did not contravene the guidelines; nevertheless he urged me not to print it because the Foreign Office was pressing him hard to have it suppressed. In the end my editor and the office legal adviser decided that the public should be told what was going on and the report duly appeared.

What neither Lohan nor I knew, as we sat at our lunch table, was that several weeks before Harold Wilson had instructed the Permanent Secretary of the Defence Ministry, Sir James Dunnett, to find some way – any way – of firing the Colonel, even though he was widely regarded as being efficient in his difficult job. The reason was that Lohan was an inveterate gossip, especially about Whitehall affairs, and he had gossiped to the wrong man. He had retailed some alleged sex scandal about a Labour Minister to the Tory MP Henry Kerby, who was functioning as a spy for Wigg and Wilson.

Kerby had first met Lohan at a party in my country home, then encountered him again at a cocktail party on 20 December 1966. He asked him if he had wind of any Whitehall scandals, and Lohan told him there was concern about a Labour Minister who was believed to be having an affair with a married woman suspected of having Communist connections. He followed up with a letter urging Kerby to publicize the scandal somehow. Instead Kerby sent it to Wigg who, sensing the stirrings of a Profumo-like situation, tackled the Minister, an old friend, and found there was no truth in it. Wigg immediately informed Wilson, and Kerby was asked to secure more information; he invited Lohan to lunch for the purpose. At his request Lohan also provided Kerby with information enabling him to table parliamentary questions; I have a copy of a letter which Kerby wrote to Lohan on 8 February 1967, thanking him for assistance in framing some of them.

Wigg then put in a report on Lohan's behaviour to Wilson, including information he had secured from MI5, which disapproved of Lohan's connections with journalists and with me in particular. Wilson immediately ordered Sir James Dunnett to sack Lohan. In a private conversation on 30 September 1967 Dunnett told me that Wilson had been trying to get Lohan dismissed more than a month before the cable-vetting row.

Dunnett and his officials tried to engineer a way of getting rid of him without revealing the reason but, in view of Lohan's prestigious position, especially in relation to the media, they could not do so. Meanwhile, at Wigg's request, Lohan was put under surveillance by MI5 – and so, I suspect was I. George Caunt, who worked for Wigg as a researcher after leaving Wilson's service, told me that he had seen records of tapped telephone conversations of Lohan speaking to friends. I spotted one rather inefficient watcher outside my flat in St James's Place, which Lohan visted occasionally.

The results intensified Wilson's determination to have Lohan removed from the Whitehall scene as a dangerous conspirator. Dunnett has told me that there were almost daily calls from Number 10 to his office, asking if Lohan had gone and if not why not. The officials remained anxious to oblige but still could find no excuse when, out of the blue on 21 February 1967, the D-Notice story broke and presented the perfect reason – Lohan had failed in his duty to stop it, perhaps deliberately to embarrass the government, in spite of the most urgent requirement to do so, not only from the Foreign Office but also from GCHQ.

The officials simply wanted to use existing Whitehall procedures to remove Lohan, but Wilson was determined to make maximum use of the opportunity. After accusing me and my newspaper in Parliament of deliberately breaching a D-Notice and inflicting great damage to the intelligence system, he moved fast to set up a Committee of Inquiry to investigate and report on the whole affair. The Foreign Office, the Defence Ministry, MI6, MI5 and especially GCHQ urged Wilson to let the matter drop on the grounds that it would be quickly forgotten, while any inquiry would only exacerbate the publicity, which they detested and regarded as particularly dangerous for a special reason: there was an ultra-secret American element.

The contents of any interesting cables were being made available by GCHQ to its American counterpart, the National Security Agency; this could increase the public outcry in Britain if it was exposed. Far more seriously, the NSA was carrying out surveillance of overseas communication by cables in an operation called Shamrock, which was especially secret because, under US law, it was illegal. There was deep Foreign Office concern that the publicity given to the cable-vetting affair could lead to the exposure of Shamrock, causing a major furore in Congress with serious damage to the President, because the process had been extended to collect domestic information on dissidents and drug-traffickers.

The danger of damage to GCHQ's operations and of the possible leakage of the American connection was repeatedly pointed out to Wilson. His Cabinet colleagues and the Cabinet Secretary, Sir Burke Trend, pleaded with him. George Brown interceded personally on behalf of the Foreign Office. Wigg assured me that he pleaded on behalf of MI5. All to no avail. Wilson induced Lord Radcliffe, a distinguished judge, and two other Privy Councillors to carry out an inquiry – confident, as he told various friends, that publication of the Committee's report would establish not only Lohan's guilt but mine.

When Wilson announced the setting up of the inquiry in Parliament he claimed that my disclosure had put men's lives at risk, which was complete humbug. Later, in his memoirs, he admitted that he had raised the issue 'gratuitously' in Parliament when there was no need to.

Once the inquiry had been set in train, the behaviour of several Government departments, and especially the Foreign Office, in trying to mislead the Committee was digraceful, as the published evidence would eventually reveal. Lohan was taken aside and induced to sign statements which he knew to be manifestly untrue on several important counts. Government witnesses were economical with the truth until conflicting evidence required them to tell it. The published evidence also showed that the Defence Ministry and the Post Office had lied while I and other journalists had been making initial inquiries about the cable-vetting. Without question there had been a full-blown Whitehall conspiracy to conceal the truth, and Wigg had been at the centre of it. Having fallen out with me over my consistent attacks on the Government, he was keen to assist Wilson to do Lohan and me maximum professional damage, as he later confessed to me after we had restored our friendship. He felt no embarrassment about it, regarding his action, like my newspaper attacks on the Labour Government, as all part of an exhilarating political game.

While I was present at the inquiry Lohan happened to raise the GCHQ involvement during his evidence. He was sharply rebuked by Lord Radcliffe and we were requested not to mention it, to which we agreed.

To Wilson's chagrin and disbelief the Committee's report came out in favour of the *Daily Express* and of me, but with strictures of Colonel Lohan, who had even altered the dates on some documents to accord with the false statements he had been required to make. Having been instructed to supply false information to the Committee, he was censured for doing so but not sufficiently to enforce his dismissal.

Wilson was furious and, against advice from everyone, with the exception of Wigg, he decided to reject the findings of the Committee which he had appointed by publishing a White Paper setting out his views and repudiating theirs. All his other colleagues could foresee the political damage that this could inflict, but Wilson cunningly arranged the relevant Cabinet meeting to suit his purpose. In his diary, Richard Crossman recorded Wilson's deviousness in timing the meeting so that Ministers would get a vast amount of reading material late on the previous night to keep their minds fully occupied, and then arranging that his White Paper should not be available until 4 p.m., when the Cabinet would have not time to amend it. He had also arranged the agenda so that the Cabinet had only half an hour to discuss it before his next engagement. Wilson dominated the brief discussion by explaining that he had to have a White Paper overturning the Radcliffe Report because he was 'so profoundly concerned about D-Notices'. This was untrue because he had been warned that his action would discredit the whole D-Notice system, which it did, irreparably. Crossman forecast: 'The White Paper as a piece of apologetics is extremely unconvincing and will do Harold untold harm.' He believed that the majority of the Cabinet was against the White Paper.

Wilson's cold-blooded ulterior motive in issuing the White Paper did not become at all apparent until the inevitable parliamentary debate about it. Before the debate began, the Tory MP Hugh Fraser told me he had been speaking to Wigg and was certain that he 'had a googly', though he did not know what it was. The 'googly' proved to be the sudden intervention of the Labour backbencher and part-time journalist Raymond Fletcher, who rose to announce that he had just returned from Fleet Street which was buzzing with rumours that Lohan had been a major source of leaks to me. My ears were closer to the ground of Fleet Street than Fletcher's, and there were no such rumours. As Crossman records, Fletcher had been briefed by Wigg to divert any parliamentary attack off Wilson on to Colonel Lohan. His statements also enabled the Prime Minister to administer the final blow. As part of his plan, Wilson had arranged to be the last speaker and at the conclusion of his speech, when nobody could question him, he told Parliament that the previous Government had reason to suspect an unduly close relationship between Lohan and myself which had caused security concern.

According to MI5 documents which had been shown to Wigg, Lohan was suspected of having tipped me off about the exchange of the two spies Greville Wynne and Gordon Lonsdale. In fact, Colonel Lohan had approached me about it only as an intermediary on behalf of the Foreign Office because he was known to be a friend of mine. MI5's ignorance of the truth underscores the extent to which the Foreign Office, which deals with MI6, was not prepared to inform MI5. The situation was rendered even more piquant by the fact that Lohan was a regular informer for MI5, with an expense account, but MI5 was still prepared to shop him with information which was incorrect. Wilson's reference to this false information supplied by Wigg was intended to suggest some kind of collusion between Lohan and myself to ensure that the cable-vetting story would be published. This was referred to in newspapers as a 'pitiless innuendo'.

During his speech, Wilson was also at pains to state that Lohan was a civil servant, which Lohan denied. His purpose was to make certain that Lohan would be required to appear before a Civil Service Board which could ensure his removal. Although Lohan had resigned in disgust at his treatment, he appeared before a disciplinary board unusually chaired by the head of the Civil Service, Lord Helsby, who joined in the kill. The confidential papers of this hearing, which lasted a day and a half, have been made available to me by Lohan's former union, then called the Institution of Professional Civil Servants. William McCall, the union's exceptionally able general secretary who represented Lohan, was totally unaware, as Lohan himself was, that the hearing was the culmination of a prime ministerial plot to get rid of him.

The board was told of Lohan's remarkable war record in highly secret operations far behind enemy lines. At one stage he had commanded the SOE in Italy. After the war he had been concerned with highly secret logistic planning including the Suez operation and had been indoctrinated on secret Cabinet Office war plans, so there could hardly have been doubts about his security. He had close relations with MI5, which on occasion, made use of him as a source.

Lohan was shown evidence that he had been shopped by Kerby. Later an MI5 friend was to tell him of 'the awful extent to which Kerby had been the eyes and ears of the Labour Government'. The board's documents also indicated the extent to which Wigg had been using Kerby as a source, no doubt feeding information he provided about the Tory Party and its members to MI5 for the benefit of its files. They also suggested that the MI5 management had been trying to use Kerby to discover what Wigg was saying about them and what he might intend to do. MI5 had provided evidence that Lohan had a key to my London flat, which was untrue, though he visited it occasionally. There was also an unsubstantiated statement that he had been involved in an 'orgy' in Soho.

The disciplinary board decided that there was no truth in Wilson's late-night smear that Lohan had been a source of classified leaks to me. The Director General of MI5 himself, Sir

Martin Furnival Jones, agreed that there were no grounds on which his reliability could be questioned. The Prime Minister had smeared Lohan on evidence which the board rejected.

Otherwise, Whitehall's revenge on Lohan and the Post Office witness who had wrecked the Foreign Office conspiracy by telling the truth was merciless. The Colonel had beaten dismissal only by resigning, which was unfortunate in a way because McCall was confident that he could have secured another post for him or considerable compensation.

It was clear to the media that the whole sorry saga had been carefully orchestrated by Wilson, assisted by his henchman, Wigg. They had not been behaving impulsively but had been abusing their power deliberately. Convinced that this was not the behaviour of a man fit to be Britain's Prime Minister, the media closed ranks with results that were catastrophic for Wilson. For the next six months his long-standing detraction by the press intensified to vilification and ridicule. Writing at the time, Cecil King recorded 'an absurd situation which has brought down on him the condemnation of all the newspapers and has made him look a fool. The result is the worst press any Prime Minister has had in my day.' Barbara Castle also referred, in her diary, to the 'mess' which Wilson had created through his handling of the D-Notice Affair. 'The evil genius had once again been George Wigg,' she wrote.

Wilson was staggered by the intensity of the criticism. As Marcia Falkender recorded in her book *Inside Number 10*, the Prime Minister had become so obsessed with the D-Notice Affair that it 'sapped his energies and his morale'. Still believing, at that stage, that his abuse of power had been justified, the whole experience deepened Wilson's fears of a media conspiracy and of my involvment in it. Had his real motive been appreciated at the time, which it was not, the media assault would have been even fiercer.

In 1978, during the hatchet-burying meeting at Lord Weidenfeld's flat, Wilson opened the conversation by apologising for the D-Notice Affair, admitting that it had been a bad mistake. He then staggered me by saying, blandly, 'It was that dreadful fellow Lohan, that I was after, you know.' Looking at the whole circumstances, this meant that he had been prepared to throw all the serious security considerations to the winds to take revenge for Lohan's relatively trivial dirty tricks on the

Labour Party. Lohan received no pension, and after a brief period as a food journalist retired to obscurity and died.

To my surprise the Government had eventually agreed that the whole of the evidence to the Radcliffe Inquiry, only slightly expurgated, should be published, even though it revealed the extent of the Whitehall lying. Wigg told me that he had pressed for publication to expose what he and Wilson regarded as 'Lohan's character defects' which had made him unsuitable for his post. Wigg seemed oblivious to his own character defects, as did the Prime Minister.

9

Plots Abounding

After Wigg's departure from Whitehall late in 1967 to become Chairman of the Horserace Betting Levy Board, Wilson's contact with MI5 ceased to be regular. He told me that he saw the heads of MI5 and MI6 so rarely that he used to confuse them. The MI5 connection was to ressurect itself, however, with a vengeance, both before and after he went into Opposition in 1970 after losing the election to Edward Heath. Meanwhile, spurred on in his fantasies by some members of his kitchen cabinet, he was to continue to concentrate his conspiratorial obsession on plots by the media and by colleagues. At least those were based on some degree of fact.

There was no shortage of attacking material for the media. With the defence cuts in full swing, a stream of leaks came my way from senior service officers and civil servants appalled by what Wilson and his Defence Minister, Healey, were doing, in the hope that premature publicity might have some effect. Some senior civil servants also leaked to embarrass some other department or individual, a fairly common insider ploy in Whitehall. While causing rows in Parliament, the leaks rarely produced any changes in policy; but in June 1970 I received a letter from Lord Mountbatten congratulating me on my 'private campaign to save the *Eagle, Ark Royal* and the Fleet Air Arm fixed-wing aviation'. He feared that Labour would have cancelled all naval aviation save for helicopters if they had stayed in office until October, but once Wilson had opted for a June election they would not have time. Mountbatten wrote, 'You realise that we were very near the point of no-return and that an October election would have written off naval aviation forever. What a triumph for all you have been working for though I must say that I don't think you could have done it without Wilson's help.'

Whether my efforts had any impact or not, which I doubt, they could not have been made without the clandestine help of informants like Lord Mountbatten.

The public joined in with letters, some signed, some anonymous, about Wilson's private life and Marcia's, most of it untrue and unprintable. One even arrived from a former member of the 10 Downing Street staff, who was deeply disappointed that I had failed to make an exposure which I simply did not believe.

The extent to which scurrilous letters about prominent people are penned and despatched in all directions is astonishing, and Peter Wright told me that one of the chief recipients is MI5. Only recently did I discover that one of my close friends had been reporting to MI5 about my activities on a regular basis: by chance, I saw a copy of a letter he had submitted giving the names of all the guests of interest at a party at my home in the 1970s, and what my connections with them seemed to be.

Denigrating Wilson was becoming almost a national sport, with some prominent private citizens even claiming to be keeping 'files' about him. Not all their efforts were aimed at the Prime Minister. Some kind reader, who signed his letter, sent me some of Harold Lever's bank statements, presumably dredged from a rubbish bin, in which he was overdrawn by several thousands of pounds – a large sum to the sender but peanuts to Lever (now Lord), a Socialist millionaire with a very rich wife. The sender's argument was, 'How can a man who is overdrawn give sound financial advice to the Government?' I returned them to Lever, who suggested I should reply by pointing out that borrowing money to use it creatively is sound advice.

Wilson reacted by stepping up his private counter-attack against individual journalists, warning Ministers to have nothing to do with them and working on their editors and proprietors to sack them. The former Labour MP and journalist Woodrow Wyatt (now Lord), has recorded, 'Several times he urged the *Mirror* to stop my column and tried to prevent my re-adoption for Bosworth.' Some of Wilson's former colleagues claim that he wasted hours of Cabinet time lecturing them about leaks, many of which, they suspected, had come from the kitchen cabinet.

The political plots from inside his own party were more serious. As early as 1963 a dining club of Labour moderates had been established with the intention of eliminating Wilson as leader and, as Lord Mayhew has recorded, it continued to meet when he was Prime Minister. Wilson's deputy, George Brown, hated him for having beaten him in the leadership election and for the way he was running Number 10. The extent to which it was reciprocated was shown when I asked one of Wilson's chief aides what the Prime Minister intended to do about George. The answer was that as long as he continued to drink as heavily as he was doing the problem would resolve itself. On 21 November 1966 Barbara Castle wrote in her diary, 'Sunday's papers are full of Roy Jenkins again. There is obviously a campaign on to run him as Harold's successor.'

In May 1968 there were reports of militant undercover activity within the Labour Party to oust Wilson. Two clandestine groups were meeting regularly at private addresses to further their intention of installing Roy Jenkins as Prime Minister before the Labour Party conference in October. In 1967 James Callaghan had made what appeared to his colleagues to be several half-hearted attempts to secure the leadership and the following year was aching for the premiership and taking stock of support, according to Joe Haines, the Number 10 Press Secretary and a well-placed observer. Hard-left Ministers and MPs held that Wilson had secured the Labour leadership and premiership by fraud – talking left and then acting right. Politicians like Benn and Foot were bitterly disappointed when Wilson retained the Polaris submarines with their nuclear missiles in contravention of his promise to scrap them.

Wilson's response to his insider opponents, according to some of them, was to leak stories about them, either directly or through his kitchen cabinet when it suited. George Caunt recalled, 'I have heard members of the Cabinet use very strong language concerning the mysterious leaks which poured out of Number 10 and were aimed at undermining their credibility.'

Of course many Tory MPs, especially those of the far Right, regarded it as their duty to denigrate Wilson. They saw him as being too soft on Communists and on politically motivated 'refugees' from places like Chile. They used the media to plant information which, in my experience, usually needed very careful checking and was often rumour or fabricated dis-information.

Members of the right-wing Tory Monday Club were savagely hostile to the Government; one of them was George Kennedy Young, the former Deputy Chief of MI6, who, as a gung-ho field officer, had been deeply involved in the successful plot to overthrow the Iranian Prime Minister Mossadeq, and in fiasco plots to assassinate Egypt's President Nasser. I lunched with Young regularly in those days and from his information, and that of other guests he brought, it was clear that he remained in touch with his old office. Among other things, he told me that certain very sensitive documents were being withheld from some Labour Ministers on security grounds because of the fear that their gossip with left-wing friends might betray sources. I suspect that many of the anti-Labour leaks which have been attributed to MI5 really originated in MI6, which had a policy of leaking both information and disinformation for operational purposes and to 'muddy the waters'.

Young had aspirations to enter Parliament, which already contained several for.ner MI6 officers in the Tory ranks, while Labour had at least two with intelligence connections. Wilson's popularity with them and with MI6 in general was not helped by a financial squeeze on the service, resulting from Labour's policy of reducing Britain's position as a world power. It meant that there were fewer slots for people serving abroad, which is a major attraction for MI6 recruits. The Prime Minister's stock inside MI6 slumped further in 1968 when he selected as its new chief, an outsider Sir John Rennie, from the Foreign Office, in preference to the inside professional candidate, Maurice Oldfield, who had to wait five more years for his turn.

While some MPs of both parties may have kept MI5 and MI6 informed about Labour's problems, Wilson continued to have his own informer extraordinary in the shape of the Tory MP Henry Kerby, who had triggered off the sequence of dirty tricks on Colonel Lohan. Later Wilson denied any knowledge of Kerby's contribution, saying he could remember only two incidents concerning approaches by him, but the great wad of Kerby's letters sent to me by Marcia Falkender were documentary proof that Kerby had been an informer from 1966 until his death in 1971.

Was Wilson lying, as many of his friends and colleagues say he was prone to do, when faced with questions about an embarrassing situation? Or was his once-famous memory already in decline? Subsequent events suggest that the latter might often have been the likelier and more understandable explanation.

If Wilson had got wind of an extraordinary incident which occurred in May 1968 he would surely have convinced himself, and the world too if he had gone public, that all his plot suspicions were fully justified. Cecil King's animosity to Wilson had peaked because, as a director of the Bank of England, he had reason to believe that the nation's financial situation was far worse than the Government was admitting: the economy was sliding to catastrophe. King's state of mind has been described by his intimate newspaper colleague Lord Cudlipp – he was suffering from delusions of grandeur and determined to do something about the situation himself. His solution was a 'Government of businessmen', a totally unworkable concept in a parliamentary democracy, and he was looking for leaders to join him.

His eye fell on Lord Mountbatten and he asked Cudlipp, who worked for him, to arrange a meeting. This took place on 8 May 1968 at Mountbatten's London residence. Mountbatten had taken the wise precaution of having a friend with him in the shape of Sir Solly Zuckerman (later Lord). The two had worked so closely in the Defence Ministry, where Solly had been Chief Scientist, that I had called them the 'Zuckbatten Axis', a description apt enough to become commonly used in Whitehall, as Zuckerman recorded in his memoirs.

Cudlipp recorded that, after King had given vent to Wilson's incapability of dealing with the economic and political situation – which would, he believed, slide into chaos with bloody insurrection, bringing the Army on to the streets – he asked Mountbatten if he would serve as the head of an alternative government. No doubt flattered, Mountbatten asked Zuckerman what he thought about the idea. Zuckerman, then serving as an adviser to Wilson, said, 'That would be rank treachery. I am a public servant and I will have nothing to do with it. Nor should you, Dickie.' Mountbatten agreed and Zuckerman left, to be quickly followed by King and Cudlipp.

This crackpot incident, which had been put on record by

Lord Cudlipp in 1976, was resuscitated recently as 'the military coup against Wilson' when it was linked with Peter Wright's book *Spycatcher*, which in fact was to throw no light on it whatever. The media rehashed it with the suggestion that MI5 had been involved. Wright was to allege that King was a 'long-time MI5 agent'. If by that he meant that his newspapers would print occasional information leaked by MI5 for their operational purposes, then the *Mirror* group was no different from any other. Otherwise King needed no MI5 input for his 'plot', which originated entirely in his mind.

Both Lord Cudlipp and Lord Zuckerman have recounted to me in the past all that happened at the meeting, which clearly was of no consequence. I was also seeing Mountbatten fairly frequently at the time, and his only concern about the Government was the way Denis Healey was handling defence issues. As I reported in the *Times*, I had several long conversations with Mountbatten in which he showed warm regard for Wilson both as a Premier and a person.

Cecil King continued with his campaign and, two days after Mountbatten's turn-down, the *Daily Mirror* announced that Wilson and his Government had lost all credibility and must go. But it was King who went. Three weeks later he was ousted by Cudlipp and the rest of the *Mirror* board in what was to be described as a 'conspiracy' by Wilson's entourage and as a 'dirty trick' by other newspapers. There was even suspicion that Wilson had been involved in it. The only certainty is that MI5 was not involved.

Sir Martin Furnival Jones, Director General of MI5 at the time, is alleged to have revealed, years later, that MI5 investigated another 'plot' in 1968 involving civil servants and military men and to have reported to the then Home Secretary, James Callaghan. I suspect that it was Furnival Jones's inaccurate recall of the King-Mountbatten-Zuckerman episode, perhaps linked in his mind with memories of so-called 'private armies', unarmed organizations set up to deal with the worst civilian consequences of a possible general strike. It is certain that nobody was charged or disciplined about it.

Wilson was not told of the still-born conspiracy as this would have served no good purpose and would have placed Mountbatten in a difficult position, especially in view of his royal connection. He learned about it only a few weeks before his resignation in 1976, when Zuckerman told him that there would be some mention of it in Cudlipp's forthcoming memoirs. His reaction then was to regard it, excitedly, as confirmation of an even more fantasist coup plot, to which he and Marcia had given credence.

In January 1974, while Wilson was out of office, the Home Office and Defence Ministry found it necessary to mount an anti-terrorist operation at Heathrow airport with a show of tanks and guns. It served both as a deterrent and as a major exercise in co-operation between the police and the Army, and was entirely in the public interest. To Wilson's mind, however, and to Marcia's, it was a potential way of staging a sudden coup by making the Government the target, especially when such exercises were repeated during Wilson's later terms of office. Marcia is on record as telling reporters how she and Wilson had wondered where the guns would be placed! The reporters were not the only ones to regard this fantasy as totally absurd and symptomatic of a wider delusion. Later, Wilson was to deny that he had been in any way perturbed about it. As Wedgwood Benn has stated publicly, 'In the end, the tragedy of Wilson was that you couldn't believe a word he said.'

10

Dismayed by Defectors

MI5 intruded itself forcibly into Wilson's life again following the defection of two Czech intelligence officers to the CIA in July 1969. They were Josef Frolik, who had served on the British desk at Czech headquarters in Prague and then in London from 1964 to 1966, and Frantisek August, who had also served in both places. The honesty of both of these men has been systematically traduced by left-wing writers for reasons that will become obvious, but reputable MI5 officers who dealt with them are satisfied that they told the truth.

Of the many allegations made by the two defectors, the one which caused the greatest alarm to both MI5 and Wilson concerned the Rt Hon. John Stonehouse, then Minister of Posts and Telecommunications. Frolik claimed that Stonehouse had been recruited by Czech Intelligence in the late 1950s after being the victim of a sexual trap in Czechoslovakia. He said that he had been pressed into service in 1965 after the arrival in London of Major Robert Husak, allegedly with instructions to 'run' Stonehouse.

There can be little doubt that Stonehouse was a Soviet Bloc target. Soviet Intelligence was particularly interested in the TSR2 bomber, and at that time Stonehouse was Aviation Minister. The Soviets were also interested in Concorde, and Frolik believed that Stonehouse had leaked technical secrets about the world's first supersonic airliner to the Soviet Bloc. When the Russian equivalent, nicknamed Konkordski, appeared in public it bore a remarkably close resemblance to the Anglo-French plane. It is possible that part of the Concorde information was deliberately leaked with in-built faults which caused the Soviet plane to crash, as it did at the Paris Airshow, leading to its abandonment; but I have never seen any hard evidence to support that belief.

When Husak returned to Prague, Stonehouse, then Postmaster General, was allegedly taken over by his successor. In his new post Stonehouse had access to communications information of special interest to the Soviet Bloc. He was also alleged to have imparted counter-intelligence information.

All the allegations were supported by the other defector, August, who was a more important witness because he claimed not only to have seen documentary evidence but to have briefed and debriefed Stonehouse during a long session in the Czech countryside. Unfortunately the documents were unavailable for examination, being in the Prague headquarters.

Because of Wilson's general ban on the surveillance of MPs, MI5 was unable to investigate Stonehouse without seeking the Prime Minister's permission. When this was sought Wilson was deeply concerned because, while MI5 clearly had to move on the information, he did not want his Minister interrogated in a hostile way which might yield some sort of confession. He therefore sent for the MI5 case officer and insisted that he should make the accusations to Stonehouse's face in his presence. MI5 had no option but to agree, and it inevitably reduced the impact of the charge.

Stonehouse was immediately produced from another room in Number 10, and it was Wilson who told him of the allegation and invited him to respond. Stonehouse admitted having met Husak in Czechoslovakia while on an invited visit in 1957, for which the Czechs had paid, but denied ever having been a spy. He agreed that the Czechs had made various efforts to establish contact on other occasions, including one in Czechoslovakia when he had gone there to sign some Government agreement. Apparently Wilson believed Stonehouse but forbade him to go to Czechoslovakia for any holidays. Any further MI5 access to Stonehouse was restricted to meetings at the suspect's club, hardly a convenient venue for interrogation.

The MI5 management was angry at the way the case had been run on Wilson's orders. They had wanted to confront Stonehouse suddenly in his office, and believed that he had been forewarned and had had time to compose himself and consider his response. When the MI5 man saw him in Wilson's presence he had little, if any, chance of securing a confession and none later.

MI5 ended the investigations at that stage, convinced that Stonehouse had lied but unable to prove it. Wilson told me in 1978 that he had simply taken MI5's word that there was 'no evidence'. Frolik was later to tell a US Senate Committee that Stonehouse had been a spy and was visited in the USA twice by MI5 officers still pursuing the case after Wilson's clearance.

Stonehouse, who was allowed to remain at his post until the general election of 1970, looked relaxed enough whenever I saw him, which was fairly frequently. When Cecil King lunched with him shortly after he went out of office he said he was relieved to be back in business, where he hoped to make some money. While he had been a Minister Stonehouse had moved in wealthy circles, and when I occasionally encountered him in country houses he made no secret of his desire to be rich in his own right.

The whole incident, which would be a serious political embarrassment for Labour if the media heard about it, was held tightly secret except for a tip which came my way that Stonehouse had been in some sort of trouble. It was to surface, however, a few years later in truly sensational circumstances.

Frolik also revealed that Will Owen, the sixty-eight-year-old Labour MP for Morpeth, had been taking £500 a month, then a substantial sum, from Czech Intelligence for many years along with free holidays in return for political gossip and sensitive information he picked up while serving on Parliament's Estimates Committee. Again Wilson had to be told and, though he had become suspicious of all allegations by defectors, he agreed that MI5 should be free to carry out the necessary inquiries. After prolonged surveillance Owen was arrested in 1970 and charged with selling confidential information. At first he denied the accusations, but then admitted having received £2300; to Wilson's relief, he was acquitted on a technicality.

Following his resignation from Parliament, when he knew he could not be retried, Owen agreed to help MI5 provided that his Labour colleague, Leo Abse, could be present as a safeguard for him. Abse agreed, and has since recorded his feelings in newspaper articles as Owen confessed to acts which meant that he had inflicted damage on the defence interests of Britain and NATO while being paid far more than he had admitted.

Frolik's and August's evidence about Owen had been true but, as it was hearsay (all relevant documents being in Prague), it had counted for nothing. The two defectors, who had travelled to Britain from America to assist MI5, felt cheated by what had obviously been a miscarriage of justice and were disinclined to co-operate further. The failure of the case also convinced MI5 that any prosecution of John Stonehouse without a confession could not be mounted.

For MI5's own purposes Wilson was kept in complete ignorance of a more important Soviet Bloc agent exposed by Frolik. This was the Labour MP and Chairman of the Labour Party, Tom Driberg, whose career had been one long dirty trick and would continue that way until his death in 1976 at the age of seventy-one.

Frolik gave MI5 a lead about a Labour MP who had worked for Czech Intelligence and had the codename 'Crocodile'. He picked him out from a spread of photographs and claimed that the Czech intelligence mission in London had been censured by the KGB because he was 'their man'. When questioned, Driberg admitted that he had sold the Czechs 'a few articles', which had in fact included details of the private lives of MPs who might be suborned. His MI5 interrogators were satisfied that he had given the Czechs anything else of interest which came his way.

MI5 could not report Driberg's admission to Wilson because for many years, on and off, they had used him as one of their own agents and he was fully aware of the strength of his position. A lifelong compulsive homosexual with the extraordinary but common requirement for 'rough trade', Driberg had joined the Communist Party as a youth 'to meet males of the working class', as he confessed in his memoirs. He was then recruited by an MI5 agent runner, Maxwell Knight, who had homosexual tendencies himself, as a spy inside the Communist Party. He proved adept at such double-dealing, which he enjoyed, until he was expelled after the KGB discovered his MI5 connection. Once he became an MP in 1942, however, the KGB wanted him back. At a party in the Soviet Embassy the British Communist Party boss, Harry Pollitt, apologised to him for the expulsion, claiming that he had been misinformed and urged him to function as a crypto-Communist inside the Labour Party.

Instead he reported regularly to MI5 on the Labour Party even while he was Chairman in 1958, being paid for his services and receiving protection against prosecution for his homosexual behaviour, which was so outrageously obvious that Churchill remarked that Driberg was 'bringing sodomy into disrepute'. When Driberg was caught by the police he gave an MI5 telephone number, which resulted in his immediate release.

He had been involved with MI5 headquarters in connection with a visit he paid to the defected spy, Guy Burgess, in Moscow in 1956. While that is outside the timescale of this book it has been made topical by a 1990 biography of Driberg, which is ill informed on the matter. The Burgess visit was utilized by MI5 to stage a dirty trick of a special kind, in which I was willingly involved.

Hollis and the rest of the MI5 management were desperate to prevent the return of Burgess because, until Anthony Blunt confessed in 1964, there was no hard evidence against him. The prospect of such a notorious defector swanning about his old London haunts, with the security authorities impotent, was a fearful prospect.

When Driberg proposed visiting Burgess – it may even have been on MI5's initiative – he was asked to induce Burgess to recall some details of the brief time he had spent in the secret Special Operations Executive during the war and to include them in the script of a book he proposed to publish and which he undertook to submit for vetting. Eventually MI5 went through the motions of warning the publishers of the book that they risked prosecution unless they removed the items which were still officially secret. They did so and I was then approached, on behalf of MI5, by Rear Admiral George Thomson, who was then Secretary of the D-Notice Committee. He asked me if I would point out, with maximum prominence, in the *Daily Express* that Burgess had committed technical breaches of the Official Secrets Act which meant that he could be prosecuted if he ever returned to Britain. I duly obliged, since it was an excellent 'story' in its own right. MI5 knew that the rest of the book entitled 'Guy Burgess – a portrait with background' was largely a disinformation exercise, since the KGB had controlled what Burgess had said and Driberg had written, but it considered that a worthwhile trade-off for publicity which might prevent the dreaded return of Burgess.

The book was, perhaps, a unique example of an intelligence exercise controlled by both the KGB and MI5 and with both aware of their different purposes. It was also an example of Driberg's penchant for playing both ends at once. The KGB had also made use of the opportunity of Driberg's visit to frame him with action-shot homosexual pictures taken with men he had picked up in the public urinals, his inveterate habit wherever he was. He claimed not to have been concerned, but publicity of the style which the KGB was to inflict on Anthony Courtney could have finished him politically.

After Frolik's exposure of Driberg, which never became public until Peter Wright revealed it to me, MI5 re-engaged Driberg in the hope of feeding disinformation to both the Czechs and the KGB. He had told MI5 that the Russians were keen to pay him well for information about the Labour Party's internal affairs. As Labour was soon in Opposition, MI5 had no objection so long as Driberg gave them the same information for their own files. The KGB provided two identical briefcases which had been bought in Britain, so that he could hand in one with his information and receive the other containing his payment. MI5 had insisted that all the money should be given in and put in the slush fund, but there could be no check on the payments and Driberg is believed to have abstracted substantial 'expenses'.

Friends of Driberg have tried to ridicule the idea that he could have been a spy on the grounds that nobody would have trusted him with a secret. The same false argument was applied to Burgess before proof of his perfidy, including the evidence of Anthony Blunt, gradually accrued. Both were arch deceivers endowed with superficial charm, an essential qualification. Driberg's friends, like Michael Foot, fell prey to the all too common self-delusion 'if he had been a spy I would have detected it'.

Lord Harris of Greenwich, the Labour peer, who was close to Hugh Gaitskell, told me that the former Labour leader had been intensely suspicious of Driberg as being involved with the KGB. Did Harold Wilson ever suspect that he was an MI5 spy or even a double agent? He was certainly aware of his pouncing homosexual activities and must have wondered why his life was so charmed. It did not stop him, though, from sending

Driberg to the Lords, which he did not deserve on any count, having been a thoroughly bad constituency MP. According to Lady Falkender the peerage had been requested by his friend Michael Foot, because Driberg was going blind. Whatever the reason, it was another monstrous mockery of the honours system. MI5 officers have told me that, while they were disgusted by the award to such an evil creature, it did mean that the service had another useful agent in the House of Lords.

Some of the information provided by the Czech defectors which was potentially most damaging to Wilson and the Labour Party as a whole concerned leaders and other senior officials of certain unions. In the Kremlin's 'long march through the institutions of the West' the trade unions had been prime targets, and a relatively small number of Communists infiltrated there had achieved a remarkable degree of power and would continue to do so. Some unions were openly led by Communists, while others were led by Communists who kept their true political allegiance secret. Among the latter was the Institution of Professional Civil Servants, which represented many of the most senior Government officials. It was led by the highly intelligent and charming Stanley Mayne, a major source of mine, who, unknown to the governments of his day, was a dedicated member of the Communist Party with access to a great deal of secret information. Through their card votes the unions, which were major financial supporters of the Labour Party, had been instrumental in pushing Labour policy increasing to the Left. The names of trade union leaders whom Frolik had alleged to be dangerously pro-Soviet were kept from Wilson but were to become public during the time of his successor, James Callaghan.

To his considerable surprise, Wilson lost the 1970 general election to Edward Heath, whose reign was to be short. During his time in Opposition the left-wing extremists who had infiltrated the National Executive of the Labour Party induced the 1973 Party Conference to abolish the Proscribed List – the Communist and Communist front organizations which Labour Party members had been forbidden to join. It meant that even MPs could join the World Peace Council, the British-Soviet Friendship Society and other outfits run essentially for the benefit of Moscow. As was intended, scrapping the Proscribed List produced a further discernible lurch to the Left which inevitably engaged the attention of MI5, charged as it was with containing revolutionary Communism in the interests of protecting democracy. Privately, Wilson had disapproved of the abolition, but he had needed to curry favour with the unions of which he had fallen foul early in 1969, when he had tried to introduce legislation to curb unofficial strikes.

That proposal had been put forward as a White Paper, *In Place of Strife*, which required a compulsory twenty-eight-day conciliation pause for unofficial strikers, who could be prosecuted if they declined to return to work during the 'cooling-off' period. With the exception of Barbara Castle, who introduced the paper, all his Cabinet colleagues, who feared the unions more than they did, deserted him. To cover his defeat Wilson withdrew the project on the transparent pretext that the union leaders had given a binding undertaking to intervene in unofficial stoppages.

One union leader who was not of the Left, Joe Gormley, President of the Miners' Union, was to accuse Wilson of duplicity during the miners' dispute while he was in Opposition in 1973. Gormley was confident that a settlement could be reached privately with the Coal Board and a national disaster – the three-day week – would be prevented. He took Wilson into his confidence, and Wilson then put forward as his own the solution which Gormley had masterminded. The ensuing publicity made the deal impossible. Wilson later claimed that the plan had been leaked by the Communist miners' leader, Mick McGahey, but Gormley did not believe him. He told Wilson that he regarded his action as a betrayal and that he would never trust him again. It is possible that Wilson leaked the plan to scuttle it so that Heath would be forced to declare an election, which he lost, but politicians are not usually that clever or so far-sighted.

While Wilson had been in office MI5 had made repeated complaints, usually through the Foreign Office, about the number of Soviet Bloc agents operating in London. There were so many posing as diplomats, trade officials, cultural delegates and journalists that the counter-espionage which MI5 could mount with its limited resources was being saturated – a KGB device used throughout the world. Wilson had declined to agree to any action. Apart from his growing belief that MI5 exaggerated everything, he was anxious to improve trade and general relations with the Soviet Bloc and knew how touchy Moscow was about suggestions of espionage.

In 1971, however, when Heath was Prime Minister, an opportunity to take action was presented by the defection of a KGB officer called Oleg Lyalin. Over the previous six months, while he had been working for MI5 as an agent in place, he had confirmed the names of some three hundred active KGB officers among Soviet officials serving under various covers in Britain. The Tory Government wanted to avoid a public row with Moscow and quietly tried to induce the Soviets to reduce their espionage effort. When this failed, the Government announced that 105 agents would no longer be allowed to remain in Britain.

Wilson's reaction to this was to suggest, ridiculously, that it was a Tory dirty trick to help them win a by-election, when in fact MI5 had hard evidence against every one of the agents. His comment caused wry smiles in MI5, as Peter Wright told me, but he was soon to take a more serious view.

Some months before he had defected, Lyalin had warned MI5 that Wilson's close friend Kagan, who had already been under suspicion, had been in regular touch with Richardas Vaygauskas, one of the most senior KGB officers among those to be expelled. Like Kagan, Vaygauskas was a Lithuanian and MI5 suspected that the KGB had posted him to London as a trade delegate to cultivate Kagan, his friendship with Wilson being well known through the Prime Minister's habit of wearing Gannex coats.

Surveillance which, according to Peter Wright, included telephone tapping and the insertion of microphones in Kagan's homes, led MI5 to suspect that Vaygauskas briefed Kagan on questions he should ask during his talks with Wilson. It was thought that Vaygauskas would then debrief Kagan and tell him what to ask next. Peter Wright recalled one incident when Vaygauskas was said to have been with Kagan when he went into Number 10 to see Wilson at about 10 p.m., and waited outside. When Kagan reappeared there was a conversation, and Kagan went back in again around midnight. MI5's inference was that Kagan had asked something on the KGB man's behalf, had reported to him and then returned to ask Wilson a supplementary question posed by Vaygauskas.

Kagan, who had recently been knighted on Wilson's recommendation, was interviewed. He admitted that Vaygauskas was a friend who visited his London office and his homes in Yorkshire, but insisted that their mutual interests were East-West trade and chess. Kagan said that he had been making arrangements with Vaygauskas to visit the Soviet Union to advise on the manufacture of Gannex under licence.

Kagan alerted Wilson, who decided that he would be wise to consult MI5. For some reason – probably because he felt he could not approach MI5 directly without Heath's permission, which would reveal his situation – he contacted Sir Arthur Young, a former head of the City of London police and a friend of Kagan, who supplied the City Police with Gannex clothing.

The MI5 officer dealing with the Lyalin case then briefed Wilson on the situation. Wilson assured him that he never discussed confidential matters with Kagan and had no idea of his friend's associations with any Russians except through legitimate trading. He insisted that Kagan had never asked anything about Government policy arising out of his relationship with the KGB man. Both Wilson and Kagan have given the same assurances to me.

The surveillance of Kagan was stepped up, and MI5 recruited several informants from among Kagan's friends and employees. MI5 continued to be interested in Kagan after Vaygauskas had been expelled, and suspected that he was occasionally in touch with other KGB officers. One MI5 officer, Tony Brooks, who used the pseudonym Colonel Tony Brewster, spent a year on the Vaygauskas case.

The experience could only have soured Wilson's relations with MI5 still further, though in the bizarre circumstances MI5 had been understandably alarmed and did no more than its duty. It certainly did not end or even lessen his friendship with Kagan, as MI5 would have preferred. The association would embarrass Wilson even more at a later date and cast further doubt on the quality of his judgement.

11

A Light-Hearted Lunch

On 5 March 1974 Wilson returned to power, having beaten Heath but by a majority of only four seats, so that a further election later in the year seemed inevitable. Marcia Falkender assured me that he did not expect to win and was almost disappointed when he did. His senior political adviser, Bernard Donoughue, (now Lord) wrote, 'Wilson had made no preparations whatsoever for victory . . . he had made quite bizarre preparations to go into hiding should he be defeated.'

To many others he seemed to have lost his zest for power. After the election results had been declared on 28 February there was a period in which Heath negotiated with Jeremy Thorpe, the Liberal leader, about the possibility of forming a coalition government. Lord Kagan told me that Wilson hoped that Heath would succeed. When he did not, Mary Wilson was so disappointed that she declined to live in Downing Street and Wilson took a private house near the Commons in Lord North Street. She hated political life, having married a young man whom she expected to remain an academic, and particularly disliked 'living over the shop'.

In the previous month Wilson had told a small group of intimates that he did not intend to stay in office for more than two years if he won the forthcoming election, being intent on retiring from active politics on his sixtieth birthday. This information quickly leaked, and I reported on 17 May that the Tory leadership did not expect him to stay long if he won. I had heard that such doubts were also common among Labour MPs, some whom were already jostling for the leadership.

His statement to one of his senior staff was more specific and much more interesting. He confided that his father had suffered from a premature senile condition which had affected his mind though not his longevity. He suspected that he might possibly go the same way and did not want that to happen while he was still in office.

Only ten days after Wilson's return, in my weekly column in the *Daily Express*, I stated that a legal document containing allegations about his previous premiership, which could be highly embarrassing if they became public, was in the hands of the Treasury Solicitor. It was a detailed statement of claim in an action against the Civil Service Department brought by fifty-five-year-old Mrs Marjorie Halls, of Barnes in London. She was the widow of Mr Michael Halls, who had been principal private secretary to Wilson at Number 10 Downing Street from 1966 until 1970, when he had died of a sudden heart attack at the age of fifty-four.

I had been alerted to the action not by MI5, as some have suggested, but by the owner of a restaurant I frequented who happened to be a friend of Mrs Halls and of her late husband. While the story created only moderate interest among other newspapers, and did not excite me all that much, it generated deep concern inside Number 10 and was to play a major role in the delusions which Wilson was shortly to entertain about MI5.

Mrs Halls, then a civil servant on the Lord Chancellor's staff, was claiming compensation of the order of £50,000 on the grounds that her husband had died because of the intolerable strain imposed by 'extremely unusual conditions' inside Number 10. She claimed that extra strain had been inflicted by having to deal with additional tensions outside his normal sphere of duty, meaning Marcia's tantrums and problems over her children. Her legal depositions, of which I secured copies, referred to blazing rows and slanging matches between Marcia and the Prime Minister, occasions which had already been described to me by George Wigg. The media, looking for further material with which to renew the assault on Wilson, did not have long to wait.

The *Guardian* was the first newspaper to be told that Wilson might have been involved in land speculation near Wigan, and the editor was prevailed upon not to print the story. The *Daily Mail*, however, was quickly on to the news and secured documents about the deals, which involved some slag heaps at Ince-in-Makerfield which became known as the 'Wigan Alps'.

Wilson's signature, which turned out to be a forgery, was on one of them. The land had been bought by Marcia's brother, Tony Field, in the hope of selling the slag, possibly as hardcore, and then developing the land. Marcia and her sister Peggy were partners in the deal. The *Daily Mail* did not run the story until a fortnight after the narrow Labour victory in the general election, so nobody could allege that it had been printed in any media drive to keep Wilson out of office.

Oddly, little notice was taken of the *Daily Mail* story until information about another deal concerning forty acres of building land on the edge of the green belt at Solihull was brought to my attention. A Birmingham businessman, of whom I had never heard, telephoned me about the deal and said he had a letter indicating that Wilson's name was involved in it. His purpose was to expose the local entrepreneur concerned, who was an undischarged bankrupt, though he did not like Wilson either. It was to be alleged that I had dredged this up in some circulation battle with the *Daily Mail*. In fact I had not even read the *Daily Mail* 'Wigan Alps' story, because it was not a field in which I was normally involved.

The entrepreneur had written to Wilson, who was not his MP, to find out about the possibilities of developing the land. Wilson, then Leader of the Opposition, had passed it to Tony Field, who had replied on Wilson's behalf. My interest increased when, on visiting the informant in Birmingham, I found that the entrepreneur had served as an agent for Mr Field, Marcia and Peggy in the slag heaps deal.

When my front-page report appeared on 3 April the *Daily Mail* responded by repeating its slag heaps story in greater detail. Both were then taken up by the media generally and in Parliament. Wilson, who was not really involved in either of the deals and should have ignored the publicity, quickly issued writs for libel against both papers but did not pursue them. Eventually he withdrew his libel claim against the *Express* and paid his own costs.

When faced with parliamentary questions, he could have truthfully denied any implication and was urged to do so but, loyally if foolishly, he felt driven to defend Marcia and her brother. So he consulted a friend, whom he would later honour with a knighthood, to ask how to deal with the situation. The friend suggested that he should insist that it was not a matter of land speculation but 'reclamation', which he did, to gales of laughter from the Tory benches and the public.

While backbenchers had fun at Wilson's expense, the Tory leadership did not pursue the land deals affair because, as will shortly be seen in another context, it did not want to precipitate another election so soon. The affair served only to addle Wilson's relations with the media still further. At no stage had there been any input from MI5, but I have little doubt that, had the police not found and prosecuted the man responsible, MI5 would have been suspected of the forgery.

The next major event to stir up press reaction to the Prime Minister was the extraordinary life peerage he bestowed on Marcia in May 1974, though it was the timing rather than the event itself which raised eyebrows, inside MI5 as elsewhere. It meant that she continued in Number 10 as a baroness when such honours were usually given only on the final retirement of a Prime Minister. George Wigg telephoned me to express his gross affront in barrack-room language, and there was little doubt that many loyal party workers who had done far more were deeply offended. The honour was publicly attacked as 'insensitive' in many political areas. Marcia explained it to me as a device to allow her to continue with a political life if Wilson failed to win the election he planned for October, but she has never really made political use of it.

Prior to the general election of February 1974, wishing to help to keep Wilson out of office, I had talked privately with a few friends – none of them from MI5 or any other secret department – about the possibility of a media campaign, using Mrs Halls' simmering legal action and other genuine topics in ways which could, I suppose, be classed as dirty tricks. Eventually I visited Lord Carrington, an old acquaintance and then Chairman of the Conservative Party, to discuss the possible issues. Politely, he made it clear that he was not interested himself and passed me to an official who made notes but did not seem to be interested either.

When I mentioned this response to my old friend the Kenyan politician Bruce McKenzie, who happened to be in England, he suggested that I should put the project to Lord Aldington, who was very close to Edward Heath. We met at the Mirabelle in Mayfair and Aldington, who did not express a personal view, agreed to tell Heath what I had told him. In short order, I received a message from Heath through an intermediary that he wanted nothing to do with dirty tricks, that he was going to win the election anyway and wanted to be seen to have won it cleanly.

Any possible private enterprise on my part was then suddenly stymied by a call to see Sir Max Aitken, who was a shooting pal as well as my proprietor. Following Wilson's call to him to visit Ian Smith in Rhodesia, he had grown to like him and had also fallen under the spell of Wilson's friend and solicitor Lord Goodman, a person of great charm and warm nature. Max told me that he had decided that the attacks on Wilson had gone too far and should cease unless there was some really important news which could not be ignored. I had little doubt that either Wilson or Goodman or both had appealed to him.

A week or two later I went up to see him about some news which I thought important to try to induce him to print it. His response was to say, 'I must get on to Goodman right away.' When I asked why, he replied, 'To warn Wilson.' On another occasion when I approached him with some genuine news he said that we could not print it because Wilson was coming to open the extension to the *Express* building called Aitken House. I had accepted a distinction called the Valiant for Truth award, but thereupon withdrew on the grounds that the truth was something I was not being permitted to print.

I was resigned to writing nothing of consequence about Wilson and did not do so until, early one Thursday morning, I was telephoned at home by my editor, Ian McColl, a most delightful and enthusiastic man with whom to work. He too had been told of Sir Max's ban, and had agreed with it on the grounds that he was bored with stories about Wilson. He asked me to join him at lunch but did not say why, though it was clearly going to be conspiratorial.

On the previous day I had met John Junor, the editor of the *Sunday Express*, going out of the office and, both being from the north and canny, we boarded a bus for our lunch appointments in the West End. On the way, as a bit of gossip, I had mentioned that, through Wigg, I had secured copies of the birth certificates of Marcia's children and had given them to McColl to keep locked in his safe against the day when they could conceivably be needed. Over our lunch McColl revealed that

Junor was more interested than he had appeared to be. He said that Junor had walked into his office and declared that, unless he printed the story about the birth certificates within the next two days, he would do so on the following Sunday. McColl decided that he could not be scooped that way and that the *Daily Express* would run it. Further, as I had been responsible for bringing the certificates in, I would have to write it.

I was horrified because the father named on the certificates, Walter Terry, was by that time on the *Daily Express* staff and I would be seen to be shopping a colleague. I took refuge in Sir Max's ban but McColl said that the proprietor was airborne on a long journey and could not be contacted, and the story had to be printed that night to beat Junor's threat.

As soon as McColl returned to the office he called Terry in to warn him what was going to happen. Understandably Terry questioned the purpose of shooting one of his own soldiers, but the editor was adamant. Equally understandably, Terry alerted Joe Haynes at Number 10. In his book *The Politics of Power* Haynes gives some idea of the deep concern inside the kitchen cabinet at this news, which was rightly regarded as yet another media dirty trick involving me.

At 6.30 that evening the chief lawyer and I were in the editor's room discussing the final proof of the story, with which it was proposed to lead the paper, when there was a telephone call. It was Goodman, who had managed to contact Sir Max and urged McColl to get himself to his office. The lawyer and I waited for his return, when he assured us that the story was merely postponed. We were greatly relieved and confident that it would never appear. It didn't, as Sir Max remained adamant.

After that non-event I received a surprise visit from a man I understood to be an emissary of Edward Heath. He was certainly very close to him and had no connection whatever with MI5. He told me that there was grave fear that Wilson was planning to spring a snap election in June to increase his unworkably small majority. Labour's stock had risen dramatically because of various concessions to the trade unions which heralded industrial peace, and soundings showed that Wilson would be returned with such a swing that some Tory Shadow Ministers would lose their seats. It was, therefore, an anything-goes situation, and any media ploys to discourage Wilson from going to the country would now be welcome. I was left in no doubt that they could include the 'dirty tricks' which had been rejected just a few months earlier. I told my visitor that I would bear the message in mind, but was rather a weak reed because of Sir Max's ban.

Shortly afterwards, on a lovely May Sunday, my wife and I were invited to lunch at the country home of Michael Sacher, a director and major shareholder of Marks and Spencer, at Greywell in Hampshire. This pleasant occasion was, without any question, the seminal source of Wilson's delusions about the MI5 plot against him. Until the events which followed it he had never expressed any serious belief that MI5 was trying to undermine him and his Government, much as he disapproved of their interest in some of his friends and colleagues.

It was a gathering of perhaps two dozen people of various ages and after lunch about half of us, mainly men, moved to the music room where one of the guests asked me what I thought about Marcia's peerage, which had recently been announced. I gave my view. I then spoke about the doubts concerning Marcia's security clearance revealed by Mrs Halls and how that and the question of Marcia's children could be raised in Mrs Halls's court case if it proceeded, as seemed likely, because the Treasury Solicitor was preparing to defend it. Spurred on by my audience I mentioned a few other possible 'time bombs', such as the land deals row and how this and any other damaging matters would probably be raised as election issues by the media and Tory politicians. I mentioned that, while Edward Heath had previously been opposed to such 'dirty tricks', I had been informed that they would be welcomed to prevent an early election. If I made any mention of MI5, which I do not recall, it could only have been in reference to the claim by Mrs Halls that there had been a problem with the re-vetting of Marcia. At no time did I suggest that Marcia or Harold Wilson were Communists or Communist-inclined, because I knew there was no evidence of any such connection, though others thought there might be. By his actions Wilson had shown, repeatedly, that he was really right of centre and Marcia supported whatever he did. I remarked that, while I expected other journalists to pursue such issues in the coming weeks, I would not be one of them because of a general *Daily Express* ban on attacks on Wilson, which I deplored.

The investigative writer David Leigh has stated, 'There had been an MI5 officer there who had spoken very freely.' Totally wrong! Nobody from MI5 was present. I was the only person who had spoken freely, and I have never been in MI5. In a previous account of the lunch I had mentioned the presence of a former senior figure from the Defence Ministry, whom Leigh regarded as 'mysterious' and 'clearly more senior than Peter Wright'. In fact it was Sir Derek Rayner (now Lord), a director of Marks and Spencer, who had been called in during the Heath Government to find ways of increasing efficiency in the Defence Ministry and was still serving on certain working parties there. He was at the lunch as a fellow member, with Michael Sacher, of the Marks and Spencer board, of which he was to become the chairman. He was also to become a member of the Security Commission three years later, but at that time had no connection with MI5.

I answered numerous questions from what must have been a predominantly Tory audience, and can recall only one claim that a smear campaign to prevent or sway an election could never by justified. This came from a man, casually dressed in jeans, whom I had never met. I learned later that his name was Martin Gilbert and that he was the historian who had secured the right to be the official biographer of Sir Winston Churchill. I had never heard of him until a couple of weeks later when he wrote to me from an address in Oxford enclosing a memorized account of my remarks and claiming that Mr Heath must somehow be allowed to disassociate himself from them. I replied, pointing out his inaccuracies, but was not surprised to receive a second letter warning me that he was sending his account to Heath and, I later learned, to Wilson, who was a friend. Whatever his motives, this was a dirty trick on me, and eventually Michael Sacher required him to apologise for breaching the confidentiality of his private household. Michael explained that he had a difficulty in that Gilbert was about to become his son-in-law!

I did not see the letter which Gilbert sent, but according to Wilson the one he received contained the allegation that he and Marcia were being accused of being part of a Communist cell inside Number 10. At least that is what Wilson told other people. Wilson had also concluded that the allegation had originated with MI5. No such allegation had ever been made by me because it was ludicrous. I can only think that Wilson assumed that my comments had come from MI5 because of his belief that I had close associations with that agency.

Wilson claimed that he was also told that I would be leading the pack of journalists – he was later to call them 'cohorts' – who would be denigrating him, when in fact I had made it clear that I would not be allowed to take part. My published output over the next few months is proof that I did not do so.

It is quite certain that until the receipt of Gilbert's letter Wilson had never complained that MI5 had been trying to undermine him, though he was angry about its treatment of his friends. From 1964 to 1974 Wilson believed that the media were conspiring to destroy him and his Government. Only when the garbled report of my statements at the lunch reached him did he begin to suspect that MI5 must have been priming the media, which, so far as I was concerned, was totally untrue. In short, the MI5 plot was a mythical spin-off from the real media plot.

Gilbert was to write and tell me that Heath had denied any suggestion that I had been approached about any media campaign on his behalf. Heath was misinformed, though it was possible that the move had been made on his behalf without his knowledge. The emissary who had visited me before manfully came to see me again to apologise for Heath's denial. I do not give his name because he is now an important political figure.

Earlier in 1974, Wilson and several of his staff were subjected to a series of break-ins at their homes and offices. These were to continue until, according to both Wilson and Marcia, they numbered more than a dozen. Allegedly, they involved the theft of tax papers from his home in Lord North Street while other tax documents, letters, photographs and tape recordings had been stolen from a room in Buckingham Palace Road where they had been stored. Marcia's cottage near Great Missenden in Buckinghamshire, had also been entered. Originally Wilson thought that BOSS, the South African security/intelligence service, of which he was extravagantly suspicious, had been responsible; so much so that when one of his senior advisers told him that burglars had stolen his long-case clock Wilson replied, 'South African without a doubt. You'll find it in the South African Embassy.' BOSS could conceivably have been involved in some of the episodes, though a former Rhodesian intelligence chief has claimed that his agents took part in the campaign to discredit Wilson by spreading rumours and may have been searching for material. Some, perhaps most, of the break-ins, had in fact been perpetrated by ordinary criminals, and Scotland Yard caught two of them.

After the implication of MI5, however, following the Sacher lunch, Wilson began to suspect that MI5 might have organized the burglaries in a search for damaging material to leak to the media. In conversations with me, both Wilson and Marcia attributed at least some of the burglaries to MI5 without any evidence. Supporters of the MI5 plot against Wilson have made the same unwarranted assumption.

It is extremely unlikely that MI5 was ever involved at all, for reasons which are obvious. When surreptitious entries are undertaken by MI5 they are so professional that they leave no trace. They do not steal documents but photograph them, leaving the originals exactly as they were. Any entry involves a substantial team with watchers in radio contact, staking out the location and keeping surveillance on the owner and on anyone else who might visit it, so that the 'raid' can be quickly called off. If there is a watchman, his movements are noted over several days, sometimes weeks. MI5 'burglars' never have to 'break in' anywhere because they have keys to every kind of lock, on which they do a complete reconnaissance first.

That is why in all the years they have been carrying out surreptitious entries they have never been caught. The size of such a team – at least a dozen people – means that the operation cannot be carried out by a couple of 'cowboys' It must have the authority of the senior management, which would never agree to an action against a Prime Minister, past or present, because of the consequences of exposure. Speaking to me in 1980, and years later on a *Panorama* TV programme, Peter Wright denied any knowledge of the burglaries and thought it most unlikely that MI5 had been involved because the break-ins were too amateurish.

12

Ungleaming Cohorts

On 14 June 1974, on the grounds that it was genuine news, I reported a further development in Mrs Halls's case against the government. I stated that, according to her, a 'certain person' had caused great difficulty to her husband when he had been on Wilson's staff over her second positive vetting in 1969. Halls had been instructed to deal with it as a special case. It was clear to any reader familiar with the Whitehall scene that the person referred to was Marcia Falkender, who had then been understandably averse to revealing the existence of her children.

It has been widely assumed that this information about Marcia's vetting problem had been put about by MI5. There is no truth in that. It had come to me directly from Mrs Halls, who had no involvement whatever with MI5. Marcia was to tell me later that she and Wilson believed that I had induced Mrs Halls to bring the claim and was prompting her moves. This was a further delusion. I had never heard of her before she began her action, and had advised her that she could never prove that her husband's death was due to anything but natural causes.

A security issue of the highest significance intruded itself into Wilson's life in the summer when Stephen de Mowbray, a former MI6 officer, presented himself at 10 Downing Street and asked to see the Prime Minister. Instead he had a long session with the Cabinet Secretary, Sir John Hunt (now Lord), and told him of his deep concern about the suspicion that a former Director General of MI5, Sir Roger Hollis, had been a Soviet agent. Hunt was not too surprised by the suspicions regarding Hollis for, a few months previously, in Edward Heath's premiership, there had been discussions about the dangers of KGB penetration. As an extra precaution, it had then been decided to appoint a Privy Councillor of unquestionably integrity to whom allegations of possible treachery might be referred for quick investigation; Lord Trend, then Rector of Lincoln College, Oxford, had agreed to take on the task should the need arise. Hunt was so impressed by de Mowbray's conviction that there had been a high-level spy in MI5 that he believed that the allegations should be referred to Trend.

The development caused consternation at the top in MI5, because de Mowbray was from MI6 and it looked like an interference promoted by the MI6 chief, by then Maurice Oldfield. A typical Oldfield 'dirty trick' was how it seemed to the MI5 management, who had assured themselves that the Hollis case was dead and buried. In fact, de Mowbray had acted entirely on his own initiative.

As he initialled the memo from Hunt, Wilson must have scratched his head when, so shortly after receiving information that MI5 thought he might be part of a Communist cell, he was being told that a recent head of that organization might have been a Communist spy! Nobody knew better than Wilson that, by keeping Harold Macmillan in ignorance about the security aspects of the Profumo Affair for so long, Hollis had contributed to his resignation and the eventual defeat of his Government.

Allegations that the Hollis Affair was withheld from Wilson are totally untrue, as Lord Hunt can confirm. In fact Wilson was later, in Parliament and on television, to claim credit for initiating Trend's inquiry. Further, after de Mowbray's visit he remarked to Marcia, who retailed it to me and to others, 'Now I've heard everything! I have just been told that the head of MI5 himself may have been a double agent.'

Hunt also told Wilson about the Blunt case, and the way that that self-confessed traitor had been granted immunity from both prosecution and publicity on Hollis's recommendation could hardly have improved his impression of MI5. Wilson told me that he had not been told about Blunt or had forgotten. Hunt is quite certain that he was told.

In late 1974 Trend was given a room on the fifth floor of MI5 headquarters, Leconfield House in Curzon Street. There for several months he spent two days a week browsing among the relevant documents, including all ten volumes of the file code-

named Fluency, which contained the results of the investigations into Hollis by a team of MI5 and MI6 officers. He made
no independent inquiries. He interviewed those officers who
were not serving abroad, including Peter Wright – at least twice
– and the senior and more balanced Christopher Phillpotts.
Both of them told me that Trend said there seemed to be a *prima
facie* case against Hollis. He did not interview John Day, who
had interrogated Hollis and who might have impressed
him most.

No new evidence whatever reached him, and at the finish he
was in no better a position than the members of the Fluency
Committee had been when they had completed their inquiries
four years previously. He was impressed by the lack of ideological background on Hollis. In the end he took a value judgement and gave him the benefit of the doubt. As a former
Cabinet Secretary, Trend had been the chief accounting officer
for the secret services, so he had a special interest in killing any
suggestions that many of MI5's efforts had been virtually nulli-
fied for thirty years.

Trend submitted his report to Wilson in the early summer of
1975. De Mowbray was seen by Hunt and briefed on Trend's
findings, which he declined to accept, but was not allowed to
see the report. Otherwise it was held secret in the Cabinet
Office.

Events which inevitably topped up the spate of bad publicity
continued to occur. Wilson awarded another controversial
peerage to a personal friend and appointed him Army Minister
in the Defence Ministry. This was Lord Brayley, who had made
a fortune in various business ventures. Brayley had a good
Army record, but unfortunately the Board of Trade was about
to make an inquiry into the Canning Town Glassworks, of
which he had been chairman, because of evidence of financial
corruption. Brayley was required to resign from the
Government and he beat a possible fraud charge by dying.
While no security issue had been involved, the incident could
only have increased MI5's wonder at Wilson's choice of friends
and colleagues.

In July 1974 several journalists, of whom I was one, received
envelopes containing a photocopy of a financial statement in
the name of Edward W. Short MP, showing deposits in the
Swiss Bank Corporation. The account was in credit by about

£23,000 and at that time, because of exchange controls, it was illegal if it was genuine. Having grave doubts about it, because such accounts are numbered and not named, I immediately took it down to the House of Commons to show it to Mr Short, who is on record as saying that this was his first knowledge of it. He declined to be interviewed but there can be little doubt that he informed Wilson that it was a forgery and, more than probably, because of the Prime Minister's recent information about the Sacher lunch, it was concluded that I might be a witting part of the action and that MI5 was involved. So far as I am aware, nobody ever discovered who concocted and sent the forgery. MI5 seems a most unlikely contender because though some newspapers – not including mine – reported the incident, it was so easy for Short (now Lord Glenamara) to prove that it was a fake that no objective could be achieved. Further, it was obvious that Scotland Yard detectives would be called in to investigate, as they were, and there was no love lost between the Yard and MI5. If the police had discovered that MI5 was involved they would, I believe, have leaked it.

Further commotion was caused that summer by the disclosure of plans to set up an anti-chaos organization, a free enterprise outfit to keep essential services going if political extremists tried to make the country ungovernable. The announcement had been given to me by the founder, the legendary David Stirling (now Sir), who had initiated the SAS during World War II and was a friend of mine. Composed of engineers, computer experts, helicopter pilots, lorry drivers and such – Stirling was inundated with volunteers – the outfit had no military overtones. Like others before it, the organization was quickly smeared as a 'private army', with the inevitable suggestion that it might be part of right-wing planning for a coup.

This derisory and totally inaccurate term had previously been applied to a similar organization called Unison, run by George Young, the former MI6 deputy chief. When I had announced its existence in January 1974, at Young's behest, he had described it as a 'vigilante group' to help protect the nation against a Communist takeover because the unions were being so militant and had brought the Tory Government down. It was a private group of ex-service chiefs, former MI6 intelligence officers, bankers and businessmen whose stated purpose was 'to help to preserve the law and the Constitution if the Government of the day fails to rise to a major threat of civil conflict' and 'to stop the sewage running down the streets'.

The organizations had no connection with the Army or MI5, which both disapproved of them, just as the police dislike vigilantes. When I had asked Young if he had any members from MI5, past or current, his reply was, 'Not on your nelly! We would never trust that lot.' It was the continuing activities of the hard leftists who were threatening Wilson's position with the breakdown of public services which had stimulated Stirling and others into action. But the 'private armies' must have stirred up anxieties about a military coup in the minds of certain people.

Wilson watched for any further developments in the expected campaign by the media or Tory backbenchers, but nothing of consequence happened until he announced the coming general election on 20 September 1974. Two days later I wrote a short item about a further development in the Mrs Halls case and Wilson assumed, understandably perhaps, that this was my opening shot in the election dirty tricks campaign. Again nothing could have been further from the truth. The ban on gratuitous attacks on Wilson imposed by Sir Max Aitken was still in force and the appearance of my brief report at that time was entirely fortuitous and had nothing to do with MI5. It merely said that the Head of the Civil Service, Sir Douglas Allen, had promised to recommend an *ex gratia* payment for Mrs Halls, which would mean that the action would be dropped. This suggested that there must be something in her claim and that she was about to be paid for keeping quiet. Mrs Halls had telephoned me with the news and wanted it printed immediately. I warned her that publicity might lose her the money, but she insisted on it and on 30 September Allen withdrew his offer.

The item, which was not given much prominence in the newspaper, seemed unlikely to cause any stir, but it sounded such alarm bells in Wilson's self-deluding ears that he ignored all advice and committed what his advisers foresaw would be a major blunder. He was due to make a speech in Portsmouth and, entirely because of that item, as Joe Haines has recorded, he insisted on inserting the sarcastic statement that 'Cohorts of distinguished journalists have been combing parts of the country with a mandate to find anything, true or fabricated, for use against the Labour Party.' This was a pre-emptive measure to blacken the press, and in his memoirs, *The Politics of Power*, Haines has described the unsuccessful efforts he made to persuade Wilson to avoid it because it was bound to alienate the media. The Prime Minister's conspiracy paranoia over-rode his judgement. As for combing the countryside, I had never moved out of my office. But Haines was right when he said in his book that my hostility to the Prime Minister was of long standing.

After he had won the election Wilson was repeatedly challenged to produce his evidence for the 'cohorts', but never effectively did so. Among evidence that he submitted to the Royal Commission on the Press, which he had set up, was the statement that a 'prominent journalist known for his virulence of opposition to the Labour Government spoke at length and had his words taken down by one of our most distinguished hisorians at a private house party about his determination to expose all manner of things'.

Wilson made no mention of MI5 to the Royal Commission, but the mythical connection between my media attacks and MI5 that was in his mind was to be revealed shortly after his resignation when he opened his heart to two young BBC journalists. He told them how he had received a statement from Gilbert following allegations made by me at a country house and added that I 'was widely believed to have first-class connections with MI5 and MI6'. Not surprisingly, since it was an ex-Prime Minister speaking, the two journalists assumed that my information had come from MI5. None of it had.

Wilson claims that he had called in the head of MI5, Sir Michael Hanley, to find out the source of the rumours. He was later to tell me, 'Naturally, I took steps to ask the Director General, Sir Michael Hanley, personally if this was true. He replied that he believed it was true but that only a small number of right-wing officers was concerned.'

This was to be denied ten years later in Parliament on Hanley's behalf by Mrs Thatcher. Whose memory was at fault? Hanley was then aged sixty-nine, but Wilson's memory was by no means accurate at that time.

In November 1974 Wilson received another security shock. While swimming off Miami beach his former Minister, John

Stonehouse, having previously taken out life insurance policies payable to his wife, faked his death by drowning in order to escape from overwhelming debt due to business calamities. (A few weeks previously he had offered to make me a director of one of his companies if I would invest in it.) His secretary, Mrs Sheila Buckley, was party to his 'suicide' but his wife was not, a situation which Stonehouse himself was to describe as 'a dirty trick'. His nastiest deception, though, was obtaining a copy of the passport of a recently dead man whose widow he had pretended to be helping. He used this passport with a forged signature to gain entry to Australia under the name Markham. In addition, he made use of a copy of the birth certificate of another recently dead man called Mildoon, a name which he also used in Australia.

While he remained missing, the evidence of Josef Frolik, which the Czech defector had also given to a US Senate Committee, was published in America. Wilson, who, like MI5, feared that Stonehouse might have defected, was then required to inform Parliament what had occurred. He said that if there had been 'a scintilla of evidence' against Stonehouse he would not have remained a member of his Government. According to Wright, however, this went further than the MI5 brief, which simply indicated that there was no evidence that could be brought into court.

Stonehouse's duplicity was spotted in Australia through his use of two names in opening bank accounts, and the police were alerted. He flew to Denmark, probably under surveillance to see whom he might meet there. It turned out to be Mrs Buckley, who joined him briefly to plan a new life together in Australia. After ten days he returned to Melbourne and was arrested on Christmas Eve. It was suggested by the police that he might be Lord Lucan, who was wanted for murder. The two were not remotely alike; it was another deception ploy. Stonehouse had been watched by Australian security men in collaboration with MI5. When he had flown to Denmark it was suspected that he might try to defect, and I understand that arrangements had been made with the Danish security authorities to prevent that.

The police discovered that Stonehouse had £90,000, a large sum in 1975, in a bank account in Zurich, held in the name of Markham and paid in only two months before he disappeared.

It was frozen after writs were issued by banks claiming that he owed them £400,000.

After a six-month battle to avoid extradition he was sentenced in 1976 to seven years' imprisonment on theft and fraud charges. The judge described him as a 'deceitful and ambitious man, a sophisticated and skilful confidence trickster.' Mrs Buckley received a two-year suspended sentence.

Lord Dilhorne, who, apart from being Lord Chancellor, had other reasons for knowing MI5's information, said to me, 'Stonehouse was in it up to the neck'; but he declined to elaborate. Though *Spycatcher*, as published, contained little about Stonehouse, Peter Wright told me that he was convinced that he had been a Soviet Bloc agent taking money. After Callaghan succeeded Wilson various MPs urged him to ask the Security Commission to investigate the case, but he did not do so.

Wilson later remarked to me, 'I never thought he was a spy but I always knew he was a crook,' suggesting that he would do things that he should not for money. Yet if that was so, why had Wilson made him a Privy Councillor?

Stonehouse was released on parole after three years and married Mrs Buckley, after which he worked hard to establish himself as a novelist. He wrote four novels, one of which he dedicated to me after we had resumed our association. He remained buoyant and even suggested that we should visit Frolik in America and jointly author a book about his accusations! He blamed anybody and anything for his misfortunes, especially the political system which had 'failed his ideals', claiming to believe that his criminal acts were the result of 'trauma he suffered from his deep disillusionment with the state of British society'. I am satisfied that his real problem was that he wanted a quick route to riches. He mixed with wealthy people, one of them being our mutual friend Geoffrey Edwards, the arms entrepreneur who had made a large fortune very rapidly through arms sales to Saudi Arabia. We had stayed together at Edward's beautiful home in Ascot and I could see that Stonehouse was rather envious. Following Stonehouse's conviction I was informed by a business friend of Edwards that, when Stonehouse had been Aviation Minister, Edwards had paid him a substantial sum to facilitate the Saudi deal.

At the end of September 1975 I was told by Lord Rothschild that the Czech defector Frantisek August, who claimed to have run Stonehouse from Prague headquarters, was coming to London from America under a false name. I now know that the original source was Wright and that he was trying to reopen the Stonehouse case – another of his deception operations. David Leigh has claimed that this minor incident was 'the most direct confirmation of the Wilson plot'. In fact it was no more than an attempt to reopen the Stonehouse case because Wright and others in MI5 believed that he had been a spy and had got away with it, even though he had been convicted for fraud.

I published the information but did not manage to find August, who had been granted a visa by the Home Secretary, Roy Jenkins, and I was unable to mention Stonehouse for legal reasons. August made the visit, which was to contact an author who was to write his story.

Stonehouse, who had great charm and retained his sense of humour, had suffered serious heart problems while in prison. He died in 1988, aged sixty-two. Following the revolution in Czechoslovakia and the new democratic Government's increasing friendship with Britain, it is possible that MI5 may be given access to the Czech intelligence files on Stonehouse. If they are, it is unlikely that their findings will ever be made public, even if they show Stonehouse to have been innocent. The same probably applies to Driberg if the files on him in Prague become available, especially as he also worked for MI5.

Early in 1975, on a visit to Moscow, Wilson offered to lend the Kremlin almost £1000 million at a low rate of interest. His main purpose was to stimulate trade with Britain, but he was also known to be anxious to make amends for the diplomatic breach caused by the previous Government's expulsion of 105 Soviet agents. The deal, which incidentally freed roubles for the Kremlin to spend on weapons, was attacked in the media and raised some wonderment in the commercial world and later in MI5 when an extraordinary consequence of it came to light. In the following November it was revealed in Parliament that the Government was admitting an unlimited number of Soviet inspectors into British factories supplying industrial equipment under the soft loan arrangements. Security-sensitive factories like Rolls Royce and Ferranti were involved, and MI5 was incensed because the KGB was likely to infiltrate agents who would throw further strain on its limited surveillance resources. It made an excellent front-page splash with suitable leader comment.

By July 1975 the economic situation was in such a plight that George Young claimed that his anti-chaos organization, Unison, had been put on alert to step in should there be a national emergency. A radio network had been formed to take over if the BBC and the Post Office were shut down by political action. A number of privately owned small planes and an airfield were to assist with communications. Arrangements had been for the production and distribution of a broadsheet newspaper to keep the public informed if the newspapers were put out of action by strikes. A document which Young showed me claimed that some chief constables were collaborating and that there was a link with Buckingham Palace which, though he remained mysterious about it, was probably no more than some Palace official. Young, who gave me all the information for publication, said that Unison's studies indicated that industrial action posed such a serious threat in the coming winter that central Government could disintegrate. He was, in fact, three years in advance of the Winter of Discontent. It was a Labour Minister, Lord Harris of Greenwich, Minister of State in the Home Office with responsibility for MI5, who redefined subversion in 1975 as activities 'which threaten the safety or well-being of the State and which are intended to undermine or overthrow Parliamentary democracy by political, industrial or violent means'.

13

Dinners of Deception

In August 1975 Lord Weidenfeld was at a dinner where he heard some discussion of the same gossip which I had retailed at the Sacher lunch in the previous year, embroidered by passage through several heads and mouths. I know that this was the same old material because the Tory MP Winston Churchill, who had been present at the dinner, had telephoned me about it that same evening to seek my opinion about the 'Communist cell in Number 10'. I had told him that is was a completely garbled account of something I had said and was untrue, as far as I was aware.

Weidenfeld told Wilson about the rumours he had heard and said that they were circulating in 'clubs, drawing rooms and country houses'. After this reinforcement of his simmering fears by the recycled stories, the Prime Minister decided that there was no point in talking to anyone from MI5. So he decided to sound out the MI6 chief, Sir Maurice Oldfield.

Oldfield's regular political contact was the Foreign Secretary and he rarely saw the Prime Minister, though in May 1974 Bruce McKenzie had told me that Oldfield had drawn Wilson's attention to the desirability of withholding top-secret information from certain Ministers and was due to see him again about it. Wilson complained to Oldfield that MI5 seemed to have been stirring up a plot alleging that he and his secretary were part of a Communist cell in Number 10 and asked him if he knew anything about it. In his usually guarded manner, Oldfield intimated that he would find out how much truth there was in the plot and report back.

On the following day, or thereabouts, Oldfield gave dinner to the MI5 officer Peter Wright at Locketts, the restaurant below Oldfield's flat in Marsham Court, near Westminster

Abbey. Oldfield turned the conversation to Wilson, disclosing that he had been called in by him to be sounded out about a plot. He said that Wilson had heard that MI5 men were talking about Communists in Number 10 and were generally stirring things up about himself and Marcia Falkender.

Wright has claimed, in his book *Spycatcher* that he then told Oldfield about the intense feelings of some MI5 officers about Wilson. Oldfield asked if the MI5 Director General, Sir Michael Hanley, knew about it. Wright claims that he said he did not. Oldfield then made Wright promise that he would tell Hanley all about the situation next morning, because otherwise there might be a scandal worse than Watergate.

Wright said that when he did so Hanley went white on learning that 'half the staff were up to their necks in a plot to get rid of the Prime Minister'. He claimed that when Hanley asked him for the names he gave them. Belatedly, Wright has since confessed not only that his story of the MI5 plot was a gross exaggeration but that he was the plotter-in-chief, possibly the only one. It is extremely unlikely that he would give the names of fictitious plotters who could be hauled up before Hanley, with serious consequences for Wright himself if faced with them. Wright has stated that Hanley never discussed the matter again, which seems remarkable if there was any truth in his story at all.

It has to be remembered that Wright's account of his dinner with Oldfield was part of his build-up of his plot story, which he has since retracted. However, there can be little doubt that the Locketts dinner did take place, nor is the reason for it in dispute. Oldfield had indeed been called in by the Prime Minister and wanted to know all that Wright could tell him, though, according to Wilson, he never did report back to him. True to form, all he did was to write to the Cabinet Secretary complaining that MI6 was becoming embroiled in the criticisms. The Prime Minister's office duly replied that MI6 was not involved in the strictures, confirming that Wilson's belief in them was real.

Only one thing in this convoluted tale is certain – I was the original cause of Wilson's fears about MI5, relayed to him, mistakenly, first by Martin Gilbert and then recycled, with good intentions, by Lord Weidenfeld. Wilson relayed them to Oldfield who discussed them with Wright and eventually was to relay them back to me with sensational consequences, as will be seen. Everybody was taking in Wilson's washing.

Wilson's suspicions were not confined to MI5. He had also become concerned about the CIA. Lord Weidenfeld told me that in February 1976, shortly before he was due to visit the USA on business, he was telephoned late at night and asked if he would see Wilson right away. The Prime Minister asked him to take a letter to a friend, Senator Hubert Humphrey, a former US Vice President, whom Weidenfeld was to visit in Washington in connection with the publication of his memoirs. Later Weidenfeld showed me a copy of the letter, which contained five questions, and the replies he eventually received.

The first requested information about CIA activities in Britain in recent years. The reply was non-committal, but suggested that there had been none. The second referred to a Dr Erskine who, it was suspected by Marcia, had belonged to the CIA. There had been nobody of that name on the CIA lists. The third asked whether CIA money had been used to arm British mercenaries in Angola. The answer was, regrettably, that it had. The fourth referred to a businessman called Grenfell-Jones and made no sense to the CIA. The fifth asked if any senior politician had been involved in the Lockheed Affair with Prince Bernard of the Netherlands. This is believed to have referred to John Stonehouse and the answer was probably no, but there was some possibility that 'something went on'.

While Weidenfeld was in New York he met George Bush, who was then head of the CIA, and discussed Wilson's fears with him. In the following month Bush made a point of calling on Wilson on his way to Germany on intelligence business. He assured him that the CIA had not been bugging him and that there was no trace of the mysterious doctor on their records. Again the fear had been fantasy and could have done nothing for Wilson's reputation with Bush.

Of course the CIA mission in London regularly reported back to its US headquarters on any Ministers considered to be possible security risks, because of the sensitivity of the Anglo-American interchange of secrets. My friend Charles Bates, the head of the FBI mission in London, had done the same, reporting directly to J. Edgar Hoover. The problem of sharing defence secrets with British governments containing far-left Ministers dated back to the first Attlee Government and it was not helped, for instance, by the circulation throughout Britain's plane and missile factories, early in 1975, of a thirty-two-page document with Wedgwood Benn's picture on the cover. It urged 'public ownership of a type radically different from anything seen in Britain so far', by putting the aircraft industry under a controlling council of workers with the power to hire and fire all management. There is little evidence that MI5, or anyone else in Britain outside the hard Left, ever took Benn seriously, but the CIA may have done so.

Wilson's suspicions about the CIA and MI5 were even exceeded by his continuing belief that agents of the South African Government were perpetrating all manner of dirty tricks against him. His behaviour seems even more bizarre at this distance in time than it did to his colleagues then. It was soon to border on the irrational.

14

A Burned-out Case

On 16 March 1976, five days after his sixtieth birthday, Harold Wilson astonished most of his parliamentary colleagues and almost all the British public by announcing his resignation. For many it remains the biggest mystery in modern British politics. It was no surprise, however, to several of his intimates whom he had assured, long before, that he intended to quit active politics, whatever his position, when he reached sixty.

The earliest recorded indication that he might leave early is in the diary of Richard Crossman for 23 April 1970. Crossman wrote that Wilson had told him, 'When I retire I shall be the youngest retired Prime Minister for 100 years and shall have plenty of time for writing.' Two years later, while in Opposition, Wilson informed Denis Healey that he did not intend to serve another full term as Prime Minister. In March 1974, when he invited Bernard Dononghue (now Lord) to head a policy advisory unit in Number Ten Downing Street, he told him that he would need leave of absence from the staff of the London School of Economics for only two years, because he would be resigning as Prime Minister at Easter 1976. Wilson wrote a letter to the Principal there, supporting the need for only two years' absence. In 1974 he also told a senior member of his staff that he had decided to retire early because of his fear of inherited premature senility.

Wilson confided in his trusted friend, Lord Goodman, round about October 1975 that he would be telling the Queen, within a few days' time, that he would resign on his sixtieth birthday. In the same week at a meeting of press barons he deliberately remarked, loudly, to Goodman, 'That thing I told you the other day. I shall be telling the Queen about it this week.' He was obviously laying down a marker so that he could refer to it later as evidence if accused in the press of resigning suddenly to escape some scandal, as he expected he would be.

There is no doubt that he did tell the Queen, who was surprised and not pleased because she liked Wilson, as most of the royal family did except the Duke of Edinburgh, who found it hard to understand how he could ever have become Prime Minister. The Queen appears to have preferred Wilson's company to that of any other Prime Minister since Churchill.

At about the same time, in October 1975, Wilson also imparted the news to the Speaker, Horace King, who later confirmed it to me. In December he informed his close friend Harold Lever (now Lord), who gave the news to James Callaghan, telling him to prepare to take over the premiership in March. Healey, who had hopes of succeeding, was not told until he met Wilson in the lavatory before the Cabinet meeting at which the Prime Minister formally announced his departure to the rest of his colleagues. This was shortly after Healey had attacked the Left in a debate in such terms that one of them walked out with two fingers in the air. His performance, which had been on Wilson's behalf, alienated left-wing support so severely that he had no chance in the leadership contest which Wilson's resignation then precipitated. Understandably, he regarded having been kept in the dark as a deliberate manoeuvre by Wilson to favour Callaghan.

All this evidence is proof that Wilson did not resign because of some sudden fear of exposure concerning any scandal, as many have believed. There is little about Harold Wilson that Lord Goodman, his solicitor and confidant for many years, does not know, and he has stated publicly on television that he is unaware of any other reason for the resignation than his stated determination to retire at sixty.

Marcia Falkender has told me that she and others applied pressure on Wilson to remain until after the Queen's Jubilee festivities in 1977, but he could see that the economy was going to be in a worse state by then and the only way he and Labour could remain in office was through a pact with the Liberals. He was not prepared to have one, while James Callaghan was.

In 1978 I drew Wilson's attention to the fact that journalists and others were still trying to discover the secret reason why he had resigned. His response was to say, 'Well, they've had two years to search and they haven't discovered anything yet, have they?' They have now had fourteen years and they have not discovered anything. It has not been for lack of trying.

Recent suggestions that various false rumours about the cause of Wilson's resignation originated in the intelligence services are without foundation. They arose in the media, in the House of Commons bar and smoking room, in the City and in the minds of ordinary people who could not believe that such a political animal would willingly relinquish the reins of power.

In futherance of the mythical MI5 plot against Wilson, Anthony Cavendish has claimed that Sir Maurice Oldfield was somehow involved in what he called Wilson's 'abrupt resignation'. It is now certain from witnesses more reliable than Cavendish that the resignation was not abrupt. Like others pursuing the scandal theory, Cavendish can produce no evidence worthy of the name that Oldfield knew anything damaging to Wilson. His suggestion that Wilson always avoided Oldfield after his retirement carries no weight whatever. Wilson did not like spooks of any description, and Oldfield had been hardly helpful to him concerning his MI5 delusion. The question nevertheless remains: Why had he so firmly decided to go when he was sixty?

Joe Haines told me that Wilson was 'burned out' long before he went. Senior civil servants close to him described him as 'totally worn out'. I have little doubt that the unprecedented media assault, sustained over so many years and which had affected him so badly, was a considerable factor. While the media generally have scant impact on specific political events against which they might campaign, sustained attrition can affect a sensitive character, as I believe Wilson to have been. Even Harold Macmillan, who was much tougher and more detached, had moments when he suspected that all the wild accusations being made against Ministers and others at the time of the Profumo Affair were 'something in the nature of a plot to destroy the established system'.

Another factor, probably not unconnected with the media onslaught, was Wilson's growing fears about his health. In January 1975, while approaching Andrews Air Force Base on a trip to Washington in an RAF plane, Wilson experienced heart flutters during some extreme turbulence, as was reported to me by a member of the crew. After a medical examination on landing he was advised to take things more easily. A year later, according to a reliable source, he told the Queen that his doctor had advised him to resign because otherwise he risked a heart attack. Some of his friends and close colleagues believe that he had already suffered a heart attack or mild stroke and had been frightened by it. His famous memory was certainly impaired because first-hand witnesses have told me that, soon after his resignation, there were times when he could not remember his exact address.

His statements to friends in 1974 predicting his retirement may have reflected his early health fears. That concern would also account for his decision to waste no time in giving Marcia her peerage, knowing that she was most unlikely to get one if anything happened to him. Historians will surely come to wonder just how ill he was by the time he resigned, for he was about to behave in a most extraordinary manner which cast the gravest doubt on the quality of his judgement.

The first evidence that his judgement seemed to be more seriously impaired was his preposterous resignation honours list. There was a life peerage for Kagan and a knighthood for his friend Eric Miller, who was soon to be dismissed from the chairmanship of Peachey Properties. The company took out writs against Miller and he was also being considered for prosecution under the Official Secrets Act concerning a confidential Scotland Yard file which was found in his office when he killed himself in 1977.

Kagan was prosecuted, for theft and falsifying accounts, after being extradited from the safe haven abroad to which he had fled. He was sentenced to ten months in an open prison and released in June 1981 after serving six months. The Queen withdrew Kagan's knighthood but removal of the peerage would have required legislation, so he was quickly back in the House of Lords.

Such awards were bound to lead to suggestions that Wilson was paying old debts. According to the Crossman diaries, he had opposed any official scrutiny of the honours list because it would frustrate his efforts to send 'unusual candidates' to the House of Lords. The Political Honours Scrutiny Committee was not told of MI5's suspicions about Kagan. Other objections were raised about certain candidates, however, but Wilson ignored them.

Even more bizarre was his behaviour, just two months after his resignation, when he called in two young BBC journalists, Barrie Penrose and Roger Courtiour, to enlighten them about his delusions concerning MI5. Wilson told them how he had heard the first version about the 'Communist cell' from Martin Gilbert, who had been present when a 'well-known Fleet Street journalist', whom he later named as me, had mentioned it, among other derogatory matters. There is no doubt, therefore, that this was the account of my performance at the Sacher lunch and was proof that I was the originator of this story in Wilson's mind. Wilson said that I was 'widely believed to have first-class connections with MI5 and MI6', indicating that the information had come to me from those sources, which were therefore the origin of the MI5 smear. He said that so many of the people who had come to hear of the campaign of denigration quoted MI5 as the source that he had 'concluded' that it must be so. This was a false assumption. Nobody connected with MI5 or MI6 had ever told me that there was a Communist cell inside Number 10. Yet Wilson told the reporters, 'They were saying that I was tied up with the Communists and that MI5 knew. The arch-link was my political secretary, Marcia. She was supposed to be a dedicated Communist.'

Wilson then told the reporters that the Tory MP Winston Churchill had also heard the story, at the same dinner attended by Weidenfeld in August 1975. Until then Churchill had heard nothing because that same evening he had telephoned me to ask if there was any truth in it. So again it was my story retold. Both Wilson's original sources derived from me.

Wilson said that he was certain that 'the MI5 faction' had been responsible for spreading the rumour that Marcia had not been positively vetted, when in fact it had been Mrs Halls. Her husband told her about the difficulty concerning the re-vetting.

Wilson suggested that he might have been under electronic surveillance and that his telephone might still be tapped. He also told the journalists of his fear that the CIA might be involved in the infiltration of the Cabinet Office, and even more of his concern about South African 'dirty tricks'. He dwelt on the strange series of burglaries he claimed that he and his staff had suffered, attributing them to the South Africans and other 'intelligence-gathering' agencies, and indicated that he expected more.

In quite extraordinary terms for a man who had just been Prime Minister, Wilson urged the reporters to investigate the forces which he believed to be threatening democracy. He promised further leads which he would give them during more confidential meetings. 'I see myself as a big fat spider in the corner of the room,' he told them. 'Sometimes I speak when I'm asleep. You should both listen. Occasionally when we meet I might tell you to go to Charing Cross Road and kick a blind beggar standing on the corner. That blind man may tell you something, lead you somewhere.'

He did meet them again, several times, to hear what they might have discovered in their inquiries and to express his fears again and his bitterness against certain journalists who had links with MI5. So he was not behaving on sudden impulse or perpetrating some kind of sick joke on the reporters, as he would later claim. I cannot imagine any other former Prime Minister making such a joke at MI5's expense or talking about MI5 at all to complete strangers.

Some of Wilson's friends, including Kagan, claimed that Wilson believed that he might be called back by the Queen when the Callaghan Government was defeated and the succeeding Thatcher Government collapsed under the onslaught from the unions. Such a cigar dream – in private Wilson preferred cigars to his public image pipe – was demolished when the two reporters went public about his attack on MI5 in 1978.

Was Wilson in breach of the Official Secrets Act? Almost surely not in legal terms. Any Minister, and certainly a Prime Minister, has the power to make an official secret no longer secret just by making it public or leaking it. The information is automatically 'authorized'. Whether this applies to a retired Prime Minister has never been established, because there had been no precedent for it. Whatever the legal niceties, Wilson's behaviour was incredible for a former Prime Minister and indicative, perhaps, of some imbalance of judgement which was not transient, for he had been prepared to prejudice the even more secret GCHQ in 1967 in pursuit of personal animosity during the D-Notice Affair.

When Wilson's statements to the two journalists came to MI5's notice, as it quickly did when they began to make inquiries, it would not have been unreasonable for the management there to wonder about his motives in denigrating the nation's security service. He certainly inflicted great damage because the plot story, which has been so widely publicized as true, has done tremendous injury to MI5's reputation with the public and to its own morale. In fact it could reasonably be argued that Wilson did far more to undermine MI5 than MI5 ever did to undermine him. Whatever his motive, it would be too charitable to think that he had just been suffering from publicity withdrawal symptoms so quickly and yearned to see his name back in the headlines.

Later, in 1978, Wilson was to claim that the statements attributed to him by the two reporters, whom he had called in and seen so often, were 'cock-and-bull written by two journalists of limited experience and with so little sense of humour that they cannot distinguish between a disclosure and a joke'. This must have caused some wry smiles in MI5 headquarters. Subsequently both Lord Wilson and Lady Falkender denied ever having said anything about MI5 and MI6 to Penrose and Courtiour, but I know that the reporters were telling the truth and that he had been making the same accusations to others.

In August 1977 Hugh Trevor-Roper, now Lord Dacre, wrote to me stating that in the previous January he had happened to sit next to Wilson at a public luncheon in Bradford. They were almost complete strangers, but when Wilson learned that Trevor-Roper had been in MI6 during the war he launched into a comparison between MI6 and MI5, saying how good the former was. He then said that MI5 had 'spied on him, plotted against him and tried to secure his downfall'. Finally Trevor-Roper said, 'But isn't MI5 under the Prime Minister?'

Wilson replied, 'Oh yes, on paper; but that didn't make any difference.'

In July 1977 Joe Haines, the former Number 10 Press Secretary, published a report in the *Daily Mirror* describing how Wilson had distrusted MI5 so much that he suspected that he was being bugged by them. Wilson had even wondered if a light-fitting behind a portrait of Gladstone might be a bug. Of course, the bugging of Number 10 is always regarded as a possibility, which is why it is regularly 'swept' electronically by a branch of GCHQ which is responsible for this aspect of counter-espionage in all Whitehall offices. According to Haines, Wilson had even employed a private agency to sweep some rooms because he no longer trusted the official agency.

Information that Wilson had been 'bugged' inside Number 10 had already come to me from Bruce McKenzie, the Kenyan politician who was a close friend of Sir Maurice Oldfield and a neighbour of mine in Surrey for much of the year. I sounded him out on it over several days and he was adamant: 'I can tell you with absolute certainty that Wilson was bugged.' I had reason to believe that he had been given this information by Sir Maurice Oldfield, who was a frequent visitor to McKenzie's homes, including those in Kenya, though it is not impossible that Wilson had also told McKenzie of these fears himself. They were such friends that when McKenzie died Wilson wrote his obituary for *The Times*. At that stage, I had no knowledge of the fact that Wilson had called Oldfield in two years previously to tell him of his fears. As Oldfield knew of my close friendship with McKenzie, I assumed that he either told him to tip me off or had no objection to his doing so.

I held on to the bugging information for some time until I was able to confirm it in a conversation with Oldfield himself. Apparently, during his talk with Wilson in the summer of 1975 the Prime Minister had also expressed his suspicion about being bugged. Olfield claimed to have followed this up, along with the general MI5 plot story, and to have confirmed it with 'informants in MI5', though he offered no names. It would seem now that his only informant had been Peter Wright, at the dinner in Locketts which I have already described. He would not have raised it with the head of MI5, Sir Michael Hanley, for fear of being accused of interference. Oldfield loved to interfere, but only at a safe distance with 'long tongs'.

The clear indication was that the bugging had been done by MI5, and it did not surprise me that Oldfield would have no objections to this being published. There was no love lost between the two services and at that time Oldfield was anxious to assure the new Prime Minister, James Callaghan, that MI6 had not been involved in any nefarious activities. So his 'leak' to me may have been directed at publicity that would put any blame on to MI5. As Oldfield's close friend, Anthony Cavendish, has written, Oldfield regarded me as a contact who could be used to plant leaks.

Having heard the information from McKenzie, whose sources in the intelligence world were so exceptional, I believed it; and when Oldfield confirmed it I published it. What better source could a journalist have than the chief of the Secret Intelligence Service? My story appeared as the front-page splash in the *Daily Express* on 29 July 1977. It stated that Wilson's suspicion that he was 'bugged' when Prime Minister had turned out to be justified.

With hindsight and further knowledge I am now convinced that it was untrue. The information was really based only on the fears which Wilson had expressed to Oldfield, and these were entirely in Wilson's head. I had retailed some Fleet Street gossip at a lunch which had reached Wilson. He eventually passed it on to Oldfield, who later passed it back to me with all his authority behind it. Had it not been so serious it would have been hilarious. Nothing had come to me from MI5 but only from MI6, and that was disinformation. I had been 'willied' by Oldfield, a 'willy' being someone who carries out an intelligence task without being aware of it.

My report in the *Daily Express* had been written in good faith and its impact was extraordinary. The early edition, which was rushed down to the Commons at about 10.30 p.m., resurrected the whole plot story, which had tended to die away. Parliament was about to go into recess for three months. Callaghan, the Prime Minister, had gone home and there were amazing all-night scenes in the Commons as MPs refused to break up for the summer until they heard from the Prime Minister in his capacity as head of the security services. They kept talking for sixteen hours until Callaghan appeared to face questions by Mrs Thatcher, then leader of the Opposition. Callaghan's difficulty was that he did not know the truth and so could not say anything positive. Inevitably it was assumed by the media that he was covering up for MI5.

Mrs Thatcher accused Wilson of breaching the Official Secrets Act. Lord Wigg, who disbelieved the report, castigated him for departing from the rules requiring former Ministers to remain silent about the security and intelligence services, whatever the provocation. Wilson eventually responded by demanding an inquiry. On 30 July he issued a statement underlining his belief that 'Mr Chapman Pincher has long been known to have close contact with certain officers of the Security Service.' He virtually denied that he had any knowledge or suspicion of having been 'bugged', though Joe Haines is a reliable close witness to that fear.

Marcia Falkender told me that Callaghan had telephoned Wilson several times late at night to say that he might not be able to avoid a security inquiry because of the atmosphere in the Commons. This was a friendly warning, but Marcia thought he was 'baiting' Wilson.

A month later Downing Street issued a statement to the effect that the Prime Minister had conducted detailed inquiries into recent allegations about MI5 and was satisfied that at no time had MI5 or any other British security or intelligence agency undertaken electronic surveillance in Number 10 Downing Street or the Prime Minister's room in the House of Commons. It also denied that there were any grounds for lack of confidence in the competence and impartiality of MI5.

As the then Home Secretary, Merlyn Rees, confirmed to me later, the inquiry had been touched off by my reports and dealt almost entirely with those allegations. It did not fully examine the general charges against MI5 made by Wilson, because they were not taken seriously. The only executive action was Callaghan's decision to break the chain of command in MI5, where normally a retiring Director General had been succeeded by another professional insider. The new head was Sir Howard Smith, a previous ambassador to Moscow whom Callaghan knew and admired.

Following publication of Callaghan's report, a well-known BBC investigator wrote to me with evidence that MI5 had put a bug into Number 10; but the details, said to have come from an MI6 source, turned out to be quite untrue. Another informant said that MI5 had bugged Downing Street, but at Wilson's request because he feared there was a spy there.

Shortly afterwards, Wilson told me that he fully agreed with the Callaghan statement and appeared to have withdrawn all his allegations about the MI5 conspiracy against him. Indeed, from 1977 onwards he distanced himself from any claims about the MI5 plot and eventually started to deny it.

During the *Spycatcher* trial, journalists were to predict that Wright would confirm in his book that MI5 had bugged Wilson, but no such statement appeared in the published edition. If it was in the original draft it was almost certainly another fabrication, inserted by Wright to prop up his MI5 plot theory, because when I questioned him about the bugging in 1980 he denied that it had occurred. Wright assured me that the only device ever found there – during a routine 'sweep' – was a microphone in Churchill's old chair. He had this installed secretly to conceal his failing hearing, having employed an outside electronics man who was later found to be a Communist!

Shortly after the Callaghan statement in 1977 I began to write a documentary book about the pursuit of power. Not then being aware of Oldfield's disinformation exercise on me I reported that Wilson's fears about a plot to overthrow him had been well founded because 'certain officers inside MI5, assisted by others who had retired from the service, were actually trying to bring the Labour Government down . . .'. That incorrect statement in the book, which appeared under the title *Inside Story* in November 1978, has been the starting point for many other writers intent on proving the plot against Wilson to be true. I apologise to them, to other readers and, above all, to Harold Wilson for the error, which was made in good faith and on the basis of what seemed to be information from an excellent source.

I should also express my regrets to Mrs Thatcher because the plot which, as John Ware said, always comes back to me, has recently been embroidered into an even more devilish conspiracy. It is fashionable left-wing practice to argue that the plot was not only real but was the start of a long-running right-wing campaign, with MI5 playing a dominant role, to get Margaret Thatcher into office long enough for her to destroy Socialism! If I have exerted little influence on the realities of history, I have certainly had an impact on its fantasies.

15

No End to It

Following the 'bugging' publicity in 1977 I received two long letters from Tenerife with the promise of a third, allegedly from a recently retired American intelligence officer holidaying in the Canaries. Enclosed with the first was a piece of card cut jigsaw-fashion, with a statement that the next two would contain similar pieces which would then all fit together so that I could be sure that they came from the same source. It was a common espionage device included to give the exercise credibility.

The letters were a mass of diffuse information, much of it scurrilous. They stated that members of the Wilson Cabinet had been put under 'wire tap' and electronic surveillance by both the CIA and British intelligence networks. US Intelligence had wire-tapped the homes of prominent politicians and trade union leaders in Britain. Though Labour politicians like Wedgwood Benn were targeted, so were Tory politicians like the late Reginald Maudling. Wilson was accused of tax evasion but, as he was out of the political picture, he was not the major target. The Soviets had allegedly set up a special department to monitor the Nationalist movements in Scotland and Wales and infiltrate them with sleepers. Security leaks had been investigated by American Intelligence at the Holy Loch Polaris base and at Edzell, a mainly American listening station. In 1971 or 1972 American Intelligence had been approached to try to find out how many English businessmen had bank accounts outside the UK, how much money was being paid into these accounts and how often. There was a great deal of wild information about the Shah of Iran.

MI5 made no sense as the source because the contents seemed designed mainly to create dissension between the

British and Americans. Though the sender claimed to be an American, this was obviously false because he wrote 'defence' instead of 'defense', which is the American style. The third instalment never materialized, perhaps because I had printed nothing of consequence about the first two. On balance it was a pro-Soviet operation, but I concluded that, though the sender was clearly knowledgeable, he was indulging, hopefully, in a dirty trick for his own purposes. It did not come off.

Eventually, after making copies of the letters, I gave the originals to Sir Maurice Oldfield for professional examination in MI6. Canny, as always, he declined to tell me the findings, but had they been of consequence I think I would have been subjected to questioning, which I was not.

In December 1977 the Tory MP Stephen Hastings (now Sir), who had served in MI6, made allegations against the leading trade unionists Hugh Scanlon, Jack Jones, Ernie Roberts and the late Ted Hill. He wanted to name Lord Briginshaw, the leader of a printers' union, but this was not permitted because he was a member of the House of Lords. The allegations were the consequence of statements about trade union leaders made on tape recordings by the Czech defector Josef Frolik. Frolik had also made the statements to a US Senate committee. The tape recordings had come my way from journalistic sources, not from MI5 or any other intelligence agency, and I had passed them to Hastings. My motive was to create a newspaper 'story' which I was able to predict with certainty, and to comment on the row in Parliament which the Hastings allegations would undoubtedly cause. I also felt, as I still do, that Frolik had been treated shabbily.

Using the privilege of Parliament, which also meant that it could be reported, Hastings suggested that there were links between such men and foreign Communist intelligence services. He described them as 'targets', indicating that there was no evidence that they had been recruited. There was a call for a full inquiry into the allegations and the extent of Soviet Bloc interest in British trade unions but the Prime Minister, James Callaghan, skilfully denigrated Frolik's evidence, suggesting that the claims had all been investigated and rejected. Little came of the operation apart from a further furore in the media.

Late in 1980 I needed to speak with Lord Wilson concerning his recollections about the Hollis case. He agreed to lunch at the Café Royal but only on condition that Marcia was present – presumably as a witness. During the meal I raised the widely reported story that he had once remarked to Marcia, 'Now I've heard everything. Even the head of MI5 might have been a Soviet agent.' I then asked, 'Was it Hollis to whom you were referring?'

Wilson looked me in the eye and answered, 'I do not remember that man's name in that connection.' While I suppressed my astonishment, he poked fun at accounts of how he had seriously considered that there could be a right-wing coup in Britain. He also denied that he had gone into any details about MI5 and MI6 with any reporters.

Shortly afterwards he left us to attend hospital for medical tests. Marcia explained that he had been suffering from diarrhoea for a year. When I asked why his doctor, Lord Stone, had waited so long for tests she simply shrugged. Nor had she any rational explanation for Wilson's statement about Hollis, merely saying, 'It must be true.' The medical tests showed that the patient had abdominal cancer and he underwent serious surgery from which he was eventually to make a remarkable recovery. One can only assume that Lord Stone had suffered from the delusion which occasionally surrounds famous patients – the difficulty of believing that a Prime Minister could be dangerously ill.

There is a widespread story that there were problems during the operation, with some resulting brain damage which is responsible for Wilson's occasional lapses of memory. On the other hand it seems possible that the memory impairment was already there and was the cause of his false statement to me about Hollis. I had thought that he had been lying especially when, a few months later, he was to stand up in Parliament and claim credit for initiating the inquiry into the Hollis case, as I shall describe. Before doing that, though, he had been allowed to refresh his memory by reading the relevant papers in the Cabinet Office.

The likelihood that his memory had failed him with his answer to me is the more charitable explanation. After all, had he simply wanted to avoid discussing the case he could just have declined to do so or used a deception ploy, as Harold Macmillan did when I tried to question him about Hollis during a visit to his home, Birch Grove.

'Hollis?' he said. 'He was a Marine, wasn't he?'

'No, that was Sir Leslie Hollis who was no relation,' I replied, as he skilfully switched the conversation to a less sensitive topic.

When, much later, I managed to raise Hollis's name again, he said, 'Ah, yes, Hollis! He was a Marine, wasn't he?'

When I asked Marcia why Wilson had insisted on claiming credit for the Hollis inquiry, on television as well as in Parliament, after his denial in front of her, she commented, 'That's just what he would do.' I think that she, too, was covering up his memory problems.

Although Wilson has continued to deny that there was ever an MI5 plot against him it has remained in his mind. When he spotted me at an Authors of the Year party a couple of years ago he wagged his finger at me and said, 'Ah, MI5, MI6!' before being eased away by his wife.

It seems to be generally agreed by his colleagues and friends that Wilson was too eccentric and addicted to fantasy ever to have been a successful Prime Minister. The view of Woodrow Wyatt (now Lord) seems to summarize the common opinion, even of those who like him, as Wyatt does: 'He was a disastrous Prime Minister, shielding the British from the inevitable meeting with reality.'

Since entering the Lords in 1983 he has taken very little part in their proceedings, though he often attends. He was spared much contact there with his old Rasputin because Wigg was suffering from a distressing illness, which impaired his speech, and died in that year. In the preceding decade Wigg had become his old idol's implacable enemy, despising him for squandering his talents and letting him and the party down.

In his memoirs, published in 1972, Wigg portrayed Wilson as a manipulator prepared to mislead the nation to preserve his position, and a Walter Mitty who confused fantasy with reality. His published criticisms would have been much tougher had not parts of the book been removed after legal complaints by Marcia and Wilson, but it still contained savage knifework on several of his former colleagues. There can be little doubt, in my opinion, that Wigg's animosity was a potent factor in reinforcing Wilson's belief that all his political colleagues were against him and that it was prudent to trust none of them.

Wigg, who detested the Israelis, found Wilson's association with them particularly offensive, especially when the Prime Minister was photographed embracing Golda Meir. Wigg had always been pro-Arab and by that time had developed a professional association with the Algerian Government. While he was chairman of the Horserace Betting Levy Board, his vendetta against Wilson was conducted mainly by his usual undercover methods, but one Labour MP felt driven to suggest that Wilson should require all chairmen of statutory boards appointed by the Government to refrain from public comment on controversial issues. The last straw for Wigg was Wilson's allegations against MI5. Previously, in his memoirs, Wigg had praised MI5 for its professionalism and integrity, noting the keenness of its members to act within the directives laid down by their political masters. He claimed to have 'steadily built up the status and quality of the Security Service,' so Wilson's damaging strictures on it are likely to be the subject of sharp comment in his papers.

In December 1976, aged seventy-six, Wigg got what many regard as 'his come-uppance'. He was accused of a breach of the peace by kerb-crawling in his car allegedly in search of prostitutes, because the police had spotted his habit of motoring round and round the Marble Arch area after 11 p.m. I appeared for him as a witness because I knew what he was really doing there. Wigg was a frustrated journalist and could not wait to see tomorrow's newspapers. He found out that some of them were on sale late on the previous evening outside the Marble Arch underground station and he was in the habit of going out in his car to collect them. As it was impossible to park outside the tube station the only thing to do, if the news vendor had not arrived by 11 p.m., was to do circuits and bumps until he came. Wigg then had an arrangement that the vendor would nip smartly over with the papers and take the money which he had at the ready. I knew that this was his habit because he had telephoned me so often at midnight to complain about something I had written in the following morning's paper.

Before appearing in the witness box I did the circuit with him, setting off from his flat at about 10.55 p.m., and the circumstances were exactly as he had described them. The news vendor had not yet arrived and as we orbited Marble

Arch tube station several times, waiting for him, I began to fear that we might both be stopped for kerb-crawling.

Statements that Wigg was convicted are wishful thinking. He was acquitted because the magistrate ended the case, having decided belatedly that kerb-crawling was not then a crime anyway and the charge should never have been brought. Nevertheless, the magistrate gratuitously and monstrously branded Wigg as a liar, indicating that he considered him guilty anyway. Several of his acquaintances, including myself, wrote a joint letter to the *Times* complaining of the magistrate's behaviour, but the damage had been done and most people who recall the case seem to believe that Wigg deserved to be damned.

Until his death in August 1983, at the age of eighty-two, Wigg remained convinced that he had been framed by the police on the orders of Harold Wilson, as an act of revenge, and told me so many times. I thought it unlikely, but I and other witnesses were surprised by the determination of the police to secure a conviction and the paucity of their evidence. Many regarded his disgrace as payment deferred, for he remained deeply detested by many Tories and some members of his own party. His memory still is.

Never having held a post which paid much, Wigg astonished his friends by leaving more than £300,000. They attributed it to his expertise on the racecourse.

16

Clockwork Banana-skin

In recent months the plot against Wilson has been resuscitated in the context of allegations made by Colin Wallace, a former information officer in the Army headquarters at Lisburn in Northern Ireland. These allegations are such that even former Labour Ministers as level-headed as Merlyn Rees, who as Home Secretary was responsible for MI5, have begun to suspect that there may have been something in an MI5 conspiracy after all. There have been more ructions in Parliament, with the Prime Minister having to admit that she had been misinformed about a certain aspect of Wallace's work which had the emotive codename Clockwork Orange. Some of the circumstances of Wallace's abrupt dismissal have been the subject of an official inquiry and will probably figure in further television programmes.

I am confident that I know the truth about this case, which has already given Wallace so much television opportunity to plead that he was the victim of a monstrous dirty trick by MI5, the police, the Army and every other department that could possibly be dragged into his extraordinary story. To understand what really happened it is necessary to know the background and nature of Mr Wallace.

He was born in Randalstown, Northern Ireland, in 1943 to a Protestant family. At seventeen he secured work with a pharmaceutical manufacturer and in the following year, 1961, he joined the local Territorial Army. His record shows that from then on he was fascinated by the Army, by its traditions and its uniforms, donning them whenever possible and delighting in being photographed in various aspects of derring-do, such as parachuting and firing weapons on ranges. Wallace would have qualified for the nickname Rambo had such a character existed at the time, though many believe that Walter Mitty would have been more appropriate.

In 1966 he joined the Ulster Special Constabulary – the B specials who were so unpopular with the Catholics, being regularly accused of brutality; eventually they were disbanded. Two years later, when he was twenty-five and still working from his home in Randalstown, a senior Army officer who had spotted his enthusiasm asked him if he would like to work as an Army press officer – a civilian appointment. On 1 May 68 he was appointed Assistant Command PRO at Lisburn barracks, his rank of information officer being the second lowest.

In 1972 he was commissioned as a captain in the Ulster Defence Regiment, thereby making himself even more of an IRA target. In the following year the new Head of Army Information Services, Peter Broderick, whom I had known at Defence Ministry headquarters in London, decided to allocate Wallace more definitively to what was known as Information Policy. This was the mutation moment in Wallace's career. He was to engage in highly secret and controversial work and was therefore given the cover title of Head of Production Services and promoted to the rank of senior information officer at the early age of twenty-nine.

Three years later he was dismissed, and after that was convicted of manslaughter and imprisoned. Since his release on parole in December 1986 he has been trying to propagate the story that he was sacked and then framed in a conspiracy by various authorities to keep him quiet – something which has certainly not been achieved.

Information Policy was a harmless-sounding codename for an intelligence operation against the terrorists of both sides. How I first came to hear about it is instructive concerning its purpose, the way it was run and as an example of a Defence Ministry dirty trick.

In 1973 I was asked by Brigadier John Stanier, then Director of Public Relations for the Army at the Defence Ministry in London, if I would be interested in some exclusive information about an Ulsterman who had gone missing, a case which had already caused some comment in the newspapers. Stipulating

(Left) The Polish Pope, John Paul II, gravely injured after being shot in St Peter's Square on 13 May 1981. *(Popperfoto)*

(Below) Mehmet Ali Agca, the Turkish terrorist who tried to assassinate the Pope, is led to prison after his failure to escape. *(Popperfoto)*.

Sir Maurice Oldfield receives his knighthood as the prestigious Chief of the Secret Intelligence Service Later he was disgraced after admitting that he had failed to reveal his homosexual practices when being positively vetted. (*Press Association*)

nuclear submarine, *Conqueror*, returns to Britain, proudly displaying her 'kill' flag after sinking the ntinian cruiser, *General Belgrano. (Press Association)*

(Above left) Lord Wigg, who as the Lab[our]
MP, George Wigg, had such influence [on]
Harold Wilson that he was knowr[n in]
Whitehall and Westminster as 'Haro[ld's]
Rasputin'. (Press Association)

(Above right) Harold Wilson's close fri[end]
Lord Kagan, a Lithuanian refugee [who]
caused deep concern in MI5 through [his]
friendship with a senior KGB officer
who was later jailed for fraud. (Ca[mera]
Press)

(Left) Colonel 'Sammy' Lohan, the D No[tice]
Secretary, whose career was destroye[d by]
Prime Minister Wilson in retaliation fo[r his]
anti-Labour gossip. (Press Association)

(Left) Colin Wallace, the former Ulster information officer, who was involved in the Army's disinformation campaign against terrorists and has received £30,000 for wrongful dismissal. *(Press Association)*

(Below left) The late Lord Rothschild, the former MI5 officer, scientist, banker and Government adviser, who has been falsely accused of being the 'Fifth Man'. *(Press Association)*

(Below right) The senior KGB officer, Vitaly Yurchenko, hailed as the CIA's greatest catch when he defected in August 1985, but who returned to Moscow three months later. *(Associated Press)*

(Above) Defector in disguise. Oleg Gordievsky, who spied for MI6 inside the KGB for thirteen years and has been condemned to death as a Soviet traitor, as he appeared on a BBC television programme in 1990. (Associated Press)

(Left) Bruce McKenzie, the extraordinary Kenyan politician and influential MI6 agent who was assassinated by a bomb planted in his aircraft in revenge for the crucial assistance he had given to the Israelis in their raid on Entebbe airport to rescue Jewish hostages held by Idi Amin. (Daily Express)

(Left) The Canadian scientist, Gerald Bull, stands under the muzzle of the experimental gun which was the forerunner of the supergun being developed for Iraq and which brought about his murder. *(Associated Press)*

(Below) Part of the Iraqi super-gun believed to be a component of the recoil mechanism seized at the Greek port of Patras. *(Popperfoto)*

The Soviet military spy known as 'Sonia' who ran Klaus Fuchs and other agents in Britain and has seen the collapse of the East German Communist society she helped to found. Really called Ursula Beurton, her British husband, Len, defected with her in 1950.

that everything depended on the strength of the information, I agreed to see a lieutenant colonel, who duly came to my office. He gave me a hand-written document with details of the Ulsterman's movements which indicated that he was an IRA terrorist, and then gave a verbal explanation, answering a few questions.

After he had left I examined the information with the intention of working it up into an item for publication, but quickly realized that so much of the material conflicted with the truth, with dates and places clearly wrong, that it was an obvious fake and a badly botched one at that. I was angry that an attempt had been made to feed me with disinformation, especially at such a level, and those responsible, including the lieutenant colonel who was a psychological warfare specialist, were terrified that I might expose the whole affair in the newspaper. After receiving profuse apologies and an assurance that no such deception would ever be perpetrated on me again, I agreed to remain silent. I realized that publicity would give the IRA a field day and I had no wish to assist those murderous thugs. I also liked Stanier, who had obviously been sold a phoney story himself inside the Defence Ministry, and had no wish to wreck his career – which would have happened had the issue been raised in Parliament. He went on to head the Army and become a field marshal and Constable of the Tower of London.

I did, in fact, reveal the story of Information Policy five years later, without mentioning Stanier, in my book *Inside Story*. Nobody took any notice, but plenty did when Wallace eventually talked about it.

The reward I required for my silence was a full explanation of what it had all been about, and in the strictest secrecy I was briefed on Information Policy. The Army needed to capture the 'hearts and minds' of both sides of the Ulster community, a phrase harking back to the successful anti-terrorist campaign in Malaya. According to some who took part there, the operative practice had been 'Grab them by the balls and their hearts and minds will follow', but that was not permissible in the United Kingdom. So the Army decided to make use of psychological warfare techniques to denigrate the terrorists of both sides. If it is fair, in the interests of the innocent passengers and crew, to use lies to foil terrorists who are planning to hi-jack a plane, then it is also legitimate to do so against the terrorists of Northern Ireland.

There was nothing secret about psychological operations, commonly called psyops, as such. In 1971 Brigadier Frank Kitson (now General) had published a widely read book called *Low Intensity Operations* which freely discussed psyops and their use, pointing out that the Joint Warfare Establishment ran short courses on the subject so that as many units as practicable could have the capacity for utilizing them should the need arise. Secrecy about their use in a particular situation was essential for their success, however, and when a small psyops cell was set up in Lisburn in 1971, under the command of a lieutenant colonel, knowledge of its existence was restricted to as few people as possible.

It was a modest operation involving only a small staff. They issued pamphlets and posters and had some facilities for producing forged documents. They sent newspapers false letters signed by non-existent people, such as 'From a Catholic mother of five', to try and wean the Catholics from IRA support. IRA gunmen were wrongly accused of raping girls. It was alleged, falsely, that the IRA were using children to plant bombs and that three eight-year-old girls had wheeled a pram containing one and left it outside a Belfast hospital.

I have not been able to establish whether Ministers were told about Information Policy. They probably were not when it was initiated, as it was a minor operational matter – although, of course, the Army chiefs in Ulster knew, and so probably did the staff chiefs in London.

Originally all counter-intelligence, of which Information Policy was only a small part, had been the responsibility of MI5, but that civilian agency had not proved competent in dealing with paramilitary terrorists in Ulster and the Army had virtually taken over from them. A modest MI5 presence remained and liaised with the Army, but did not have much clout, and Information Policy was very largely an Army and Defence Intelligence Service operation.

The obvious and most direct way to distribute the disinformation was to feed it to the media, as had been attempted with me. The main media targets were in Northern Ireland itself, but attempts were also made to use the London national papers, radio and TV networks. The skill was in convincing the media that what they were being fed was true, and this involved the establishment of good long-term relationships with journalists by feeding them accurate information as well.

Wallace was not the only Army information officer to serve as a conduit with the media, but he probably became the main one at Lisburn. This meant close daily liaison with the psyops people and necessary access to much secret intelligence, the common lot of senior Defence Ministry public relations staff, who all have to sign the Official Secrets Act. There has never been any serious doubt that Wallace was required, as part of his duties, to give unattributable briefings to journalists and that these would include some disinformation. Contrary to the recent media view, Wallace was not much good at inducing seasoned journalists to swallow the disinformation and print it in good faith. Most of the correspondents came to distrust it so much that the Army Press Office became widely known as the Lisburn Lie Machine.

Wallace did, of course, have some success in placing disinformation passed to him. In the summer of 1972, for example, he told several correspondents that IRA bomb-makers were using French sodium chlorate, which was unstable as explosive. The idea was to force the IRA to find a substitute, which would hold up the campaign; the information, which was false, was printed in several newspapers. Another story, successfully planted, claimed that static electricity from women's nylon underwear could prematurely detonate bombs. Another suggested that some bomb materials being used could cause cancer.

According to Wallace, quoted in a book by Paul Foot, I am supposed to have published in the *Daily Express* in March 1972 some of his faked information, suggesting that American ex-Vietnam soldiers might be recruited to fight with the IRA as mercenaries. I have no record of it, but if I did run such a story it was given to me by a Defence Ministry source in London for I never met Wallace or had any contact with him or with the Ulster office.

Wallace had folders of documents which contained notes and printed forgeries and were shown to visiting journalists, and he may have concocted some of these himself in what he regarded as line of duty. For example, on one of the documents Wallace had written that Denis Healey was an ex-Communist

Party member and that Tony Benn had links with Czech Intelligence. Army psyops could have had no possible motive in distributing such information. It is certain that Wallace was involved in the rather crude concoction of a diary of a disaffected IRA man, supposed to have been secured in a raid on an IRA house.

While some correspondents needed to be given occasional exclusive leaks to establish good relations, evidence of Wallace's zeal in that practice has come to light. At the end of July 1972 he gave Angus Macpherson, the Defence Correspondent of the *Daily Mail*, 'full details – down to troop numbers and dates – of the top-secret Operation Motorman'. Some five thousand soldiers were to clear the no-go Bogside area of Londonderry where the IRA were established in force. Had Macpherson used this scoop Motorman could have been seriously prejudiced and lives could have been lost. After discussion with his editor, the information was rightly suppressed. Why had Wallace leaked it, and what would have happened to him then had the authorities learnt what he had done? Was it to scare the IRA out? Was it to induce the IRA to stand and fight and suffer heavy casualties? By the time the Army moved in the IRA had mostly gone anyway, presumably having learnt of the operation in advance.

While such a leak may have been outside Wallace's remit, every kind of permissible activity was certainly required. The situation in Ulster was grim. Internment without trial had begun in August 1971 but did not reduce the level of violence. Instead, bomb explosions soon exceeded the 100 mark, with many people killed. On the day after 'Bloody Sunday', 30 January 1972, on which thirteen men had been killed by paratroops, I attended the press conference mounted by the Defence Ministry. The colonel who briefed us insisted that no Army unit had fired lethal bullets until its soldiers had been fired on by terrorists or were seen to be in danger of immediate attack by gunmen or bombers. All the Army's shots before that time had been fired from riot guns using rubber bullets. The colonel said that the thirteen men who had been killed were all of military age, which would have been unlikely had the soldiers been firing indiscriminately. Four of them were on the 'wanted' file of IRA members, and the Army had received an intelligence warning that the IRA intended to exploit Sunday's massive

Londonderry Civil Rights Association march.

On the following day the Army said that probably only twelve men were killed. The thirteenth was the body of a seventeen-year-old youth killed on the previous day and dumped by the IRA on the scene to create a situation in which the troop could be accused of killing a boy, even if there had been no other casualties.

I wondered at the time how much of this might be disinformation, but there was no way of checking it and it was reported as the Defence Ministry's interpretation of events. The IRA responded with a massive campaign of shootings and bombings. The Stormont Parliament was dissolved and Northern Ireland was put under direct rule from London.

The IRA then notched up a propaganda victory against what it regarded as another British Army dirty trick. A reconnaissance force of about four dozen soldiers, trained by the SAS, had been patrolling the streets in taxis and other innocent-looking vehicles. One of its ingenious deception operations was the Four Square Laundry, a washing and dry-cleaning service offering cut prices to attract custom. Its vans were used for general surveillance but the main object was to secure clothes which could be tested for traces of explosives. The IRA rumbled it, raided its headquarters and shot up one of the vans in October 1972, killing the driver.

In the following year the headlines were seized by what became known as the Littlejohn Affair, which was certainly a deception on somebody's part. Kenneth Littlejohn, a convicted criminal who had previously served in the Parachute Regiment, was on the run in Ireland, where he had links with the IRA. His younger brother, Keith, also a convicted robber, had met Pamela, Countess of Onslow, a prison visitor who remained in touch with him after his release from jail. He told her that his brother had valuable information about the IRA and, acting in the national interest, she reported the offer to Lord Carrington, the Defence Secretary, who was a personal friend. He arranged a meeting between the Littlejohns and the Army Minister, Geoffrey Johnson-Smith (now Sir), at Lady Onslow's home. By that time, owing to the collapse of a robbery case, the police had lost interest in Kenneth Littlejohn and both brothers were then able to claim that, through their criminal contacts, they could provide intelligence about the source of new Russian arms and so save the lives of British soldiers. Among other things Kenneth said he knew was that the IRA was out to kill a tough Ulster politician called John Taylor.

When Littlejohn declined to see the police he was put in touch with an MI6 officer called John Wyman. Shortly afterwards, when an attempt was made to kill Taylor, Littlejohn was contacted and named one of the men responsible as Joe McCann, who was duly shot dead by an Army patrol soon afterwards. From then on, having established their apparent reliability, the Littlejohns' brief was to cause trouble in the Irish Republic that would be blamed on the IRA and lead to tougher measures against them there.

In October 1972 the Littlejohns were arrested in Britain following a raid on a bank in Dublin. They were extradited to Ireland and received heavy sentences, their claims that they had been working for MI6 cutting no ice. Latching on to the party political possibilities, Harold Wilson and others suggested that there was a Watergate smell about the way Ministers had received information about the IRA from the Littlejohn brothers, though all previous Governments had operated on the principle of using criminals as informants when it suited. As Army Minister Johnson-Smith was justified in meeting Littlejohn, who had insisted on seeing a Minister whom he could recognize. Equally, Lord Carrington was justified in agreeing to the meeting. Once contact had been effected Littlejohn had been passed to MI6, which was then involved in operations in Ulster.

I established to my satisfaction that the Littlejohns were never recruited as properly paid agents, as they claimed in the hope of securing mitigation of their sentences. No offer of protection was made to them in the event of their being caught. Is it credible that any Minister or senior MI6 officer would have said, 'Rob the bank and if you get caught we'll get you off somehow and you can keep the money'?

On 13 August 1973 Robert Carr, the Home Secretary, answering parliamentary questions, admitted that Kenneth Littlejohn had been in touch with an officer of MI6, having inadvertently named that unnamable organization in a letter to Lord Wigg which was quickly made public. The letter also confirmed that MI6 was operating in Northern Ireland, which had not been officially admitted before. When the MI6 officer, John Wyman, was arrested in Dublin under the Irish Official Secrets Act I, among other journalists, was asked to keep his name out of the newspaper. The editor agreed to do so.

After the Littlejohn scandal MI6 was largely replaced in Ulster again by MI5 in what was becoming almost a game of musical chairs. Wallace claims that with the advent of MI5 he became involved in Clockwork Orange. A senior officer has confirmed to me its existence as a tactical psyops operation directed solely against terrorists and their supporters to stem the rising tide of sectarian assassinations.

It was essentially an intensified attempt to publicize the names of IRA personnel and the way they were organized by concocting and planting media stories. It included forgeries and other devices providing information about their personal lives, if necessary. False statements that individual members of the IRA were informers or MI5 agents were planted ingeniously and sometimes successfully, leading to their execution or mutilation by their own side. Genuine gunmen of both factions were named as being responsible for sectarian killings.

Clockwork Orange attempted to link the IRA with the KGB and other foreign intelligence agencies supplying weapons and explosives. Wallace, for example, had the task of planting a false story that a Soviet submarine had been seen off the Irish coast and had landed three Russians. While the story was a fake there was no doubt, from intelligence sources, that some IRA terrorists had been trained by Soviet GRU explosives experts in Europe.

Wallace was to claim that in 1974 Clockwork Orange was 'escalated' and directed against Labour politicians. It is inconceivable to me that it ever would have been. The Army has never been particularly opposed to Labour administrations, as the Navy and RAF may have been, because Labour usually ended up spending more on conventional weapons, which is what the Army prefers.

Wallace claims to have seen documents 'relating to scandal about politicians of the Left or who were soft on terrorism' and alleges that they came from MI5; but, if they existed, he had no proof of that. His files apparently contained a copy of a forged letter to Merlyn Rees implicating him, quite incredibly, in contributing to the IRA fund Noraid. He showed it to journalists, but there is no evidence that it came from a British official source. It could have been an IRA forgery, because that organization was busy with its own disinformation and other dirty tricks. In April 1974, for instance, I was presented with documents purporting to be part of a long internal IRA memorandum disclosing a most dastardly plot by the British. It warned that large quantities of 'doctored' ammunition were being manufactured at Royal Ordnance Factories to be funneled to the IRA. When fired, it would explode, blow up the gun and kill or injure the gunman. IRA commanders were warned to examine all rounds carefully and even to weigh them before issuing them to gunmen. The memorandum warned that the British were also doctoring Russian, Czech and American ammunition, which are used by the IRA.

The purpose of this fake was to show the British as being prepared to stoop to any depths and to enable the IRA to blame the British when one of their own devices blew up. As I will explain, this particular deception operation was, in fact, barred on UK soil on policy grounds.

Clockwork Orange, about which Wallace and his supporters have made so much, was actually of such small significance that little could be recalled of it in the Defence Ministry. It is those intent on exploiting its political potential who have built it up into a mystery which the Tory Government is trying to conceal at all costs.

Concerning Clockwork Orange, Wallace claims that he wrote down details of the instructions and information he received from higher authority, mainly MI5, in Army issue notebooks which are said to relate to the first six months of 1974, probably beginning before the February election of that year. There were, apparently, thirty-two pages of such notes but eleven are missing, a loss which Wallace cannot explain. What remain have been put forward as grave evidence that MI5 was making use of Wallace and his position to undermine the Labour Government and even Tory politicians regarded as being soft on terrorists.

One note expresses his view that the next general election would be dominated by personality factors, and that every effort should be made to exploit character weaknesses such as financial, sexual or political misbehaviour. It was followed by names including Wilson, Heath, Maudling, Pym, Rees, Benn and Foot. The idea that anyone in MI5 would have put his career on the line by giving such false information for Wallace to toss around with his media contacts beggars belief. The names may have been no more than people of whom Wallace, who was politically naive, personally disapproved.

Another of his notes states: 'It is estimated that between 20 and 30 Labour MPs are members of the Communist Party.' Such information did not have to come from MI5. It was common knowledge in Fleet Street and elsewhere that there were secret Communists posing as Labour MPs.

Another paragraph refers to the Soviet intelligence officer called Richard Vaygauskas, who had been expelled in 1971 along with 104 others. It claims that, through Vaygauskas, Wilson and Heath were under Soviet control and that Wilson had received about £60,000 from East German sources for campaign funds. Again, the idea that anyone in MI5 would give such a dangerous and totally unsubstantiated statement to Wallace to push around is incredible in my opinion. The connection between Vaygauskas and Wilson's friend Kagan was well known to Fleet Street and TV investigative journalists at the time, but was not used for fear of libel actions by Kagan. Wallace did not have to be in touch with MI5 to hear of it, especially in the garbled form in which he wrote it down.

Paul Foot, in his highly subjective book about Wallace, argues that information about Paul Rose, a Labour MP with alleged Communist connections, could only have come from official intelligence files. But detailed information of that nature was being circulated to journalists anonymously by several freelance anti-Communist groups.

Another note refers to Marcia Williams's alleged refusal to submit to positive vetting. Paul Foot attaches great importance to this on the grounds that it could only have reached Wallace through MI5. Not so. News of the alleged PV problem arose out of the Mrs Halls case, and I published it in June 1974. I did not give Marcia's name for libel reasons, but anyone in Fleet Street or Whitehall who was interested knew to whom I was referring. Further, I spoke about it to press officers in the Defence Ministry, people with whom I lunched regularly. The story could also have been floating round Whitehall because the Treasury Solicitor had Mrs Halls's full statement. Finally, Mrs Halls spoke to other journalists too.

Yet another note states: 'Murder of Hugh Gaitskell to assist Wilson to power?' While MI5 had investigated this possibility, as Peter Wright disclosed to me in 1980, the remote possibility had been widely rumoured because it was known that, shortly prior to his fatal relapse, Gaitskell, who had appeared well enough to visit Moscow, had visited the Soviet Consulate to secure a visa.

Wallace's notes also state: 'Stonehouse – shielded by Wilson for his protection?' This question too had been widely asked after Wilson made a statement to Parliament about John Stonehouse on 17 December 1974, replying to allegations, which had been made previously in several newspapers, that Stonehouse had been spying for the Czechs while holding ministerial office. The allegation had come from the Czech defector Frolik. Again, Wallace could have noted down the question without need of any information from MI5.

In a further note Wallace stated that Wilson was under Soviet control through Lord Rothschild. Paul Foot then argues that this reference shows that Rothschild was 'suspected by at least some people in Intelligence of being a Soviet agent'. This conclusion is totally unwarranted. Rothschild has never been suspected by anyone in MI5 or MI6, as I will show in a later chapter. The suspicions have all originated with journalists who did not know him, because of his long friendship with Anthony Blunt.

Wallace claims that his MI5 contact, who used the pseudonym John Shaw, was asked to produce an analysis of the likely consequences if Ian Paisley was assassinated. This would have been a reasonable request if 'Shaw' was thinking of Paisley's possible assassination by the IRA, but Wallace seems to have indicated to Paul Foot that MI5 was planning to do it. He claims that as part of the 'exercise' he received details of a forged bank account in Paisley's name – indicating, again, that MI5 had produced it. There is no evidence for any of the assertions, which could be fantasy.

When the Heath Government realized that internment on suspicion without trial had failed to stem the violence, it began to release internees piecemeal in 1973. Then when Labour was elected the number of releases increased, to the understandable dismay of the Army authorities, who suspected that many of them would soon be back in IRA units murdering soldiers and policemen. It is more than likely that the Army let its objections be known through its PR officers, including Wallace, so that they could spread it around, but that was no evidence of serious intent to undermine Ministers. Such moves have been standard practice with all the services during defence reviews, for example: each service would try to influence the media with propaganda to gain support in 'fighting its own corner'.

It has been suggested that the whole of the notes in Wallace's hand were written recently in an attempt to bolster his frame-up story. Even if they are genuine, they are worthless as evidence of any MI5 plot against politicians because they could all be his own private observations. I would have had no difficulty in building up a better Clockwork Orange document from my own inside information, none of which came from MI5, and from the daily press summaries which Wallace always saw.

Evidence of Wallace's state of mind is contained in an essay, 'Ulster – a State of Subversion', which he admits he wrote himself. His own conclusion was that

> Government information policy in Northern Ireland has been weak, ineffective, uncoordinated and defensive – like their security police as a whole.. . . Given such a situation it must be clear to all reasonable people that the present government's apparent lack of moral courage in dealing with the unrest is not simply the lack of resources or will and that there must be more deep-rooted causes behind this sinister abdication of responsibility. In their worthy socialist thinking they see the solution as a red shamrock United Irish Workers Republic. Their answer, however, ignores Ulster's religious divisions and social conservation. Contemptible and risible as such blatant Marxist thinking is, their part in fomenting the present campaign of violence is considerable.

This was Wallace's own thinking. He loved the Army and hated seeing it fighting the IRA with one hand tied behind its back and sustaining casualties. Many officers up to and including the rank of general had a similar view, but would not have been prepared to do anything out of line. Wallace wanted something done about the situation and he seems to have set about doing it himself, waging his own war against the IRA and against anyone whom he felt was not totally committed to it or was interfering. As I have mentioned earlier, he frequently demonstrated his vanity by posing for photographs in various military situations, and could further have inflated his importance by showing journalists classified documents and some of his own manufacture. The sense of power which knowledge gives feeds on itself.

While the Information Policy exercise was in progress the Chief of Public Relations at the Defence Ministry in London, John Groves, had not been regularly informed by the Army about it. When he got wind of the way his staff were abusing their contact with journalists to plant disinformation he objected, verbally and in writing, to the Civil Service chief at the Defence Ministry, Sir James Dunnett, and to the Secretary of State for Defence, Lord Carrington. He pointed out with considerble force that the purpose of the press officers, of whom Wallace was one, was to issue the truth and that any involvement with disinformation would damage their credibility and that of the Ministry's public relations as a whole. At that stage, both Dunnett and Carrington declined to interfere. Groves was to persevere with his objections.

Only one official statement about Clockwork Orange has been made at the time of writing – by Archie Hamilton, the Minister for the Armed Forces, in a written parliamentary answer dated 30 January 1990. He said that two documents dating from 1975 had been found containing brief references to a *proposed* project of that title. 'It appears that this title was given to a project contemplating the dissemination of an account of the organisation and activities of the Provisional IRA. The documents show that Mr Wallace was involved in the project. The documents also state that the project was not cleared.' Mr Hamilton continued: 'No evidence has been found that, before work on the Clockwork Orange project was stopped, it had been extended to cover Protestant organisations and individuals or to include Northern Irish and British politicians as Mr Wallace has alleged.' He reiterated the Prime Minister's assurances that an inquiry carried out on her behalf by Sir Anthony Duff, when head of MI5, had shown that any allegations by Wallace, Wright or anybody else that MI5 had been engaged in a plot to destabilize the Wilson Government were false.

Hamilton's statement strongly suggests that the project had not been given ministerial approval or official clearance for action and was not in operation for long before it was stopped. The commanders involved at the time, General Sir Peter Leng, who was keen on psyops operations, and General Sir Frank King, have been quoted by a Defence Ministry spokesman as saying that they were not aware of anything called Clockwork Orange. John Groves has assured me that he never heard anything about it. On the other hand I have established that one or two senior Army officers were aware of it but regard it as being of no great consequence.

Mrs Thatcher has, however, admitted having given a misleading statement to Parliament concerning the use of 'black propaganda' – disinformation – in Northern Ireland. When she made it she had been misinformed by the Defence Ministry about the existence of any relevant papers after such a long interval. The Labour Opposition tried to make party political capital out of the admission by suggesting that, as the Prime Minister had been wrong in that respect, Parliament had probably been misinformed about the whole Wallace Affair.

All that had happened was that some written evidence about information Policy, which also showed that Wallace had been involved with it, came to light in a routine search of Defence Ministry archives. The Ministry has conducted an inquiry into the matter and reported that the file which mentioned Clockwork Orange – one codename among many – had been stored separately from the main papers in the archives, which are very large.

Meanwhile, at the Government's request, an independent inquiry into aspects of Wallace's dismissal was carried out by David Calcutt QC, the Master of Magdalen College, Cambridge. The Commons all-party Defence Committee decided to hold its own investigation into aspects of the way Wallace had been dismissed but, at the request of Tom King, the Defence Minister, the inquiry was delayed until after Calcutt's report had been received. Wallace did not endear himself to the Committee by complaining that its Chairman, Michael Mates, should be disqualified because he had served, as a soldier, in Northern Ireland. Mates had not served in Ulster since 1970. I offered to give evidence about Information Policy if needed. The clear implication of the Government's statement, made by Archie Hamilton, was that Wallace's claims about the Clockwork Orange plot were untrue.

What is not generally known but is quite certain is that Wallace was believed by senior officials to have been responsible for so many unwarranted leaks of classified information that Army Security began to take an interest in him. He was put under surveillance for several weeks to see whom he was contacting and what he might be doing with classified documents. His telephones at home and in his office were tapped. He was also followed and watched. Extracts of his conversations were sent to his superiors in London. Some recorded him saying, with some pleasure, that there would be a hell of a row about this and that. Some of the leaks seemed so pointless that Major General John Woodrow, another friend of mine who was in charge of Army Security at the time, was concerned about Wallace's motives. Army Security worked in close contact with MI5, which would have known that Wallace was under surveillance, so it is inconceivable to me that MI5 was authorizing his activities.

Almost certainly, Archie Hamilton could have told the House about the surveillance of Wallace had he wished to, but preferred to leave it to Calcutt. If Calcutt does not mention it in his report it is because of someone's unwillingness to admit to it. I know that he was told about the surveillance.

In explaining the reason for his own dismissal Wallace claims that at the end of September 1974, when Harold Wilson had called another election, he saw his MI5 contact and told him he was not prepared to do any further work on Clockwork Orange without proof that the project had been approved by a Minister. He says that he became concerned about the salacious material he was receiving about Wilson and Marcia during the election in October and handed over his Clockwork Orange files to his MI5 contact, whom he never saw again.

What really happened is very different. In the middle of September Sir Frank Cooper, the Civil Service chief at Stormont, had taken a decision that Information Policy must stop and, in particular, that Wallace must be removed. Cooper had been under sustained pressure from John Groves, the Defence Ministry's Chief of Public Relations, and had also received reports about Wallace's conduct from Army Security. He held a meeting with Sir Michael Carey, the Defence Ministry's Permanent Secretary, and Groves, in Carey's office in London; agreement was reached that the Army should revert to its proper role in support of the civil power and should not be allowed to go on 'doing its own thing' in the disinformation field.

The reasons for Wallace's removal were considered to be fully justified by those concerned. The tapping of his telephone had convinced his Army superiors that he was grossly mismanaging the information supplied to him. The possibility of a prosecution under the Official Secrets Act was considered, but it was decided that such a scandal would bring comfort to the IRA. His departmental chief, John Groves, then had to decide how Wallace should be withdrawn without letting him know that he had been under surveillance and still was.

It is normal practice for information officers to be moved after two or three years, so in December 1974 Wallace was told that he was required for interview in London. He went there on Christmas Eve and saw Grove's deputy, Tony Chinneck, who told him that he was being posted away because his life was in danger. This may have been true but it was also an excuse to induce him to leave Ulster, which he did not want to do, without telling him the real reason. By that time Groves had found that there were two possible vacancies in Wallace's rank – at North West District, near Preston, and at South West District, in Taunton. Eventually Wallace chose Preston and was not replaced in Ulster. On 4 February 1975 he left for his new appointment, but before he did so he inadvertently sealed his professional fate.

After putting his luggage on a ship he drove to see Robert Fisk of the *Times* at Fisk's cottage near Hillsborough. Fisk was out, so he left an envelope containing a restricted document of several pages – a script for a study day in which representatives of the Army, the RUC and Ulster Defence Regiment were to be briefed on the latest situation concerning Information Policy. The document, marked 'Restricted', was picked up off the doormat by Fisk's daily help. Her husband happened to be an RUC policeman and she is said to have handed it to him. On the other hand I have established that the 'watchers' responsible for the surveillance of Wallace were following him in a car and saw him deliver the material. So the 'authorities' would have demanded to see it anyway.

As Information Policy was regarded as a highly secret subject and the RUC was involved, RUC headquarters took the matter seriously once the material was read there. Wallace, however, claims that the contents were innocuous, and I have been told by an official source that they were 'not all that important'. The RUC sent detectives to see Wallace in London, where he was spending a few days acquainting himself with his new position. The confrontation took place in Groves's office and Wallace was rather shattered when told about the documents. He admitted that he had passed information to Fisk, but claimed that he had been authorized to do so. Verbal briefings about classified information were his entitlement, but Whitehall and its outstations have always been sensitive about documents.

On 11 February 1975 Wallace was suspended from duty in Preston on the grounds that he might face a charge of serious misconduct by retaining a document he should have handed in and giving it to an unauthorized person. On both counts it was, technically, a breach of the Official Secrets Act. He should have remained at home, but continued to frequent the office to the annoyance of those Army men who knew the circumstances.

On 18 May he received a letter from the Defence Ministry listing charges of breaches of discipline, the main one being that he had retained a document which he should have given in and had passed it to someone who had no authority to see it. A fortnight later Wallace went to London and put his case to John Groves and R. T. Fairbairn, another senior civil servant. All the interview did was to prove the main charge, because Wallace admitted delivering the document, as the two civil servants reported to higher authority.

On 25 June he received a letter from a Deputy Under Secretary saying that a most serious view was taken of the breaches and that it had been decided that he should be dismissed. The full-time legal adviser to MI5, Bernard Sheldon, now retired, had been consulted about the action because it was a security matter, and had agreed with it. This suggests that MI5 could not have been too worried about anything Wallace might reveal about Clockwork Orange to any appeal inquiry.

My inquiries have convinced me that Wallace's posting and his dismissal were quite separate incidents and not part of a preconceived plot. It had been decided to get rid of him from Northern Ireland, and then his chance action in trying to pass the Restricted document to Fisk had offered an opportunity to get rid of him altogether. The authorities seized it.

Wallace's fate was inevitable after the cleaner had handed in the documents to the police. He had taken a chance and been unfortunate. Nevertheless he decided to appeal with the backing of his union, the Institution of Professional Civil Servants. At the Civil Service Appeal Board hearing in October 1975 Wallace repeated his claim that he had been authorized to pass on the documents, though he had already signed a statement confirming that he had handed in all classified papers. The Defence Ministry's case was presented by John Groves.

The Board concluded that the Defence Ministry had been justified in dispensing with his services but, because of his record of service, suggested that he be allowed to resign. This meant that he received an extra six months' pay. Regrettably, the union's papers on the Wallace case were destroyed after five years because it was not regarded as an important issue likely to arise again.

Seemingly unable to desist from meddling, Wallace says that in July 1976 he wrote to Airey Neave, the MP who was later assassinated by the IRA in the precincts of Parliament. He claims that speeches which Neave made were based on material he had supplied. This was a copy of his essay 'Ulster – a State of Subversion'. It is common practice for MPs to seek material from knowledgeable people, and much has made out of nothing by Labour MPs and others because of Neave's previous connections with wartime intelligence.

On 5 August 1977, after reading the row caused by my report of the alleged bugging of 10 Downing Street, Wallace wrote to Lord Wilson assuring him that his fears that MI5 was trying to discredit him and undermine his position were justified, and claiming that he had been part of the plot. He gave examples, and claims that he asked for an interview with Wilson. He received no reply.

In April 1980 the *Irish Times* published a series of three articles, one of which claimed that, according to an 'intelligence source', MI5 had been working against Wilson. The source was Wallace, who could not properly be described as an Intelligence source – which implies membership of MI5, MI6, GCHQ or Defence Intelligence.

In the summer of 1980, while working in Arundel, Sussex,

Wallace was accused of murdering a friend with whose wife he was having some kind of romance. He was eventually convicted of manslaughter and sentenced to ten years' imprisonment, being released on parole in December 1986. The details of the circumstances are not relevant to this study.

It is always possible that Wallace was the victim of a miscarriage of justice in the Arundel case, as is claimed for so many convicted people these days, but to suggest that several Departments of State were involved in framing an innocent man to shut him up by sending him to prison shows total misunderstanding of how they work. Too many people would have known about it, and such a conspiracy is beyond the limit of dirty tricks in this country. An innocent man was killed in the incident and, had MI5 been prepared to resort to murder, it would have been much simpler to have killed Wallace and let the IRA be blamed for taking revenge. That would really have shut him up, which the alleged conspiracy did not.

In my view, after many years of dealing with the departments concerned – the Defence Ministry, MI5 and MI6 and the police – the idea that Wallace was framed for murder is paranoid in itself. Nevertheless Paul Foot, who claims to be a serious researcher, really seems to believe that MI5 took revenge on him by setting him up as a killer! His book, which set out to examine the question: Was Colin Wallace framed? ended up, without any proof, entitled *Who Framed Colin Wallace?* Some believe he was set up by the police for reasons even more Machiavellian.

Wallace and his supporters seized on Peter Wright's 'disclosures' about an MI5 plot against Wilson as proof of his own story, but Wright has since retracted this plot myth as being essentially a device to sell *Spycatcher*. There is nothing credible in Wright's story that supports Wallace. Yet various Labour MPs, such as Ken Livingstone, have been trying to make capital out of the so-called coincidence that Wallace's and Wright's allegations fitted each other. The only way the allegations are alike is in that they each originated in the minds of fantasists, being based on nothing more than office gossip about Ministers and others who were disliked for what they were doing or not doing. The two men were also alike in their bitterness about the way they believed that MI5 had treated them. The extent to which Labour MPs, of both front and back benches, have latched on to the Wallace Affair, as they did with *Spycatcher*, is a symptom of desperation after eleven years in the wilderness.

In what I believe to be the biggest disinformation ploy of his strange career, Wallace has continued to insist that the whole operation of his removal was to 'stitch him up' for his alleged refusal to continue with political 'dirty tricks' to undermine leading politicians in the 1974 Government, including, of course, Harold Wilson. He maintains that the authorities had needed to discredit him in case he blew the story to Fleet Street. I can find no evidence whatever for this and it makes little sense because he could still have exposed it, especially as Foot maintains that the way he was sacked supports his whole story.

The Government asked Mr Calcutt to investigate the possibility that the Board which heard Wallace's appeal had not been given all the relevant facts and that, as a consequence, its confirmation of his dismissal might have been unfair. This arose from the discovery of the document proving that disinformation had been used by the Army to counter IRA propaganda and that it had been part of Wallace's 'job description' to disseminate it through 'unattributable briefings'.

Calcutt submitted his report to the Defence Ministry in September 1990. In his opinion, the Ministry had been at fault on two counts. Certain of its 'representatives' had been in private contact with the chairman of the Appeals Board in advance of the hearing, which was irregular. What these representatives told the chairman has not been revealed but, if they were from Army Security or MI5, they may have disclosed that Wallace was under surveillance and the reason why.

The Ministry had also failed to disclose the full nature of Wallace's authorised work at the hearing. The brief document giving the full description of Wallace's task was classified because it mentioned his involvement in disseminating disinformation, though without any mention of Clockwork Orange, and the Board members did not have the security clearance to read it. So they were told only that he was responsible for producing posters and leaflets to counter IRA propaganda and was empowered to brief the media with due regard to national security.

Calcutt believed that the behaviour of the Ministry's officials probably affected the outcome of the appeal. So, while Wallace had erred, neither dismissal nor enforced resignation had been a reasonable penalty. Calcutt therefore concluded that the mode of Wallace's dismissal had not been completely fair and recommended that he should be compensated by the payment of £30,000. The Ministry agreed.

Inevitably, Wallace and his supporters alleged that the Appeals Board had been 'nobbled' and that there had been a conspiracy to pervert the course of justice. Some MPs also claimed that since Wallace appeared to have been right about his dismissal he might also be right about the MI5 plot. They renewed their calls for a full judicial inquiry into his allegations of a 'dirty tricks campaign by the security services'.

The Government maintained that the Calcutt inquiry had changed nothing regarding its denial that any such plot or campaign against Ministers or MPs had ever been mounted.

What the Wallace Affair demonstrates, above all, is that in Britain, if a case is anti-authority, there will be no shortage of people to champion it on television and radio or through articles and books, irrespective of the facts.

17

Deceiver by Profession

In 1988 John Ware, of the BBC *Panorama* programme, visited Peter Wright in Tasmania with a TV camera crew to interrogate him about his allegation of a treasonable plot against the Wilson Government by MI5. His claim that about thirty MI5 officers had been involved and that he had been responsible for stopping the plot had been given international publicity and was widely believed, especially by Labour MPs.

To Ware's surprise, Wright specifically denied that up to thirty MI5 officers had approved a plan to leak damaging information about Wilson. When asked why he had put that false figure in his book he tried to blame his ghost-writer, Paul Greengrass, for the error, but when faced with the fact that he had checked the proofs he admitted that he had left it in because it would help to sell the book. He had taken the trouble to alter other details, but not that one.

When asked how many MI5 officers had really been involved in any plot, Wright said that the maximum number was probably eight or nine and sometimes it had been only three. Ware then insisted on knowing how many had been really seriously interested in joining the plot, and Wright answered that the number might have been only one other apart from himself! So from thirty MI5 officers, which would indeed have been a formidable conspiracy and had caused such a furore, he was down to two – himself and one other chatting about Wilson in the office or in the nearby pubs. The original number had never made any sense to those who knew how MI5 works. As I had pointed out repeatedly in TV and radio interviews, it would be impossible for so many officers to be involved in a plot without the management becoming aware of it. And no senior MI5 officer would be prepared to put his head on the block to further such a crazy scheme, because one day it would be likely to leak.

Wright then confessed to Ware that he himself had been the originator and ringleader of the plot, which was in sharp contrast to his claim that he had tried to stop it. His plot to unseat Wilson, whom he still insisted on calling a traitor, had at best been a 'cowboy' operation – Lone Ranger Wright assisted by some Tonto as yet unidentified, if he existed.

The *Panorama* programme was shown at the usual peak time on 13 October 1988, but this abject admission that his plot story, which had generated such outrage, was a monstrous fabrication was virtually ignored by the other media and it is surprising how many people are unaware of it. Some of the newspapers were undoubtedly embarrassed because they had projected Wright's original story and appeared to have accepted it, accusing the Government of trying to cover it up. Some had even been to court to defend their right to publish Wright's claims and suddenly were seen to have been defending lies. No newspaper likes admitting that it has been conned.

Nor was Wright's confession taken up in Parliament. Labour MPs who had swallowed the plot story simply stopped talking about it until they got the chance to recycle it through the even wilder claims of Colin Wallace. Neil Kinnock had been demanding an independent inquiry into Wright's allegations and the collapse of Wright's story proved how right Mrs Thatcher had been to resist one, with all its unnecessary expense.

Throughout his professional life Peter Wright had been dedicated to the technical art of the dirty trick – the probe microphone, the long-distance 'bug', the eavesdropping camera, the surreptitious entry and the plausible lie – so presumably it had been no problem to him to perpetrate this particular deception on his old service, his former colleagues, the British Government and the world at large. It was only the last of a long succession of dirty tricks which he had generated following my chance meeting with him in his retirement in 1980, which was to lead to a quite extraordinary succession of deceptive actions involving some of the highest people in the land.

Early in September 1980 I received a telephone call from the late Lord Rothschild, an old friend who said that he had an interesting man staying with him who wanted to meet me. He sent a chauffeured car to take me to his home at Cambridge where I was to spend the night. Because Victor Rothschild had been a wartime member of MI5 and had retained his fascination with secret affairs I was not surprised to find that the man was a retired MI5 officer, Peter Wright, whom I had never met or even heard about before. He had written ten chapters of a book about the Soviet penetration of the British intelligence services, which he proposed to call *The Cancer in Our Midst*, but was so chronically ill that he feared he would die before it was completed. More urgently, he needed £5000 within three months to save from bankruptcy an Arabian horse stud which he had set up in Tasmania.

He proposed that I should finish the book with material which he would supply and that we would share the royalties. He had a list of names including Philby, Blunt, Burgess, Maclean, Driberg, Blake, Hollis and others I had not heard of, and said that he had secret information about all of them. I was fully aware, as Lord Rothschild must have been, that what he proposed was a blatant contravention of his oath of secrecy and that no officer of any British secret service had ever behaved so treacherously. For, though there was truth in his claim that his prime purpose was to expose security scandals so that weaknesses could be rectified, there could be no doubt that his immediate motive was money.

A better man might have declined to assist him and even found some way of alerting MI5, but I could not resist the opportunity of at least discovering what he had to tell, even if I could not use it, and I do not know any other investigative writer who would have done so. I suppose that I had been looking for someone like Wright for forty years, and I agreed to go out to Tasmania to be briefed by him.

Because Wright was so anxious to keep our collaboration secret Lord Rothschild, who had been associated with him on security and intelligence ventures for many years, eventually organized confidential banking arrangements for him to receive his share of the royalties, which would be paid directly by the publisher and never through me. At that time Rothschild was a banker and Wright could legitimately ask him to make such arrangements, which I understand were quite legal.

I do not know and I never found out why Lord Rothschild had brought us together. It was out of character for him to do anything which would prejudice official secrecy, but he did it in Wright's interest rather than in mine. Because of rigid Treasury rules Wright had a miserable pension and was living in penurious circumstances which Rothschild regarded as grossly unfair.

Five years later, in a total deception proclaimed on oath, Wright was to repay his debt by assuring an Australian court that it was Lord Rothschild and myself who suggested the idea of a book to him, thereby 'corrupting' him by offering him money for secrets. Wright was also to claim that we had corrupted him at the behest of MI5, which wanted to use him as a vehicle for releasing all the skeletons in its cupboard. Broke, ill and embittered in the shack that was his home on the other side of the world, Wright had corrupted himself before he ever met me. Displaying all the symptoms of what excessive service in the deception game can do to the mind, he had certainly become vindictive and may even have become deluded.

I spent nine days with Wright in Tasmania while he unburdened himself of almost every major secret he could recall. On my return to Britain, using much secret information which I already possessed, I worked up Wright's revelations into a book which I called *Their Trade Is Treachery*, a title which some might say applied to Wright and myself, though it was intended to mean those traitors and suspected spies exposed within. In our modest way my publisher and I utilized what deceptive techniques we could to keep the project secret from the authorities but, being concerned about possible prosecution under the Official Secrets Act, we took one other man into our confidence to secure his wise advice. The full text was made available to him on the understanding that he would not show it to anyone else but, sensing danger not only to us but to national security, he secretly passed it to a friend who also happened to be the Chief of MI6, Sir Arthur Franks.

This could be construed as a deception, and the publisher and I would certainly have called it that had we known about it at the time. However our friend, who still requires to remain anonymous, had secured an undertaking that we would not be prosecuted for having secured the information, which in itself was an offence under the Official Secrets Act. The authorities, who were deeply perturbed by the news of my book, could not move without seeing it and they had no means of seeing it without the agreement. I suspect that when this agreement was given the authorities had no real idea of the extent of the information in it, and I know they were horrified when they read it. But by that time they had given their undertaking and were to stand by it. Our friend's deception, which had extraordinary consequences, proved to be most welcome because it was to save both Lord Rothschild and myself from possible arrest and prosecution in 1987.

Sir Arthur Franks passed the text of my book to MI5 where the legal advisers took the view that, as it was essential never to reveal the identity of the man who had kindly supplied it, no steps could be taken to suppress it because in any court action, which we might defend, his name might emerge. While secret sources are the lifeblood of any intelligence service, this was a strange decision because the man had assured the MI6 chief that if the authorities had any objection to the book he could take action to prevent its publication. The publisher and I had agreed to abide by his advice, so all that was needed was a telephone call to him.

This crucial information was never passed to the Prime Minister or to her Cabinet Secretary, Sir Robert Armstrong (now Lord), as the latter has confirmed. When they met in secret with William Whitelaw, at Number 10 Downing Street, they all wanted my book suppressed, but finally agreed that they had no alternative but to accept the MI5 advice that it could not be. That decision was to lose the Government its case against Wright and his *Spycatcher* book six years later in a blaze of adverse publicity; in all the circumstances, I regard it as something of a deception operation by the secret services on Mrs Thatcher.

The next event was a deception operation by Sir Robert Armstrong, which rebounded in damaging allegations in the Australian court. On the day that a newspaper began to serialise *Their Trade Is Treachery* my publisher was telephoned by Sir Robert, who said that he urgently needed a copy of the book because the Prime Minister would, no doubt, be required to make a statement to Parliament about it. We were still unaware that the full text of the book had been in his hands for so long that Mrs Thatcher's statement had already been prepared. She had even written to Harold Macmillan warning him that the book would be coming out and that he would be mentioned in it, but he replied that he did not propose to read it because of difficulty with his eyes and that he preferred to stick to Scott and Dickens anyway.

My publisher immediately sought my advice, which was that we should supply a book only on receipt of a written guarantee that the Government would not prevent its publication – an undertaking which I believed would not be forthcoming. The publisher then telephoned the Cabinet Secretary, who to our delight sent round a guarantee by hand in the form of a letter signed by him. Either the Prime Minister agreed to this deception or Sir Robert believed that she would approve of it. This letter was to have such far-reaching impact that my publisher has preserved it as something of an historic document. During the trial Sir Robert was to admit that the letter was a deceptive device to cover the Government's possession of the script and, while denying that it was a lie, made his now famous comment that he had been 'economical with the truth'.

Their Trade Is Treachery duly appeared in March 1981, providing the first authoritative look inside MI5 and its guilty secrets, the main one being that its former Director General, Sir Roger Hollis, had been so seriously suspected of being a KGB agent that he had been recalled from retirement for interrogation. A majority of the MI5 and MI6 officers who had investigated Hollis maintained that the 'preponderance of probabilities' indicated that he had been a spy.

A further deception operation to counter the book, and the Hollis case in particular, had already been devised in the form of a statement, agreed to by MI5, MI6 and GCHQ, which Mrs Thatcher delivered from the Despatch Box in Parliament on 26 March 1981. It was a damage limitation exercise to rubbish the book in the minimum number of words and give the impression that at best it was all speculation, when in fact they knew it had all come from prime sources. Security disasters which Wright and his colleagues had attributed to Hollis were debited to Philby or Blunt despite the fact that they had no access to secrets in the late 1950s and 1960s when the main problems had occurred. By referring only to the war years the statement gave the impression that it was all ancient history, and it was so misleading in other ways that officers who had investigated Hollis regarded it as deliberate disinformation fed to her by MI5. One of the leading officers of the Hollis investi gation, Christopher Phillpotts of MI6, who was much senior to Wright and of unquestionable integrity, being shocked by Wright's behaviour, told me that, had he known the statement would be so inaccurate, he would have done his utmost to induce Mrs Thatcher to avoid making it.

The statement was brilliantly handled by the Prime Minister. Because she had been so forthcoming about the treachery of Anthony Blunt she was widely believed, and the parliamentary mechanics were so arranged that she could not be asked any difficult questions. Though scores of backbench MPs rose when the Prime Minister sat down only three questions were allowed from each side, and those MPs chosen by the Speaker could be guaranteed not to be controversial. The Labour leader, Michael Foot, had been consulted by Mrs Thatcher and had a strong interest in throwing doubt on the book, which for the first time revealed the treachery of Tom Driberg, a former chairman of the Labour Party, and other Labour MPs.

Having denied to me, in front of Lady Falkender, that he had ever heard of any doubts about Hollis, Harold Wilson stood up to claim credit for having set up the Trend inquiry. He asked: 'Will the Rt Hon. lady confirm that, although Sir Roger Hollis operated during seven premierships, including my own, I was the first to set up an independent inquiry?' Mrs Thatcher did so. I have already given a possible explanation for his behaviour.

After her brief knock-down of the book the Prime Minister had pre-empted further parliamentary curiosity by announcing the first independent inquiry for twenty years into the efficiency of the safeguards against any future penetration of the secret departments by foreign powers. It was to be carried out by the Security Commission. As had probably been anticipated, many MPs assumed that the inquiry would cover the cases which my book had revealed. They were misled. The remit to the Security Commission specifically banned it from making any such investigations. But the existence of the inquiry meant that MPs could be fobbed off until the Commission reported, which would obviously take some time.

Mrs Thatcher promised Parliament that she would publish the Commission's findings, subject to security considerations, but she was to renege on that. She also told Parliament that an inquiry into my sources was already under way, in terms suggesting that it was something special and might lead to my prosecution. In fact it was simply the inquiry inevitably being made by MI5 and, apart from the fact that it soon identified Wright, no more was heard of it.

At a press conference I predicted that Mrs Thatcher would come to regret her statement. Although I had no idea at that stage that Wright would eventually produce a book of his own, her brusque dismissal of the Hollis case was to stimulate Wright to continue with his campaign, which resulted in *Spycatcher*. All the Prime Minister needed to have done was to say that Hollis had been suspected and investigated and that, while there was no proof of his guilt, the case, like all similar intelligence cases, remained open.

The Security Commission did not report until May 1982 and Mrs Thatcher then declined to publish its long statement, claiming that the text would have to be heavily expurgated for security reasons and that this would give 'a seriously misleading impression'. Because the Falklands War was in progress MPs showed no interest whatever in the thin résumé which was published. It listed a large number of security improvements and referred to others so secret that they could not be mentioned. There were so many, causing major changes in the running of MI5, MI6 and GCHQ, that it seemed crazy that they should have had to wait on the chance publication of a book by an investigative writer.

18

The Truth about the Spycatcher *Affair*

I remained in touch with Wright by letters sent to accommodation addresses until the spring of 1983 when he ended the correspondence. He had formed a new and more promising association with a TV producer called Paul Greengrass, who was eventually to 'ghost' *Spycatcher*. Wright would maintain that this book had been written because *Their Trade Is Treachery* had failed to produce a proper inquiry into the Hollis case but, as it contained no significant new evidence in that respect, it was essentially a commercial venture which was to make him into a millionaire.

In the hope of avoiding a court action, his publishers sent a copy of his lengthy typescript – some 637 pages, according to one source – to the Attorney General, Sir Michael Havers, hoping that, given the chance to remove a few especially sensitive passages, he would pass the rest for publication. Havers found it 'dull and repetitive'. There were a few shocks which had not appeared in *Their Trade Is Treachery*, such as the technical details of bugging friendly embassies, like that of the French, and mischievous information about interception operations involving other countries. These allegations did not worry Havers because many of them had occurred during Labour administrations and Wright's charges about Wilson's friend, such as Kagan, were far more damaging to Labour than to the Conservatives. Havers and MI5 were relieved to find that Wright admitted that, while the evidence seemed strong, there was no proof that Hollis had been a spy.

The major difference between *Spycatcher* and *Their Trade Is Treachery* was Wright's account of an MI5 plot, involving about thirty officers, to undermine Harold Wilson and his

Government. When I had visited him in Tasmania we had discussed the relevant parts of my previous book, *Inside Story*, which had contained my mistaken account of a plot. He declined to confirm my assertion, insisting that any MI5 actions against Wilson or his intimates had been in the normal line of duty. In particular, he denied that Wilson had been bugged and that, because of security arrangements peculiar to Number 10 Downing Street, it would have been impossible for MI5 to have organized it. John Ware encountered the same reluctance to confirm any plot when he had visited Wright in 1984.

I greatly doubt that Wright was holding his plot story back for a later book of his own, because he genuinely did not believe that he would live long enough to write it and wanted to maximize the impact and financial success of *Their Trade Is Treachery* to resolve his desperate need. So why would he have denied the Wilson plot then had it been true?

Havers was assured by MI5 that the plot was completely false, but the book was rejected on the principle that it was a breach of the confidentiality which Wright owed to the Crown through his secret service. Mrs Thatcher and the rest of the Cabinet were determined to establish the principle that all officers and retired officers of the secret services owed this confidentiality, and that to breach it was a crime. To do anything else would open the floodgates for other secret service officers with even more interesting and more dangerous stories to sell. On retirement Wright had signed a form accepting that such breaches were offences under the Official Secrets Act, even if committed abroad.

The case to enable Wright to publish his book in Australia was based on the fact that, essentially, *Spycatcher* would only be repeating information already published in *Their Trade Is Treachery*, which the British Government had failed to suppress when it had the opportunity to do so. Wright's Australian lawyer, the ebullient Malcolm Turnbull, had realized that if the issue could be diverted to the question of secrecy rather than confidentiality then it could be won in an Australian court. He then devised the concept of a secret deception operation in which MI5 had conspired with Rothschild and myself to induce Wright to part with official secrets so that my book could be written and published. This was Turnbull's explanation of why the Government had not suppressed my book.

Wright knew that there was no truth whatever in this crackpot conspiracy. The idea that the MI5 top management, which is constitutionally opposed to revealing anything ever, should suddenly want to reveal the skeletons which had been concealed for so long is preposterous. At no time when I was with Wright in Tasmania or during our long correspondence did he ever suggest that MI5 had been involved in such a way. Instead he underlined the need for the utmost secrecy from MI5, stressing that the organization would kill the book if it learned about it in advance. He also feared that MI5 would stop his pension. Nevertheless he claimed, under oath, that he felt he was being 'drawn into a deniable operation' by Lord Rothschild. It was a myth which was to dominate the proceedings, even though the judge eventually dismissed it as incredible.

Realizing that *Spycatcher* would look like a tame rerun of *Their Trade Is Treachery* unless it included something new and sensational, Wright inserted the story of a plot by thirty MI5 officers to destabilize the Wilson government. This deliberate use of information which he knew to be false also enabled Wright and his supporters to claim that the Thatcher Government was trying to suppress the book to prevent exposure of this scandal, even though it had occurred while Labour had been in power and been responsible for MI5.

Before the trial proper began Turnbull was in touch with me by telephone and told me that as the Government was 'playing it dirty' – of which I could see no evidence – he would be playing it dirty too. 'We have to play dirty because we have to win this case,' he told me.

The first dirty trick was the release to the media of confidential letters which I had written to Wright. These revealed my social associations with senior personalities like Sir Michael Havers and Sir Arthur Franks and enabled Labour MPs to make party political capital out of them. As Turnbull was to reveal in 1988 in his account of the trial, he decided to 'stir up the Opposition in London with calls to prosecute Rothschild'. He told Wright: 'The Government will have to respond by saying they are going to investigate. Rothschild might defend himself by telling the truth.'

Turnbull also warned me by telephone that certain Labour MPs would be calling for the prosecution of myself and Lord

Rothschild for corrupting Peter Wright by an offer of money to part with official secrets. In November 1986 an obscure backbencher with no hope of preferment, Dale Campbell-Savours, did so. Prolonged inquiries by Scotland Yard were to prove that neither of us had done any such thing. Campbell-Savours and others who supported Turnbull had been 'willied' into taking part in a deception exercise.

Wright had readily agreed to this operation to discredit Rothschild, the old friend whom he professed to admire so much. When told by Turnbull that this was the best way of winning the case Wright put down his whisky glass and said, 'Oh well, poor dear Victor. Throw him to the wolves!'

In the deception campaign, masterminded from Sydney, various MPs in London swallowed lie after lie and regurgitated them in Parliament. For example, under the protection of parliamentary privilege Campbell-Savours referred to allegations that Harry Wharton, a distinguished MI5 officer, had been a 'leading conspirator' in the 'plot' to bring down the Wilson government. He asked if disciplinary action was to be taken against him. Yet there was no such claim in Wright's book when it eventually appeared. Campbell-Savours was to admit in Parliament that the main objective of his interventions was to destroy the case in the Australian courts.

Though grateful for that assistance against Britain's interests, Turnbull wanted someone with greater political clout. The TV producer Paul Greengrass, who, incredibly, was being allowed to assist Turnbull in the court while having a secret vested interest in *Spycatcher*, said, 'David Leigh's the man. He knows Kinnock.' After talking to Leigh, a reporter for the *Observer*, Turnbull telephoned Neil Kinnock, the Labour leader, who duly intervened in Parliament. Turnbull has recorded, 'There was no doubt I was using Kinnock, in the sense that his questions assisted my endeavours to extract the truth from Armstrong.'

Members of former Labour Governments then latched on to the mythical plot charges as excuses for their past failures – the inference being:'How could we have succeeded when we were being secretly undermined?' Kinnock, Campbell-Savours and the rest were serving as puppets in a disinformation campaign for Turnbull, who pulled the strings when he wanted to. It was also a brilliantly successful advance PR campaign for the book.

At the same time the most sensational claims alleged to be in *Spycatcher* were leaked to British and American newspapers. The main object, apart from keeping the issue alive in the media, was to induce journalists and MPs to claim that the Government was trying to ban the book to prevent disclosures which would damage its reputation and that of MI5. Both the media and tame Labour MPs obliged. Sensational allegations which were not in the book at all were peddled as though they were. Some of Britain's leading newspapers were misled, as were the broadcasting media. The *Times*, for example, reported that in addition to Harold Wilson, Lady Falkender, Lord Goodman and Bernard Donoughue had been illegally bugged. It claimed that Wright would reveal an unsuccessful MI5 attempt to lure Anthony Wedgwood Benn, then a Labour Minister, into a sex trap. MI5 was also alleged to have released a file on a homosexual relationship between Jeremy Thorpe, the former Liberal Party leader, and a friend, Norman Scott. None of these assertions, which were all untrue, appeared in *Spycatcher*.

When I saw Wright in Tasmania in 1980 he gave me a list of important people who were suspected of being Soviet agents but had never been named publicly. Copies of this list, which could only have originated from Wright or his associates, were left, anonymously, at newspaper offices in London in the hope that they would be followed up and used.

The Government construed all this activity as 'a conspiracy orchestrated from Australia'. It was not an exaggeration. Both MPs and journalists had been deceived by a dirty tricks campaign of unprecedented proportions based on myths and lies.

Throughout the court case Wright was projected as a frail old patriot who had been forced into exile because he wanted to expose treachery and inefficiency. He had not been forced into exile but had emigrated to Tasmania because he had a daughter living there and, perhaps, to get himself out of the reach of the British Official Secrets Act, which has no extradition clause. Sir John Bailey, the Treasury Solicitor, told me that he had been advised that Wright should not be cross-examined in the witness box because he might drop dead and then the Government would be held responsible. In fact Wright was certainly capable of withstanding cross-examination physically, and his evidence could have been demolished.

To diminish this danger Wright submitted a thirty-page affidavit which eventually was to be investigated, statement by statement, by Scotland Yard detectives. They proved it to be essentially a massive deception on the Australian courts and the world at large. Here are some of the statements it contained and the real facts behind them as checked out by the Metropolitan Police.

1. Wright told the court that in September 1980 Lord Rothschild and I induced him to part with secrets so that I could write a book. He claimed that he had not suggested the idea of a book.

Fact: In November 1976 Wright wrote to Lord Rothschild stating that he was going to write his memoirs. Lord Rothschild wrote to the Director General of MI5, Sir Michael Hanley, to warn him. In June 1980 Wright wrote again, stating, 'I am writing a book whose tentative title is *The Cancer in Our Midst*. It is about the penetration of our society by the Russians and how the Soviets have used it to manipulate us and achieve their ends.' When he arrived in England three months later he brought with him the first ten chapters of his book and showed them to Lord Rothschild.

2. Wright claimed that money had never been a major incentive but just an incidental benefit.

Fact: His immediate motive for wanting me to write the book was his imminent bankruptcy and desperate need for £5000. His letters and cables pestering me to expedite his payments proved that money was a major motive. He repeatedly stressed his need of it and put up suggestions for making more.

3. In closed session Wright told the court that I had sent him £5000.

Fact: Scotland Yard established – and told me so – that I had never sent any money to him. Every penny he received had been paid by the publisher.

4. Wright alleged that I was 'an agent of MI5 and a double agent', presumably for the Soviets.

Fact: Wright himself told me that MI5 had considered trying to recruit me, but decided against it because I would not be 'controllable'. All my professional life I have done all I can in newspaper articles, broadcasts, books and speeches to expose the subversive activities of the KGB.

5. Wright indicated that Lord Rothschild had given me a great deal of information about the Hollis case.

Fact: Lord Rothschild pretended to know nothing about the case. My information had come from the Tory MP, Jonathan Aitken, who had received it from MI5 officers early in 1980, as Wright knew.

6. Wright assured the court that he had not taken any material from MI5 when he had retired.

Fact: On 3 November 1976 Wright had written to Lord Rothschild about Anthony Blunt, stating, 'I have still got all my notes of my talks with him.'

7. Wright stated that Lord Rothschild had sent him a first-class return ticket to London which he exchanged for two economy-class tickets so that his wife could accompany him.

Fact: Scotland Yard detectives established, from the ticket agency concerned, that Lord Rothschild had sent him one economy-class ticket. Wright must have paid his wife's fare. His false statement to the court made him look a poor man who could not afford to do that.

8. Wright indicated that he had met me in the past, giving the impression that we been in some sort of previous collusion.

Fact: I had never knowingly set eyes on Wright until I met him in Cambridge in September 1980.

9. Wright told the court that Mrs Thatcher had discussed intelligence matters with Lord Rothschild at his London flat.

Fact: Police inquiries and examination of diaries from Number 10 Downing Street showed that she had never been there.

10. Wright explained that one of the reasons he had written *Spycatcher* was because he was so disappointed with my book as it had not called for a searching inquiry into the existence of more moles in MI5.

Fact: Wright never expressed any disappointment to me. It was Wright who gave me various reasons why MI5 was no longer harbouring any high-level moles after 1971. In 1980 he was opposed to a major inquiry into MI5, as had happened with the CIA, because it could wreck the service.

11. Wright claimed that he had come to disapprove of the surreptitious methods used by MI5, which contravened civil liberties.

Fact: In 1980 Wright had been vainly proud of these methods, some of which he had invented. His alleged conversion was advantageous to the presentation of his case in securing the sympathy of the court and promoting the eventual sale of his book.

12. Wright's affidavit stated that the secret banking arrangements made by Lord Rothschild for the transfer of the royalties to him were to protect the identities of Lord Rothschild and me.

Fact: They were entirely to protect Wright's identity because he was afraid of losing his pension if MI5 could prove that he had been a source for my information.

The police report showing that Wright had given so many false statements to the court must have shocked the Director of Public Prosecutions and the Attorney General when they read it, because they must have realized what a blunder had been made by the failure to cross-examine Wright in the witness box.

The Government lost the case in the Sydney court mainly, in my opinion, because it had failed to make a proper reconnaissance of the Australian system of justice, assuming that it would be broadly the same as in Britain. Instead Turnbull was permitted to make the wildest accusations and to browbeat Sir Robert Armstrong into making apparent admissions, some of which were untrue, because he had been ineptly briefed before leaving London. The so-called 'tall poppy syndrome' – the Australian delight in chopping any distinguished person down to the grass-roots level, especially if he is British – was much on display.

Sir Robert did himself great damage by his statement that, when pretending that he did not have an advance text of *Their Trade Is Treachery*, he was just being 'economical with the truth'. In a British court the judge would probably have received this remark with some humour, knowing that economy with the truth – revealing the minimum of information without actually lying – is standard practice in Whitehall and Westminster. One can almost hear such a judge – 'Ah, Edmund Burke, I believe.' Those listening in the less sophisticated Australian court affected to be deeply offended. 'It brought a gasp of disbelief from the courtroom,' Turnbull recorded. Sir Robert's credibility as a witness slumped disastrously.

Publication of the American edition of *Spycatcher*, with

worldwide publicity for its contents, was timed to do maximum damage to the Government's appeals in the Australian courts by showing that, as the horse had bolted, any action to restrain it was pointless. The book was only 382 pages long because the American publisher required the removal of material unsuited to the general US market. Wright's book, as he wrote it, has never been published anywhere.

The cover of the American edition bore a description of Wright as 'Former Assistant Director of MI5', giving the impression to many that he had been Number 2 in the organization. In fact Assistant Director is a modest rank, which was one reason why he left with such a small pension. A journalist from the prestigious *Sydney Morning Herald* who interviewed Wright in 1988 went away convinced that Wright had been 'the number 2 man at MI5' when he had barely been number 32. He assured the journalist that the most important thing he achieved against the Germans in World War II was the sinking of the German battleship *Tirpitz*. He claimed to have used submarines which he had rendered invisible to German radar by electronics. 'I planned the whole operation,' he said. In fact, the actions which first crippled the *Tirpitz* were planned by senior Navy and Fleet Air Arm officers in the Admiralty. The *Tirpitz* was sunk, months later, by the RAF using special bombs designed by Sir Barnes Wallis.

To counter Wright's allegations against Lord Rothschild and myself I published an account of what had really happened in 1987 under the title *A Web of Deception*, changed to *The Spycatcher Affair* in the paperback edition. It answered the questions raised by the Wright trial but was virtually ignored by the media, which by and large preferred to give credence to Wright, his being a 'better story'.

It so happened that in the final result, in the federal appeal court in Canberra, all the tricks and deceptions counted for nothing. The British legal advisers had held high hopes that the High Court there would rule that publication of the book would be against Australia's interests as well as Britain's. Instead it awarded the case to Wright and his publisher, almost summarily, on the grounds that it should never have been brought because any legal action under the British Official Secrets Act was unenforceable in the Australian courts. Clearly someone on the legal side in Britain had made a gross error in failing to appreciate this in advance and the cost to Britain, apart from the embarrassment of the defeat in such a blaze of publicity, was some £2 million.

The demands by Labour MPs for the prosecution of Lord Rothschild and myself, which was a non-starter because it was based on a totally false accusation, eventually overbore the Attorney General, Sir Michael Havers. Admittedly he was not well at the time and had been subjected to a barrage of hurtful allegations about his integrity in the Australian court, but a more robust law officer would have resisted the demands, which could only waste more public money. There was never any possibility that MI5 or the Government would countenance the appearance in the witness box of Lord Rothschild, who knew so much about MI5's secret machinations. He was also too ill to testify. Additionally, there could be no case without cross-examination of Wright, who had been warned by Havers through an intermediary that he would be prosecuted if he ever returned to Britain. Further, any prosecution of me might reveal the name of the man who had supplied Sir Arthur Franks with the text of my book, and Sir Robert Armstrong had endured massive indignities in the Australian court to prevent that.

Nevertheless, Havers consulted the Director of Public Prosecutions and instituted criminal inquiries by the Serious Crimes Squad of the Metropolitan Police. The remit of the two senior officers allotted to the task was to investigate the allegations which Wright had made in his affidavit to the Australian court. One by one Lord Rothschild and I, who also agreed to be interviewed, demolished them.

At an early stage of my interrogations, which totalled at least twelve hours, I predicted to the police that they would reach a point in their inquiries where they would be called off because they would not be permitted to question certain witnesses. It was clear to me that they could not complete their evidence without interviewing Sir Arthur Franks. This could never be allowed because even the police could not be told secret MI6 matters. That was exactly what happened and in July 1988 the Attorney General, then Sir Patrick Mayhew, made a written parliamentary statement that there was no evidence to justify any proceedings against Lord Rothschild or myself.

There had been one action on my part which could be

construed as a dirty trick. At the end of their interrogations the police suddenly produced a search warrant and demanded to see my private files. I was sick of being harassed to satisfy the whims of negligible backbenchers and of being part of what I knew to be no more than a political pantomime on the Government's part. When documents were selected for the police to take away I ensured that they included files about certain individuals containing information which, I was confident, would make any prosecutions totally impossible. They must certainly have raised some distinguished eyebrows and I suspect that they resulted in at least one major political action, for which I have no regret.

Most people and the media seem to believe that the Government was completely vanquished in the *Spycatcher* Affair and that Wright's victory was total. That is not the Government's view as expressed by Lord Armstrong in the *Times*. Various judgements on consequences of the case involving newspapers were given in British courts and, with some justification, Armstrong regards them as a victory for the principle for which the Government had fought on the nation's behalf. The Law Lords were unanimous in deciding that present and former members of the security and intelligence services have a lifelong obligation of confidence owed to the Crown in respect of information derived from their work. So none can follow Wright's example with impunity. It was also the Law Lords' view that any who behave like Wright are guilty of treachery, their conduct 'reeking of turpitude'.

At the time of writing Wright, now seventy-four, is still living in seclusion in his shack, to which he has added an extra room. In spite of the Government's view of him it cannot legally withdraw his pension, nor has the Queen seen fit to cancel his CBE, which has angered some of his old colleagues. Though still able to move around, he is increasingly frail; so apart from money, which he is too ill to enjoy, what did he get for his pains? In Australia he is regarded as something of a folk hero for having beaten the British establishment, but his confession that he had faked the Wilson plot torpedoed any reputation for veracity or honesty of purpose. His original book was never published. *Spycatcher* took the Hollis case no further and there was little else new in it. In the British courts and in Parliament he has been called 'treacherous', 'a traitor' and 'a skunk'. In the House of Lords he was called 'that infamous and treacherous character' by Lord Annan, while Lord Mayhew spoke of 'traitors such as Wright and Philby'.

Inside MI5 he is the example to recruits of everything a secret service officer should not be. His name is perpetuated in 'Wright's disease' – the exorbitant suspicion which can lead to dangerous and damaging excesses. Former colleagues have publicly called him 'a liar', 'a shit' and 'a renegade'. During the recent sale of a former MI5 outstation in Marlborough Street, London, a prospective buyer asked the old man at the reception desk what he thought about Peter Wright. He answered, 'He was a bastard then and he's still a bastard.' Wright was an intelligence supergrass, and like all supergrasses some of his information had been intended to settle old scores. Even his sister, Elizabeth, has branded him publicly as a liar and a vindictive mischief-maker prepared to betray secrets for money. By and large, while the British public had some sympathy for Wright, they did not approve of their security secrets being sold for private gain.

Apart from the motive of money, what made him behave as dirtily as he did? It was Harold Macmillan's view, as expressed to me, that the world of MI5 was so peculiar that anyone who spent more than ten years in it was likely to be weird or even mad. The regular use of lies and deception is bound to contaminate and corrode character. People like Wright become intensely suspicious and reluctant to trust others, but the real world is based on trust. They end up unable to believe that two and two could possibly make four because it could never be that simple. They also tend to despise their colleagues, so that few spooks have a good word for any others. Wright was affected by all those susceptibilities.

There can be no doubt that in one major respect the Government snatched a major triumph from the *Spycatcher* Affair in the shape of its tough new Official Secrets Act, which makes new inquiry and publication about the secret service almost impossible. Without the Wright case it is unlikely that the Government would have attempted to push such a draconian act through Parliament. After Wright's behaviour it was able to claim that such legislation was urgent and, in the face of the facts, parliamentary opposition was feeble. The legal bill of £2 million has been cheap at the price, and the media have not yet fully appreciated what is liable to hit them if they offend the secrecy restrictions as freely as they did in the past.

When the late Reginald Maudling was Home Secretary I once ribbed him about his reluctance to abolish Section 2 of the Official Secrets Act. He told me that I and other campaigners against the Act were stupidly short-sighted. 'You always seem to find ways of getting round the Act and we have no wish to change it because whatever we do will be unpopular. But I warn you that if you ever do force a Government to abolish it you will get something you will always regret – an Act with teeth in it.' He was absolutely right. The new Act has stripped the secrecy away from Ministries like Environment and Education but clamped it much more firmly on the Defence Ministry and the Foreign Office as well as on the secret services. Revelations of the kind I made in *Their Trade Is Treachery* are a criminal offence and, whatever MI5 might or might not advise, prosecution would now be virtually automatic.

The main objection I have to the new Act is that it can now be an offence to publish material about secret affairs even if it has been published before. Writers and journalists have always worked on the principle that, libel apart, what has been published once can be published again. I find it hard to object to the fact that a defence of public interest is no longer possible because the majority of the public want its secrets kept. It is the media and a few Labour MPs, who would sing a different song were they in office, who make all the noise about the democratic need to know.

The new Official Secrets Act was only part of Wright's legacy of legislation and change. After the disclosures in *Their Trade Is Treachery* and further security disasters the Prime Minister got her Cabinet Office intelligence co-ordinator, Sir Anthony Duff, to take control of MI5 so as to reorganize and revitalize it. He also conducted a thorough inquiry into the allegations by Wright, Wallace and others that there had been a plot by security service officers to bring down the Wilson Government. As the Prime Minister told Parliament on 6 May 1987, the allegations were shown to be false. Duff had overseen a comprehensive review of all the papers. All the officers interviewed, including the Director General at the time, Sir Michael Hanley, denied taking any part or even having any knowledge of activities or plans to discredit Wilson or his Government when he was Prime Minister. Hanley also denied having told Wilson that he knew of a disaffected faction inside MI5 and said he had no reason to believe that such a faction existed. As Duff was not a professional MI5 officer, with no responsibility whatever for the past and no personal interest in promoting a cover-up, there could be no doubt about his integrity.

One of Wright's legitimate bleats was that when he suspected senior colleagues of treachery there was no other senior person whom he could approach for advice in absolute confidence. In the autumn of 1987 the Government appointed Sir Philip Woodfield, a former senior civil servant, to serve as an Ombudsman – officially Staff Counsellor – to the secret services including GCHQ. Staff can approach him in secrecy to air any grievance without prejudicing their careers.

The Government's first legal response to the *Spycatcher* Affair was a Security Service Act which became law in April 1989 and established a legal framework for MI5. It made the Director General responsible for 'ensuring the continued political neutrality of the Service' while not admitting that any previous DG had ever been anything else. It looked progressive but was essentially a cosmetic operation, and MI5 will largely function as before. Then, later in 1989, the new Official Secrets Act became law. Peter Wright is likely to be judged harshly by history, but he certainly has his place there.

Since Wright's abject admission about the Wilson plot and his false statements to the court it has been suggested that the information he gave me in 1980, including the secret material about Hollis, might also have been untrue. I have several reasons for knowing that this was not so. In the first place I was able to check out his information with other sources who had been involved in the various enterprises, and the Hollis case in particular. Secondly, he had no motive for giving me any false data. On the contrary, he wanted to make *Their Trade Is Treachery* a continuing success to resolve his financial difficulties. Apart from the Wilson plot allegations his factual disclosures in *Spycatcher* have not been seriously challenged, and they confirm what he originally told me.

Since the Hollis case could still generate charges of deception by the Government if the guilt of the former Director General should ever be proved, a brief summary of recent developments will not be out of place here. The view of most of the intelligence officers who were involved in the case, and some others who have studied it, remains that there was a spy at high level in MI5 during the 1950s and 1960s and that the preponderance of probabilities is that it was Hollis.

In the year in which he died, 1987, William Casey, head of the CIA, told an American Senator friend of mine that he was convinced that Hollis had been a spy. They had been discussing counter-intelligence and Casey seemed so sure that my friend suspected that the CIA must have received some new information about Hollis – possibly from a new break in the recorded wartime messages transmitted by Soviet Intelligence, which are still being patiently processed with the help of super-computers.

Shortly before Sir William 'Intrepid' Stephenson died he claimed that Hollis had been a double-agent, and Wright seized on a conversation with him to say that he now had proof of his guilt. I was in touch with Sir William over several years, and the most he would ever say was that he had been advised not to trust Hollis and to watch him while he was visiting the USA because he was anti-American. He assured me that he had no other evidence on which to base an opinion about Hollis's loyalty. So it is likely that the conversation with Wright was just another of his burgeoning fantasies.

There is slowly growing evidence of Hollis's far left-wing leanings which date from his years in China before joining MI5 in 1938. He was certainly in touch there with a leading Communist revolutionary and recruiter called Arthur Ewert. One of his first wife's close relatives, who knew him well, is on record as saying that he was 'very Red' when he returned from China and, in his opinion, could have been a spy.

The Hollis family has reason to believe that it can claim descent from Peter the Great and this link could explain the fact that a defector, Igor Gouzenko, claimed that the spy whom he knew to be in MI5 had 'something Russian in his background'. Nobody else fitted that peculiarity so exactly.

In a film shown on British television in May 1990 the former KGB officer Yuri Modin, who ran the Cambridge Ring, made great play of the fact that none of them had ever been prosecuted, thanks to the KGB's efficiency. The only reason that one of them, Anthony Blunt, escaped prosecution was because Hollis arranged immunity for him. So Modin may have been making the subtle suggestion that Hollis had organized it on the KGB's behalf. This could, of course, have been no more than deliberate disinformation. Philby also declined to clear Hollis when given the opportunity to do so during interviews with the journalist Phillip Knightley shortly before his death.

The recent KGB defector to Britain, Oleg Gordievsky, has stated on television that he does not believe that Hollis was a Soviet agent. He claimed to have had access to records while service in KGB headquarters in Moscow but, when originally questioned by MI6, all he said was that he had been given no information about the Hollis case and had not been aware that the KGB had ever had a British source at such a high level.

While Hollis's supporters are keen to regard this as proof of his innocence, there are two serious weaknesses in Gordievsky's evidence. If Hollis was a spy there can be no doubt that he was recruited by the GRU, not the KGB, as I have shown in detail in my book *Too Secret Too Long*. Secondly, the existence of such an important asset would be held closely secret to a very few people, even after he had ceased to function. It is the view of intelligence officers whom I have questioned that if Hollis had been a spy his file would not be in general circulation. It seems that Gordievsky did not see any file on Hollis, yet there must have been one in the KGB counter-intelligence records simply by virtue of his long service in MI5.

The secret services and the Government have a vested interest in permitting Gordievsky to state publicly that, in his opinion, Hollis was not a Soviet agent. One wonders if he would have been allowed to appear if he had evidence of Hollis's guilt.

The private papers of Harold Macmillan, who had dealings with Hollis, especially during the Profumo Affair, have revealed only that the former Prime Minister had a poor opinion of him. According to his official biographer, Alistair Horne, Macmillan regarded him dismissively as an 'insignificant man'. In Volume 2 Horne wrote, 'Judging from MI5's inept performance during the Hollis years, Hollis – an unforthcoming, reticent and retiring man – had at least a great deal to be reticent about.' He left the question of Hollis's loyalty open, though Macmillan doubted that he had been a traitor.

Much has been made of a memorandum on Soviet Communism by Hollis dated 25 June 1942 and found recently in the

Public Record Office by a researcher. Addressed to the MI5 Director General, Sir David Petrie, and circulated in Whitehall, it warned that while Britain should obviously co-operate with the Russians in the war effort, care should be taken to watch what the Comintern was doing. It stated:

> In the past, the Communists have made a regular practice of ganging up with the lesser enemy until the major enemy is defeated. Germany is obviously the major enemy at present but I see no reason to think that we and the United States are not lesser enemies to be dealt with later as occasion offers. If we are not, the USSR has changed its spots and has become the Socialist State instead of the International Revolutionary . . . If Russian Communism has become merely a domestic matter, Stalin ought to call off his bloodhounds.

This long memorandum, which continued in the same vein, has been put forward as conclusive evidence that Hollis was a hard-line anti-Communist but, as head of the MI5 branch responsible for overseeing the Communist threat, what other kind of memo could he have written without raising eyebrows? He submitted the document from his sickbed, having been away from work for three months with a recurrence of tuberculosis, presumably to remind his chief that he was still active. It also promoted the case for having an MI5 section to counter Communism after the war, with himself heading it as the authority on the subject.

Like his chief, Hollis was aware that the document would have little, if any, impact on Foreign Office relations with the Soviet Union. It was the kind of document which Philby would have written, just as that same traitor joined the Anglo-German Fellowship to cover up his true allegiance.

Inquiries by the BBC have established that there was a copy of this memorandum in the relevant MI5 files, which were all available to the MI5 and MI6 members of the Fluency Committee who investigated the Hollis case. Clearly, its existence had little impact on them.

In 1990 the Hollis case was given further prominence by the reappearance of an eighty-three-year-old Soviet agent, with the codename Sonia, who is suspected of having been a wartime courier for Hollis while MI5 was stationed at Blenheim Palace. Sonia is a rare example of a female professional deceiver who had come to England in 1941 under the cover of being a Jewish refugee from Hitler. She repaid Britain's hospitality by serving as a courier for several Soviet spies, including the atomic scientist Klaus Fuchs, during her nine-year stay before fleeing to East Germany in 1950.

I recognized her while watching some television interviews of Communists in East Berlin during the revolution there, in January 1990, and alerted a newspaper, which sent a reporter to track her down. Sonia, whose real name is Ursula Beurton, declined to say anything of substance beyond stating that she had never known Hollis. She continued to do that in a later television programme and when interviewed by other newspapers.

According to her own memoirs she was a career officer in the GRU, and presumably is a pensioner of that military organization. If so, or almost in any event, she would be required to seek Soviet permission before commenting on any of her espionage activities, either positively or negatively, so little credence can safely be given to anything she says.

In particular, she continued to preserve her cover story about why the GRU had posted her to the Oxford area early in 1941, claiming that her parents had been evacuated there. My researches have shown that they were never evacuated to Oxford and that her posting followed the evacuation of MI5 to Blenheim Palace, near Oxford. She has confirmed that she was soon transmitting information to Moscow, and while some have doubted that she could have done this for long when there was a radio-detection station close by, at Arkley, it now transpires that some of her traffic was intercepted. The senior officer to whom such intercepts were passed has assured me that he handed them on for decoding either to Hollis or Philby, who invariably told him that they had never yielded to decipherment. Her transmitter was never tracked down.

Regarding Sonia or any other Soviet agent interviewed by journalists, the KGB and the GRU have manifestly taken the view that, in spite of any warming of East-West relations, no gratuitous assistance is to be given to the intelligence agencies of the West. On the contrary, they are to be allowed to stew in their doubts about Hollis, the 'Fifth Man' or any other suspected spy.

From her comments on television it was clear that Sonia

remains an unrepenting, hard-line Communist, along with her traitorous husband, the Communist Briton, Len Beurton, who defected with her to the new East Germany in 1950. It must be extremely sad for such people to realize that they have devoted their lives, uselessly, in following a misguiding star, and some Communist apologists insist that they deserve sympathy because they were striving to form a new kind of society. So was Mussolini. So was Hitler.

There is one dirty trick of particular general interest on which Wright threw some genuine light in *Spycatcher* – the deception of the Queen by MI5 concerning Anthony Blunt's confession that he had been a Soviet spy while serving inside MI5 during the war. Early in 1964 Blunt was 'blown' to the FBI by Michael Straight, an American whom he had briefly recruited to the Soviet service while both had been at Cambridge. Blunt was still attached to Buckingham Palace as Surveyor of the Queen's Pictures, so MI5 faced the immediate question of whether or not the Queen should be informed and, if so, what advice she should be given. Largely because the public exposure of the traitor would be such a scandal for MI5 itself, the Government had agreed that he, and any others he might unmask, should be given immunity to prosecution. The official argument was that Blunt would co-operate only if immunity was granted, and this was given as the explanation when the Queen's Private Secretary, Sir Michael Adeane, was called to a meeting with Hollis and the chief civil servant at the Home Office in April 1964.

Adeane was told that, in Hollis's view, Blunt should be allowed to continue in the Queen's service because otherwise he might not be helpful and the Russians might learn what had happened. Blunt could easily have been required to retire on grounds which would not have raised suspicion, but when Adeane passed the MI5 advice to the Queen she accepted it, embarrassing though the occasions when she encountered Blunt might be.

I discovered that the Queen had been told about Blunt's treachery before I published *Their Trade Is Treachery* in 1981 because she had admitted it in front of a friend of mine who was not a Palace official but met her socially. There was no further confirmation of this, however, until 1987 when Wright revealed in *Spycatcher* that, after he took over the interrogation of Blunt, Adeane had called him to the Palace. Adeane assured him that the Queen had been fully briefed about Blunt, but his main purpose was to warn Wright not to pursue any information which the traitor might give him about a mission in Germany which he had undertaken for the Palace at the end of the war.

There is no doubt that the mission involved the recovery of documents which could be embarrassing to the royal family, if published, but there is still no certainty about their precise nature. The Queen had been subjected to a deception which kept a traitor in her service for a further fourteen years to save MI5 embarrassment, but the mysterious German mission may have made Adeane more amenable to recommending it. Such are the manoeuvres of the secrets world.

19

Hounded Hero

The most venomous character assassination campaign in recent times with the least evidence to support it has been that mounted against Lord Rothschild, who died in March 1990. It could be argued that, as a power-hungry politician affecting all our lives and with no lack of opportunity to retaliate, Wilson was fair game. As a private person ham-strung by the security restrictions of having worked in MI5 and the Cabinet Office, Rothschild was not. Nevertheless, over many years he was subjected to snide innuendo and false accusations, often based on parliamentary questions, designed to brand him as a traitor. Though entirely without foundation, we may not have heard the last of the vendetta for, just as many people still believe that some skeleton in Wilson's life will one day be exposed, many also suspect that Rothschild was not all that he seemed.

Such a phenomenally gifted man – biologist, linguist, mathematician, counter-intelligence expert, bibliophile, county cricketer, golfer and outstanding jazz pianist – was bound to generate envy, especially with a family name which, almost uniquely, attracts universal interest. He was also likely to attract enmity, for nobody suffered fools less gladly or had such a low boredom threshold. While loaded with charm, which some less sincere men can turn on, he could turn it off, at a second's notice, giving him a reputation, probably deserved, for arrogance.

His misfortune was to have been at Cambridge University – at Trinity, by scholarship – in the 1930s, where inevitably he had been friends with other stimulating characters who were not only Communists but were secretly recruited as Soviet agents. It has been a literal instance of guilt by association. The two chief offenders were Guy Burgess and Anthony Blunt. In addition he was also a friend of Michael Straight, the rich American who was recruited by the Soviets but recanted and eventually 'blew' Blunt to the FBI and MI5.

As Victor Rothschild often explained to me in our long friendship, the trouble was that if you were intellectually curious as an undergraduate you tended to know everybody else who was. So he was invited to join the now almost infamous Apostles Society which harboured a number of Communists, including Blunt, who had impressed him with his outstanding intellectual abilities, especially in art and mathematics. As a letter to Maynard Keynes, the economist, shows, Rothschild was not much of a supporter of Marxism-Leninism: 'We talk endlessly in the Society about Communism which is rather dull. We need your presence.'

Rothschild, impressively good-looking when young, was also exciting to know. He drove a Bugatti and set a long-standing record time for the then tortuous drive to London, demonstrating a natural facility for risk-taking which was to serve him well during the coming war. Yet, while leading a fuller social life than most students, he was intensely serious about his scientific work.

In 1931, at the age of twenty-one, he obliged the family by trying his hand at banking; but he returned to Cambridge after only six months to be a full-time scientist, specializing in the intricacies of egg fertilization. On the outbreak of war he was invited to join the fast-expanding MI5 by Guy Liddell, one of its senior officers. Initially he was concerned with identifying key points in the United Kingdom which needed protection against enemy saboteurs while also working in the commercial espionage unit, where his family business contacts were so useful. Blunt was to be in a different section of MI5 and Rothschild was in no way responsible for his entry, as has been maliciously suggested. There is a letter in Rothschild's papers which disproves that falsehood.

Among later tasks, Rothschild dismantled dirty-trick sabotage bombs camouflaged in all sorts of ways, 'in a teapot, or as a lump of coal or in the pocket of a raincoat', as he recorded. Operating in various parts of the world of British interest, such as the Abadan refinery at Iran, and on ships, he took about a hundred booby traps apart, remarking later, in his bland way,

'It is only with a new one that it is stimulating.' He was given permission to reproduce his chilling telephone talk-back to base as he gingerly dismantled a crate of onions which had been dropped by the Luftwaffe – in fact a vicious booby-trap containing many pounds of TNT. His explosives expertise also involved him in the famous Double-Cross operation which 'turned' captured German spies to work for the Allies. He was given the job of examining cigars and other presents given to Churchill to ensure that they were not booby-trapped or poisoned. All the cigars were X-rayed to prove that there was no explosive device inside and others were sampled for poison by tests on mice. Food such as hams, and drinks like cognac, presented as gifts to Churchill had to be tested for poison without his knowing it. Among sundry additional tasks, Rothschild investigated the Liberator air crash at Gibraltar which killed General Sikorski, the Polish leader, and was thought to be due to sabotage. In 1944, when he held the equivalent rank of colonel, he was upbraided in the street by an acquaintance for not being in uniform and, true to form, offered no explanation. Next day it was announced that he had been awarded the George Medal for his cold-blooded courage.

In the same year it became necessary to impart some highly secret and complex technical knowledge to the American forces. Rothschild was chosen for the task and briefly joined the US Army. To conform with routine regulations he was required to take an intelligence test and was found to have an IQ of 184, a level which had been recorded only once before.

Rothschild had married in 1933 and he has been accused many times of letting rooms in his wartime London house in Bentinck Street to Blunt and Burgess and of being involved in 'orgies' there. The facts are that Rothschild and his wife wanted to dispose of the lease and offered it to two former Cambridge friends, Patricia Parry (now Lady Llewelyn-Davies, the Labour peeress) and Tess Mayor. They could not afford the rent, and as the accommodation was on three floors it was agreed that they could sublet to friends. They were both friendly with Anthony Blunt, then in MI5 and above any suspicion. He suggested his friend Burgess as another tenant.

In 1946, having parted from his wife, Rothschild married Tess Mayor who had become his assistant in MI5 and was awarded an MBE for her dangerous work. He told me that he proposed to her and was accepted in a bunker. I assumed that it was on a golf course, but it may have been a protective bunker used in their bomb disposal operations.

After the war he took his seat in the Lords on the Labour benches and returned to biological work at the Cambridge Zoology Department, pioneering further research into the process of reproduction. He told me that while working at a French marine biology laboratory he was pushing a glass tube into some resistant rubber tubing when it broke and slashed into one his fingers, severing an artery and a nerve. While first aid was being administered, a scientist lit a cigarette and put it into his mouth to help him overcome the shock. He was a chain-smoker ever after and when told, in his seventies, that it had fatally ruined his health, he took out his slide rule and calculated that he had smoked 21.6 miles of cigarettes.

Though so successful in the field of science that he was elected to the Royal Society in 1953, he missed the peculiar excitement of the undercover life, suffering withdrawal symptoms, as many do when they quit the secrets world, and he did what he could to remain in touch with it through continuing friendship with permanent officers. The secret world had also left its mark. He had become intensely security-conscious and remained so. Whenever we spoke confidentially, unless it was deliberately outside in a garden, he would either assure me that his room had been 'swept' that morning or would put a couple of cushions over the telephone.

Rothschild retained some genuine fears that the KGB might take some form of revenge, even assassination, for his activities against them, though I never believed that to be realistic. If going abroad he would always say, on the telephone, that he was going to Wales, though this was mainly because he was a target for Palestinian terrorism. In the Jewish family tradition he had done much for Israel's benefit. While he always denied any connections with Mossad, the Israeli secret service, I took that as part of his security armour.

To some extent he became the victim of his own inscrutability. Because he said little, people suspected he might be hiding much. What that might be was first rumoured following the defection of Guy Burgess to the Soviet Union, along with Donald Maclean, in 1952. However, I have established that when Maclean first became suspect as a Soviet agent in 1950 eight other Britons, most of whom had been at Cambridge, were put under some degree of surveillance by MI5. Rothschild was not one of them. No British or American intelligence officer ever put forward Rothschild's name as a member of the Cambridge spy ring, but some armchair espionage aficionados did.

His outstanding intellectual ability – 'Lord Razorsharp' was one affectionate name I had for him – brought many demands for committee work and he took on the chairmanship of the Agricultural Research Council from 1948 to 1958. Three years later he joined Shell as a science adviser. It was then that his second misfortune befell him. He met Peter Wright.

According to Rothschild, that happened when he realized that one of the Shell scientists had special qualifications which might be of use to MI5 in the preparation of new secret inks and anti-corrosive greases to protect equipment, like radios, buried in the ground. He told Sir Dick White, then head of MI6, who arranged for Wright to see him. They became friends, and Wright used him as a sounding board for thinking out and refining deception operations and solving other problems apparently beyond the capability of those inside MI5. This relationship, which put Rothschild back in touch with highly sensitive secrets, would never have been permitted had there ever been any doubts about his loyalty.

In 1964 Rothschild was devastated by Blunt's confession that, throughout the war, he had been a KGB 'mole' inside MI5. He had drifted away from Blunt after 1950, though his wife had remained in touch with the traitorous art historian who by that time was Surveyor of the Queen's Pictures and Director of the Courtauld Institute. Like the rest of Blunt's close friends, Rothschild was interviewed by MI5 and gave valuable assistance in the search for the Fifth Man, Philby and Blunt being established as the third and fourth members of what had obviously been a Cambridge ring of spies. At no time was he suspected of having been a member.

While Blunt's confession was kept secret, along with the immunity to prosecution granted to him, Rothschild feared the possible backwash if it ever became known. His close friendship with Blunt, and that of his wife, would obviously be far more likely to raise doubts in the public's mind than his university association with Burgess.

In 1971, having retired, aged sixty, from the Royal Dutch Shell Group where he had been Research Co-ordinator, and not relishing the idea of joining the family bank, he was suddenly invited by Edward Heath to set up and run the Government's 'Think Tank'. Officially called the Central Policy Review Staff, it was a group of independent thinkers available to consider any aspects of Government policy. That meant access to Cabinet secrets of the highest sensitivity, especially for its chief, and before Rothschild's appointment was announced he was subjected to the positive vetting procedure. Because of his association with Blunt the process was particularly stringent, with a major input by MI5, which takes a particular interest in Cabinet Office appointments.

Nothing could be found to suggest that Lord Rothschild was not a fit person to have access to documents of the highest secrecy. Had there been any doubts, he would have been quietly barred. This, surely, is the most telling public evidence that he had never at any time been the subject of internal suspicion, as all the four proven spies of the Cambridge ring had been.

Inside the Cabinet Office he teamed up with his old friend Sir Dick White, a former head of both MI5 and MI6, who was serving as Co-ordinator of Intelligence there. They remained close friends until his death.

Shortly after Rothschild left the Think Tank in 1974, Harold Wilson wanted to reduce the size and scope of the Aldermaston nuclear weapons establishment and he set up a high-powered committee to examine the problem. Those appointed to it needed MI5 security clearance at the highest possible level because the work required access to the most sensitive atomic secrets. Rothschild was one who passed that test without any difficulty, and served on the committee.

He was also selected to serve in various important investigations such as the Royal Commission on Gambling, of which he was chairman. Mrs Thatcher was later to call him in from time to time for advice and he did some work for the Environment Ministry. Such services would not have been open to anyone with the smallest taint of disloyalty.

Rothschild had maintained his connection with MI5, but Peter Wright's retirement in 1976 and emigration to Australia effectively ended his operational relationship. Then three years later, when Blunt was publicly exposed as the 'Fourth Man' of the Cambridge spyring, the media began looking for the Fifth. Rumours and innuendoes quickly reached his ears and, fearing that he might be driven to take libel proceedings, he wrote to Wright in June 1980 saying

> Things are starting to get rough. I cannot see that it would be a breach of the Official Secrets Act for you to put on a piece of paper, *but not send to anybody*, a detailed account of your relationship with me, including *all* details, and let me have it by a method which I shall let you know in due course. There certainly is a need to know and you would only be telling someone something that, memory lapses apart, he could put down himself.

Wright responded with a three-page letter headed 'Victor Rothschild's help since 1951 to the Security Service'. It concluded, 'I do not believe it is conceivable that either Victor Rothschild or Tess Rothschild have ever been Soviet agents. I am willing to testify to that effect in any way deemed suitable.' The date 1951 referred to the assistance that Rothschild had given to MI5 concerning the defection of Guy Burgess.

Wright's list still remains unpublished – even by Wright himself, presumably because it did not fit in with his defence during the *Spycatcher* court case. The left-wing writer David Leigh saw the list when he was covering the case. Previously he had been highly critical of Lord Rothschild and seemed prepared to believe the fifth man accusation but, after reading the list, he described both Victor and Tess Rothschild as 'entirely innocent patriots'.

I have already described the manner in which Rothschild introduced me to Wright in the autumn of 1980. It was a major error of judgement which he was greatly to regret, though he never said so to me. He never explained to me, or, satisfactorily, to the police, why he had taken such trouble to bring me together with Wright when he already knew that the MI5 man was to proposition me about writing his book. One lawyer whom he consulted understood that Wright had made it clear to Rothschild that he intended to get his material published somehow. Rothschild, the lawyer asserted, was aware that I knew a great deal already, and believed that if he brought me into the picture Wright would realize that I would be publishing it anyway and he would then abort his book. That does not fit the facts at all and can be discounted.

One of his former Cabinet Office colleagues thinks that Rothschild realized that if I wrote the book he would not be mentioned in it while another writer might concentrate on him. That would accord with the fact that Rothschild induced Wright to give him the chapter he had written about him and that I was never shown it. On the other hand, Rothschild never asked me to keep him out of the book, which he would have done had he been greatly concerned. I did not mention him in the text because, so far as I knew then, his activities had little relevance to those I was describing and I also wanted to avoid drawing attention to any part he might have played in its origin.

The most credible explanation in my view is that Wright had made it clear that he was determined to find an author, and if that failed he would somehow finish the book and publish it under his own name. Rothschild realized that this would give its contents enormous credibility, while if they appeared under a journalist's name they could be dismissed by the authorities as speculation. He already knew that I was interested in the Hollis case and he could trust me not to reveal either Wright's name or his own. In short, bringing me into the picture was a damage limitation operation. When I put this to him at the height of the Scotland Yard inquiries about us, his typical response was: 'A very interesting hypothesis!'

I have also thought it possible that if Wright had failed to find an author he might, in desperation to prevent his bankruptcy, have sold his material piecemeal to Australian newspapers, where it could have appeared under his name. This would also have given it far more credibility and, in Rothschild's eyes, been far more damaging in security terms.

There is no doubt that Rothschild felt sorry for Wright in his financial predicament and miserable standard of living and had tried hard to induce the Treasury to increase his pension, even securing the support of Edward Heath. The Treasury's adamant refusal may have been a factor in his decision to assist him. The only certainty is that he must have given the matter the deepest thought before involving me, because he never did anything impetuously.

When I published a large book, *Too Secret Too Long*, in 1984, presenting the case for some external supervision of the secret services, he seriously suggested that a committee should be set up to investigate the need for it and that he should chair it. It was an unlikely appointment because, by that time, MI5 had discovered his involvement in *Their Trade Is Treachery*, but he was one of the few with security clearance high enough for the task.

I was not present when Wright left Rothschild's house after his visit to Cambridge, but it would seem that they did not part on good terms. Wright is on record as saying that his host told him that he never wanted to see him again, and they never communicated. In preparing his case for the Australian court, Wright rounded on Rothschild. These facts raise the possibility that Wright was able to lean on his host, perhaps in connection with the chapter he had written about his MI5 operations. In return for suppressing that chapter Rothschild may have been required to assist him.

Rothschild suffered a mild heart attack during the three-day-week winter crisis of December 1973. It was the first serious sign of generalized arterial damage which he would come to accept as entirely due to smoking.

Rothschild's connection with Wright and me was leaked to the media and to Labour MPs after Wright and his lawyer, Malcolm Turnbull, had agreed to 'throw him to the wolves' in order to win their action. Inevitably it gave journalists and MPs a field day, and the old story that Rothschild had been the so-called Fifth Man of the Cambridge spy ring was resurrected and hyped up by a completely ludicrous suggestion. It was argued that he had encouraged Wright to give me the information about Hollis so that the former MI5 chief would be exposed as the Fifth Man – a move which would draw suspicion away from himself. This was a particularly stupid 'think-piece', which had originated with Turnbull in Australia, because the Fifth Man could not possibly be Hollis. The Fifth Man had to belong to the spy ring which operated at Cambridge in the 1930s. Hollis was at Oxford in the 1920s. Wright, of all people, knew that Rothschild had been involved in so many successful operations against the KGB that he could not possibly be the Fifth Man, and had produced a three-page statement to that effect, but he still went along with Turnbull's disinformation.

Had he wished to do so, Rothschild could have promoted the

Hollis story through me without bringing Wright from Australia. I already knew a great deal about it and he could have told me more, knowing that I would not reveal the source. Instead, when I attempted to secure information from him he tried to put me off the scent by sending me a letter suggesting that the allegations were untrue. I have little doubt that before sending it Rothschild had taken advice from his friend Sir Dick White, who was anxious to keep the Hollis Affair secret.

The Rothschild and Hollis cases cannot be sensibly compared in any way. There was never any internal evidence to point suspicion at Rothschild. The Hollis case was based on a mass of intelligence evidence which convinced most of the MI5 and MI6 officers involved in the investigations that there had been a high-level Soviet spy inside MI5 in the 1950s and 1960s and that the 'preponderance of probabilities' pointed to Hollis.

Apart from a 'good story', what motivated the media to impugn a public figure whose many contributions had been so beneficial to society? Firstly he was a Rothschild and an establishment figure, near the top of Whitehall's list of the 'Great and Good' who are recruited for service on Royal Commissions and committees. The tall poppy syndrome is not peculiar to Australia, and what a specimen to cut down! Those who disliked him for his arrogance relished his discomfiture, and, with some, there may have been a factor of anti-Semitism.

Though he had at one time been a Socialist peer, Labour backbenchers saw him as Heath's former Think Tank guru as well as a symbol of rich Tory privilege. In the long-running pantomime of Parliament there are always members queuing for the role of Jack the Giantkiller, and he was a heaven-sent target for demolition by all the processes available under their privilege, the freedom from legal redress protecting them in law whatever they might say in the House.

MI5 remained silent and would do nothing to help their former servant by making any sort of statement when his homes in London and Cambridge were being besieged by reporters and photographers, who even tried to bribe the milkman to let them drive his vehicle past the security arrangements to the front door. At the age of seventy-six he was knocked down in a media melée outside Rothschild's Bank.

I had suggested that he should release Wright's list to me for publication, but he believed that this would have been a breach of the Official Secrets Act and was not prepared to do it. I did my best from my own resources: in newspaper articles and, when opportunity offered, on television, listing those achievements of which I was aware.

Apart from his counter-sabotage work he had provided the lead which had given MI6 its first hard evidence that Philby had been a Soviet spy. While visiting the Weizmann Institute in Israel he overheard an Englishwoman, Flora Solomon, declare that she had known for years that Philby was a Communist and Soviet agent. When they were back in London he induced her to repeat her statement to Sir Dick White, then head of MI6. Counter-espionage officers from MI5 then interrogated her and she confessed to having kept silent about Philby's treachery until he had started attacking Israel in newspaper articles. It was on her reluctant evidence that Philby was confronted in Beirut and confessed to having been a spy.

He also gave the lead to Alister Watson, a close Communist friend of Blunt and Burgess who had become an Admiralty scientist. Watson was interviewed and, while denying being a spy, confessed to having faked his positive vetting form by falsely denying that he was a Communist. He was quietly transferred to non-secret work. A wily interrogator, during World War II Rothschild had been chosen to break down tough targets like Otto Skorzeny, the man who rescued Mussolini.

Through more than one intermediary he now asked MI5 to come to his assistance with some sort of statement, either directly or through the Cabinet Office, but he expected no result and got none. His view of the MI5 management, when those who have helped them are in trouble, was, 'They will see you dead before they will help you.'

Eventually, when the situation worsened, with his homes and office besieged, he decided to try to force MI5's hand. He asked Max Hastings, editor of the *Daily Telegraph*, to visit him and receive an exclusive statement which appeared on the front page of the newspaper on Thursday, 4 December 1986. Addressed to 'The Editor and Readers', it state:

> Since at least 1980 up to the present time there have been innuendoes in the Press to the effect that I am 'the 5th man', in other words a Soviet agent. The Director General of MI5

should state publicly that it has unequivocal, repeat unequivocal, evidence that I am not, and never have been, a Soviet agent.

The Director General of MI5 did nothing apart from bleat to the Cabinet Office about the difficult position in which he had been placed. Two days later the Prime Minister, who had been irritated because Rothschild had not first cleared the matter with her office, issued a press notice saying that the Government had no evidence that he had ever been a Soviet agent – a far cry from what he had requested.

Some of his friends thought his letter was unwise, because the negative can never be proved and any statement could not go further than saying that no evidence existed. But he was much more seriously ill than they knew and he could take no more, being also anxious to protect the good name of Rothschild.

Sadly, there was worse to come. Wright's misleading evidence that Rothschild and I had corrupted him, along with other machinations in Sydney and in the British Parliament, which had been a massive deception operation, led to investigations by the police. Rothschild was advised by one eminent lawyer to refuse to see them, as was his right, and he could certainly have declined on medical grounds, but his curiosity got the better of him. During the investigations he underwent a 'scrape-out' of one of his carotid arteries, a serious operation which can lead to brain damage. On recovering consciousness, to convince himself that his mind had not been impaired he correctly repeated the first fifteen prime numbers, to the puzzlement of the nurses, who thought it must have been. In spite of such spirit he became very depressed and fearful that he might be prosecuted, which would smear the family name. I found it hard to convince him that he was untouchable on several counts. To cheer him up Sir Robin Butler, now Cabinet Secretary and a great admirer of Rothschild, organized a party of old colleagues.

The case against both Rothschild and myself had collapsed by April 1987, the police being forbidden to continue with it, but neither of us was told. For their political convenience, the 'authorities' wished to defer any clearance until after the coming general election in the autumn, possibly to avoid any hustings jibes. Fortunately Rothschild's MP in Cambridge, Robert Rhodes James, made public the undoubted fact that the whole Rothschild family were suffering intolerable distress because of the continuing uncertainty. This was followed by a brief statement from the Attorney General, in the form of a written answer to a parliamentary question to the effect that the allegations against us both had not disclosed evidence against either of us to warrant proceedings.

The media showed minimal interest and Parliament showed none. The cowardly Labour backbenchers who had forced the police inquiries, while sheltering behind the privilege of Parliament, remained silent. Had the statement been made orally, questions could have been asked in our interest, but the Government wanted to avoid the suggestion that the inquiries had been a waste of public money and police time spent in chasing the fantasies of Peter Wright and the backbenchers.

To what extent did Wright's false statements and harassment contribute to Lord Rothschild's death from a massive heart attack in March 1990, while he was listening to the late news in his armchair at his St James's Street flat? Mental stress is often a contributory factor to heart attacks, and Rothschild had been severely shaken by Wright's allegations and the consequent police inquiries. For two years he had also been undergoing treatment for throat cancer, though none of his friends knew it.

The Prime Minister, Mrs Thatcher, attended his memoral service, announcing to Parliament pointedly and most unusually that she was leaving to do so. William Waldegrave, Minister of State in the Foreign Office, and an original member of Rothschild's Think Tank, gave a laudatory address stating that he *knew*, from his position that Rothschild 'had served his country as signally in secret as he had done openly'. Two former Prime Ministers, Callaghan and Heath, were there along with many former Ministers and service chiefs. Sir Dick White represented MI5 and MI6, and there was a massive turn-out of the 'Great and Good'. Few, if any, of these would have been present if the deceased had ever been a suspect spy.

Many will continue to ask: If Rothschild was not the Fifth Man, who was? The question makes sense only in the context of the fifth person to be recruited to the Cambridge spy ring and to become an active spy himself, with a position where he had access to secret information and had passed it on to the

Soviets. It is not applicable to suspects like Sir Roger Hollis who were never at Cambridge.

A KGB defector, Anatoli Golitsin, claimed knowledge of a 'ring of five' Soviet agents recruited at Cambridge and there is previous evidence that, in its early days, the KGB encouraged rings of five Communist conspirators. There is no doubt, however, that the Cambridge Ring eventually involved more than five, as Blunt and the others recruited more.

In *Their Trade Is Treachery* I was able to name one man who had confessed to being a member, John Cairncross, who worked in both MI6 and the forerunner of GCHQ during the war. In *Too Secret Too Long* I gave full details of his damaging treachery as a major member of the Cambridge Ring, including his leak to the Russians of the most secret 'Ultra' documents, which were believed to have been inviolate.

Nine years later the Soviet defector, Oleg Gordievsky, named Cairncross as the Fifth Man with the false claim that it was the first public exposure of his importance. This was used to sustain the argument that, as Cairncross was the Fifth Man, Sir Roger Hollis could not have been. Yet no serious student had ever suggested that Hollis was the Fifth Man, which was an impossibility. The Fifth Man had to be at Cambridge in the 1930s. Being at Oxford in the 1920s, Hollis belonged to a different generation.

Wright had told me of another strong suspect, Alister Watson, who worked in a secret Admiralty laboratory and had confessed to being a secret Communist while denying being a spy. Wright also described the case of Leo Long, another Cambridge undergraduate who had been exposed by Blunt and had then confessed to having committed frank treason.

Another certain member of the Cambridge ring was James Klugmann, an open Communist who recruited Cairncross and others and penetrated SOE so effectively during the war that he played a major role in the plot to put Yugoslavia under the control of the Communist dictator, Tito. New details of Klugmann's baleful influence on the history of Yugoslavia became available in 1990 through tape recordings made by an important SOE officer, Major Archie Jack. They confirm the extraordinary dirty tricks which Klugmann and others, when based in Cairo and in Bari in Italy, perpetrated to ensure that General Mihailovitch, the leader of the Royalist Yugoslav freedom fighters, the Chetniks, was undermined to ensure Tito's accession. Ammunition and supplies intended for the Chetniks were diverted to Tito. Sabotage successes achieved by the Chetniks against the Nazis were attributed by the BBC to Tito's forces. Even Winston Churchill was deceived through fake radio reports transmitted by Klugmann's subversive group.

Klugmann, who died in 1977, could well qualify to be an earlier member of the ring than number five. He might even have been number one, though that dubious distinction is usually accorded to Philby. Several other Cambridge men have been mentioned as possible members of the ring – an undoubted New Zealand spy, Paddy Costello, the American Michael Straight, who admitted being recruited, and the Canadian Herbert Norman, a secret Canadian Communist who became an important diplomat.

Various Cambridge dons have been named as recruiters, but they do not qualify as Fifth Man because they did not have access to secret information and could not be spies. They include Peter Kapitza, a Soviet scientist from the Lenin Polytechnic Institute, who had been refused entry visas to both Germany and France on suspicion of being a Bolshevik agitator, but had been admitted to Britain. As a member of Lord Rutherford's outstanding atomic physics team at the Cavendish Laboratory in Cambridge he could qualify as a technological spy, as he made frequent visits to Leningrad and could also have been a KGB recruiter.

The police questioned Lord Rothschild about Kapitza and other names bandied about by Wright in the Sydney court. All that emerged with certainty from those inquiries was that the Fifth Man's name had not been Rothschild.

There is one intriguing possibility which does not seem to have been given any attention – that the Fifth Man was a woman. There are credible candidates, some no longer living.

20

High-Tech Sting

The susceptibility of MI5 and MI6 to penetration by traitors serving as Soviet agents, with all the publicity which ensued, raised continuing doubt in the USA about the wisdom of sharing American intelligence secrets with Britain. Fortunately, the British contribution to the partnership had become so valuable that the American authorities had little option but to forgive the security disasters. The main input had been supplied by the organization known as GCHQ (Government Communication Headquarters), centred on Cheltenham in Gloucestershire, and where no evidence of espionage had arisen – though it was obviously a target.

GCHQ is essentially an electronic eavesdropping agency with outstations in many parts of the world – a unique legacy from the imperial past. Since 1947 it has been run in partnership with the much larger American National Security Agency (NSA) with total exchange of information. Together they form an intelligence-gathering machine of such high-tech sophistication that the truth surpasses anything that has been written about them.

The GCHQ staff, unofficially estimated at twelve thousand, with five thousand of them in Cheltenham, the rest in outstations, intercept secret radio messages transmitted, usually in code, by other Governments communicating with their embassies and sometimes with their spies. Arrays of the most advanced computers decode and analyse what they can and store the rest against the day when some error or sloppiness on the part of the KGB or Red Army enables a code-break to be made. The harvest of intercepts make a major contribution to

225

the regular intelligence reports which the British Prime Minister and US President regard as essential for the conduct of both foreign and domestic affairs.

At the same time GCHQ is an aggressive centre for intricately ingenious deception operations – what might be called technological dirty tricks. Even its siting at Cheltenham was the result of a mild deception, as Professor R.V. Jones has recently recorded. The senior RAF officer first appointed to head it after World War II happened to be an ardent betting man and stipulated that he must have plenty of time for meetings, without saying that he meant race meetings. He then chose Cheltenham as the site because of the racecourse there.

Among GCHQ's simpler operations are underground tunnels driven to connect with cables carrying secret messages, such as those now known to have tapped into Soviet military traffic in Vienna and Berlin. Those involving radio, radar and satellite techniques are much more complicated and so productive that events thousands of miles away can be witnessed and overheard in quite astonishing detail.

With the advent of large spy satellites and over-the-horizon ground radar stations, the Americans and British, working in combination, found themselves able to monitor Soviet missile tests and so deduce the performance of new nuclear weapons long before they went into service. This was possible because when a missile is test-fired the propulsion unit and the dummy warhead send back a stream of information to the research scientists on the ground by the process called telemetry. Devices fitted to them record and signal back to base the data, like velocity, acceleration, engine performance and aerodynamic details, needed to assess and improve the performance of the missile. Such espionage operations took a major step forward in the 1970s with the introduction of satellites with enormous unfolding aerials which could take photographs and transmit them and the other data to centres in the USA and elsewhere almost immediately.

The Russians guessed what was going on but there was little they could do about it until the means to do so was provided, secretly, by another British traitor – the first, so far as is known, to have penetrated GCHQ. He was a signals technician, ostensibly of small importance, called Geoffrey Prime. Having qualified as a Russian translater while in the RAF in West Germany, he had been bribed, or possibly blackmailed through sex deviation, into working for the KGB and then wormed his way into GCHQ in 1969. During the eight years he remained there, mainly in the London outstation but with the last year at Cheltenham, he gave the KGB such detailed information about the Anglo-American missile eavesdropping operations that Soviet scientists were able to stage the ultimate in technological stings.

Knowing the code-keys to the American satellites, they fed false information into them over a long period. It was scooped up by GCHQ and the NSA and misled American intelligence analysts into seriously underestimating the true state of Soviet missile development. Prime also kept Moscow informed of the extent to which the Americans and British were being deluded, so enabling the deception operation to be continued with maximum effect. The high-tech robot spy in the sky, believed until then to be inviolate, had been outwitted through a low-grade human spy on the ground.

Coupled with other ingenious deceptions which appeared to confirm the false data, this technological sting gave the Soviets a crushing lead in nuclear missiles, while the Carter administration cut back on long-range missile development, believing that the USA was in front. Had it suited the Kremlin to order a surprise nuclear attack, the Soviet advantage might have been decisive.

The true situation was revealed only when Prime and other spies operating in the USA were exposed in 1982. When President Reagan eventually learned the extent to which the Soviets had leaped ahead he set about restoring the balance as quickly as practicable. The cost of the damage which Prime alone had inflicted was officially estimated by the Pentagon as 1 billion dollars – easily Britain's most expensive spy disaster.

Prime was eventually sentenced to thirty-eight years' imprisonment, but the manner of his arrest only served to raise American distrust of British security precautions to a new high. He was caught only when the police became interested in him because he could not resist masturbating in front of little girls. Even then, his treachery came to light only because of patriotic action by his wife.

The ensuing circumstances raised intriguing questions, which have been asked before and since in connection with other cases. Is the wife of a dangerous spy who betrays him to the authorities to be admired for choosing the right priority? Or is the wife who knows that her husband is a spy and does nothing demonstrating a greater loyalty, which is enshrined in the legal tenet that a wife can never be required to testify against him?

When Prime confessed his sexual obsession with small children to his wife, Rhona, after being questioned by the police, he also admitted that he had been a Russian spy at GCHQ. Next day he gave himself up to the police on the sex charge but said nothing about espionage. Mrs Prime agonized for three weeks, because she had regarded the marriage as happy and Prime had been a good stepfather to the three children she already had by a previous husband. During that time she discovered equipment which was obviously for spying and letters addressed to East Berlin, indicating the extent of his treachery, so she denounced him, fully appreciating the consequences.

At Prime's Old Bailey trial she told the court, 'I could not live with myself as a committed Christian if I did not go to the police and I did so. I can only condemn the terrible crimes he has committed but I know, in my heart, that I can forgive him because he is totally repentant.' Prime informed the court that he bore her no malice, but then it was too late for any other view and she had promised to stand by him.

The circumstances were complicated by what the Security Commission, commenting on the case, thought about another woman, Dorothy Barsby, who had been a friend of Prime's previous wife. She had been told by that wife that Prime was a spy for the Soviets, but she still acted as a character referee for him when he was being positively vetted – an act which helped him to spy so damagingly for another nine years.

Again, in making a judgement, the dirt is in the eye of the beholder. Mrs Barsby thought it would have been unpardonable for a woman to denounce her friend's husband because of the consequences for the friend. Mrs Thatcher took a different view, siding with the Security Commission, which considered it 'tragic' that she had not denounced Prime in 1973, before he had done his worst damage. Mrs Barsby and her supporters ended up claiming that MI5 and GCHQ were playing a dirty trick on her by making her a scapegoat for their failure to detect Prime's treachery.

In any event the damage had been done and Prime will always be the type specimen of the high-tech spy. The Pentagon went out of its way to tell the Security Commission the huge cost of his various deceptions, and, as most of this money had been spent by US taxpayers, the extreme anger of their representatives in Congress and the Senate at the ineffective security at GCHQ was not surprising. It even led to a visit to the Cabinet Office by an American delegation headed by a senior representative of the Senate Intelligence Committee to demand improved precautions at GCHQ, which they regarded as essentially an arm of the NSA. Whether as a result of that visit or not, the Prime case altered the Government's whole attitude to the official secrecy which had always surrounded GCHQ and those who work in it.

As with MI6, successive Governments had managed to avoid admitting that GCHQ existed, other than as a communications outfit, largely because they did not relish having to admit that it intercepts other nation's private messages in peacetime. They were particularly loath to admit that it was run by the Foreign Office, which concentrates on maintaining friendly relations with other states and could be tainted by any of GCHQ's dirty tricks that might go wrong. In the early 1980s, however, the worldwide publicity given to the Prime case, and especially the Security Commission's revealing report on it, changed the situation so drastically that the Government decided to seize some advantage from the calamity in a way which was to cause another political uproar likely to reverberate again when it suits Mrs Thatcher's opponents. Some of GCHQ's employees, many of them scattered in outstations in Britain, West Germany, Cyprus, Hong Kong, Turkey, Gibraltar, Oman, the Ascension Islands and elsewhere, are convinced that in the process the Government, and the Prime Minister in particular, perpetrated a particularly nasty trick on them.

In a time of crisis the interruption of the flow of intelligence information from GCHQ could be damaging, and in the event of impending war disastrous. When such an interruption was caused by a union-sponsored strike in 1981, during the time that President Reagan was shot by a would-be assassin, the Government was greatly dismayed, as were the American defence chiefs. Previous intelligence had established that the killing of the US President could be the first move in a surprise

Soviet nuclear attack and, while the strike lasted, the Government was half-blind to events. There had been previous disruptions at sensitive times, such as the Soviet invasion of Afghanistan.

There was particular concern about the angry American response to the strike because, while Britain has no spy-in-the-sky satellites of its own, the vast amount of information gleaned by the American satellites through photography, radar and other means is all made available to GCHQ and to the Defence Ministry. Loss of that material would be catastrophic for Britain, so as soon as the strike was over the GCHQ director, Sir Brian Tovey, prepared a plan to bring GCHQ into line with MI5 and MI6, which have never been unionized, and submitted it to the Joint Intelligence Committee. There was no evidence of any serious left-wing infiltration of the GCHQ unions, but there was always the possibility of a left-wing union leadership at a later date; the prospect, however remote, of a politically motivated strike at GCHQ during a time of emergency was frightening. So it was secretly recommended that unions should be banished from GCHQ, whether the staff there approved or not.

Mrs Thatcher's own Intelligence Steering Committee advised that the deunionization of GCHQ would not justify the ensuing hassle, but the main reason for shelving it in 1981 was that the inevitable union reaction would expose GCHQ to publicity and the Foreign Office would probably be driven into admitting what GCHQ does and accepting responsibility for it. At that time few people knew what GCHQ really did.

Two years later, however, when the Prime case had not only publicized GCHQ's functions but forced the Foreign Secretary, Sir Geoffrey Howe, to admit responsibility for them, there was little to lose. So deunionization was resurrected and a firm decision was taken to press ahead with it. Apart from the belief in MI6 and MI5 that the move was long overdue, it would show Washington that the Government was taking every step it could to prevent a further security disaster. The security authorities even went through the motions of threatening to introduce the polygraph – the 'lie-detector' – which was a standard adjunct in the positive vetting of Americans. The US authorities had been pressing for its introduction into all British departments with access to American secrets.

The deunionization decision was kept secret from the unions until representatives of those concerned were summoned to see the Cabinet Secretary, Sir Robert Armstrong, in January 1984. Not knowing why they had been called, the union leaders were appalled when told that the Foreign Secretary, Sir Geoffrey Howe, was already announcing the deunionization of GCHQ in the House of Commons, along with the admission that it was run by the Foreign Office. As an inducement, which the trade union leaders called a bribe, every member of GCHQ who renounced union membership, including those who had never joined a union – about half the total staff – was to be paid £1000. The furious union leaders believed they had been deceived as well as outmanoeuvred, and immediately announced a campaign to fight the ban on membership.

At the unions' request, Mrs Thatcher agreed to meet a delegation led by William McCall, general secretary of the Institution of Professional Civil Servants. They met in the Cabinet Room and the Prime Minister was flanked by a big-gun team of Ministers and officials. McCall offered an alternative solution incorporating the safeguards she needed, including a no-strike deal in each employee's contract so that any strikers knew that they would be fired. The Prime Minister went through the motions of agreeing to consider the offer.

Sir Robert Armstrong and other senior officials favoured the deal, but by the time of the next meeting a big majority of the GCHQ staff had accepted the £1000 offer. Mrs Thatcher was therefore in a position to take a much tougher line and said there was unbridgeable gap between the Government and the unions and that the ban on membership would stand. The trade union leaders attributed the Prime Minister's intransigence to her dislike of unions and to increased American pressure, which had been intensified by the introduction at Cheltenham of some new interception devices especially sensitive to strike action. The banning caused outrage throughout the trade union movement as a slur on the loyalty and integrity of the GCHQ staff, and the Labour Party is committed to reversing it, though whether it would face up to the American objections to doing so is doubtful.

The £1000 inducement set a bad precedent. In 1990 certain civil servants in central London, where there has been difficulty in filling certain posts which give regular access to top-secret information, are now being given large cash bonuses to compensate them for the intrusion into their privacy when they have to be positively vetted!

At GCHQ the staff have been granted a further consolation prize. In spite of the disappointment it would cause in Washington, the plan to introduce the polygraph was quietly abandoned on the grounds that a trial had proved it to be unreliable. In fact, the long US experience has shown it to be not only a deterrent but a valuable guide, not to indict anyone on that evidence alone but to indicate where further inquiries might be advisable. The real reason for dropping it was the Government's disinclination to stir up the unions any further.

It did not, however, signal any reduction in Mrs Thatcher's determination to get her way, as evidenced by a semi-domestic event which occurred around that time. The Prime Minister happened to be in the Cabinet Office with Sir Robert Armstrong and noticed two elegant table lamps which were Government property and took her fancy. She made it clear that she would like to see them in Number 10. Nothing happened, in spite of odd reminders, until the lady appeared in the Cabinet Office and told Sir Robert, 'I'll carry this one. You bring the other.'

The GCHQ union battle was not the only public evidence of the determination of Western Governments to ensure that, in the nuclear missile age, nothing can be allowed to interfere with the constant gathering of electronic intelligence. The ousting of Gough Whitlam, the Prime Minister of Australia, in 1975 had all the signs of being another expression of the awesome power of the intelligence community.

When the anti-American Whitlam became head of a Labour Government in 1972 he ended the co-operation of the Australian Security Intelligence Service (ASIS) with the CIA, which he greatly distrusted. He believed that the CIA was spying on Australians, a claim he was also to make against the British.

Two years later he set up a Royal Commission to inquire into the intelligence services, as he had promised he would. He replaced the heads of both ASIS and the Australian Security Intelligence Organization (ASIO), further moves which worried the American and British but were tolerable. But when he threatened not to renew the lease on a super-secret establishment called Pine Gap, in the desert near Alice Springs, there was serious alarm.

Pine Gap, officially known as the Joint Defence Space Research Facility, is largely financed and run by the CIA and the NSA to receive signals from American satellites stationed over the Pacific and to serve other crucial surveillance functions. Britain eventually receives the processed information through its Anglo-American intelligence agreements.

Whitlam was opposed to renewing the lease on the grounds that it made Australia a Soviet target. So, with British support, because of GCHQ's abiding interest, the USA retaliated to Whitlam's threat to deprive it of its main surveillance base in the Southern Hemisphere by threatening to cut off all intelligence links with Australia; this was not welcomed by the Australian intelligence chiefs. At the same time the British and American Governments planned further secret action.

Exactly what was done has never been disclosed, but in 1975 the Australian Governor-General, Sir John Kerr, used his powers to dismiss Whitlam in the name of the Queen. He may have had quite different reasons for his action, but Whitlam's removal came only days before the treaty enabling the CIA to keep Pine Gap going was due to expire.

The official explanation was that Whitlam had narrowly lost a majority in the Senate and therefore could not guarantee to pay the Government's bills. To many observers the dismissal looked like the end result of a deception operation, which Whitlam himself would probably have called a dirty trick or worse – though, apart from wrongly predicting that Kerr would suffer for his action, he accepted his position remarkably quietly.

21

Judge Not!

While American intelligence officials and some Senators and Congressmen had been bitterly critical of Britain over the Prime case, events were soon to show that it never pays to be too superior about security. Unknown to them, the National Security Agency already had its Prime and he had been right inside its headquarters at Fort Meade in Maryland.

Ronald Pelton was, like Prime, a low-level, run-of-the-mill member of the agency's forty thousand staff but had access to secrets every bit as damaging, though in a different area. What matters most in the world of secret treachery is not rank but access. The way he had escaped detection was even more reprehensible than in Prime's case for, being in severe financial difficulties, he just walked in through the front door of the Soviet Embassy in Washington in January 1980 and offered to sell secrets. The FBI is supposed to have the Embassy under permanent watch, but it missed out on Pelton. It had taped his telephone call seeking how to make contact, but had failed to identify the voice.

Pelton was uncovered only by the dirty trick which all spies fear – betrayal by a defector. One of his contacts in the Soviet Embassy had been Vitaly Yurchenko, the KGB security officer there from 1975 to 1980. After returning to Moscow to work for several years at headquarters there, Yurchenko defected to the CIA during a visit to Rome on 1 August 1985. A flamboyant, mustachioed figure then aged forty-nine, he had been chief of the counter-intelligence directorate responsible for rooting out spies inside the KGB. He immediately betrayed Pelton as an American traitor who had sold secrets to the KGB.

The case, which was conducted in extreme secrecy, was of major interest to Britain, a fact also suppressed. Pelton, who had worked for fourteen years in the NSA, had spent six of them, between 1966 and 1972, either at GCHQ in Cheltenham or at Menwith Hill, the joint NSA-GCHQ station near Harrogate. There is no doubt that some of the secrets he peddled prejudiced British operations, including naval activities of extreme sensitivity.

Pelton had recently resigned from the NSA when he committed his treachery, travelling to Vienna several times to be interrogated in detail by the KGB about every area to which he had access. Although they paid him only £23,000, the information he gave them was staggering.

The KGB's immediate interest was in a joint NSA-Navy operation codenamed Ivy Bells, which had been proceeding with highly satisfactory results for several years. NSA scientists had devised a 'black box' which could be clamped on to a telephone cable submerged on the sea-bed and, by induction, would record on tapes for at least a month any messages passing through it. The clamps were designed so that the black box would fall off if the cable was raised for repair or inspection.

Using free-ranging robots operated from submarines, the US Navy had been able to attach and remove the black boxes to and from cables in deep water. In daring operations many had been fixed and successfully recovered on Soviet cables carrying military messages, some of them inside Soviet harbours. As the Russians used plain speech or low-grade codes on the cables, believing them to be untappable, the Americans gained valuable intelligence which was shared with the British. It can also reasonably be assumed that British intelligence agencies were making use of the black box technology in other marine areas. Before Pelton's betrayal there had been no incidents to alert the Soviets about Ivy Bells, but in 1981, after Pelton had blown it, the Russians recovered at least one of the black boxes and not only ended the operation but knew its secrets, so that they could use it themselves if they wished.

Pelton, who turned out to be a far more damaging spy than has been publicly appreciated, exposed several other equally sophisticated and valuable operations being mounted jointly with GCHQ. The extent of his treachery was reflected in the sentence imposed when in June 1986, at the age of forty-four, he was convicted on various counts to three life sentences plus ten years.

The NSA's awareness of its own vulnerability to Soviet penetration helped to soften the impact of the Prime disaster, and any general American sense of superiority regarding security was shattered by the exposure of further treachery on an unprecedented scale. This was the case of a naval espionage ring run by a former naval warrant officer called John Walker. His brother, his son and a close friend were involved with him in the sale of secrets to the KGB literally by the sackful. The son, Michael, for example, who was on the aircraft carrier *Nimitz*, was in charge of the bags of decoded secret messages which were supposed to be burnt but instead were handed to his father, who hid them in woods for the KGB to pick up while leaving money in payment. Like Pelton, Walker had simply entered the Soviet Embassy and offered his services, which lasted seventeen years. Like Prime, he and the rest were caught and heavily sentenced in 1986 only because his wife betrayed him.

The British authorities were even more perturbed by the Walker case than by Pelton's because, while the Royal Navy's codes were different, the American traitors had revealed secrets about NATO naval plans and tactics, especially against submarines, which affected them. They made no public comment, however, not only because of its extreme sensitivity at a time when some real East-West détente with Gorbachev seemed likely, but because the Pelton case drew public attention to an aspect of the secrets world which has been kept surprisingly quiet in view of the extent to which it is practised – the use of military means to acquire intelligence in peacetime.

Britain has its own separate Defence Intelligence Service which controls the work of the Naval, Military and Air Attachés and a great deal more besides. In my experience the Defence Ministry, of which the Defence Intelligence Service is part, is responsible for more deception operations than any other department. It is closely linked with GCHQ units at Cheltenham representing the Navy, Army and RAF.

For obvious reasons it is deeply concerned with the monitoring of foreign military communications. At the present time there is continuing need to monitor the Soviet war machine to ensure that it is being switched to a defensive from an offensive posture, as the Kremlin leadership claims it is. If the claim is genuine, a pronounced difference in training methods should soon become observable by the various clandestine eavesdropping systems as well as by agents on the ground. The spy satellites should show a reduction of airborne forces and airlift capabilities and a noticeable reduction of the Soviet naval presence in the Atlantic and Pacific. Defence Intelligence is particularly on the look-out for any reductions in the Soviet Spetsnaz forces – the commando-style troops trained to be infiltrated into a target country in disguise, prior to an assault, to blow up defence installations and assassinate political and military leaders. The pride of the GRU, the vast Soviet military intelligence machine, the Spetsnaz forces have been greatly expanded in recent years and there is bound to be strong military opposition to pruning them.

Inevitably, the bulk of British Defence Intelligence operations has taken place on and beyond the inner German border between East and West Germany, because that was the line of confrontation between the forces of NATO and those of the Warsaw Pact. It was mainly there that operations have been staged to withdraw Soviet Bloc individuals who had signalled a wish to defect, to rescue an agent in distress, to plant eavesdropping devices or to secure choice specimens of defence equipment. The disappearance of this border with the unification of the two German states will create considerable tactical problems because, while East Germany will become NATO territory, its border will be with Poland and Czechoslovakia. Any intelligence infringement of the neutrality of these two independent states, which are unlikely to join NATO, would be fraught with political penalties.

Through GCHQ the Defence Intelligence Service collects and stores electronic intelligence about the radar transmissions of possible adversaries so they can be used in counter-measures. To accomplish this it sends out 'ferreting' aircraft and submarines so that possible adversaries turn on their counter-measures which can then be recorded and analysed. Electronic gadgets, disguised in various ways, are also planted on adversary territory to relay information of interest.

The Navy's nuclear-powered hunter-killer submarines do far more than routine practice patrols, and so far have not come to grief as the Russians did in the celebrated 'Whisky on the Rocks' episode in October 1981. A Whisky-class submarine engaged in a surreptitious probe near a naval base in southern Sweden ran aground and was unable to extricate itself. During the ten days that the Swedes courageously held the vessel for inspection the Soviet dirty trick departments moved into counter-action. They falsely accused Sweden of carrying out radio signalling operations on behalf of NATO and floated forged telegrams referring to a secret agreement between the USA and Sweden about American use of the naval base.

In spite of this embarrassing exposure the Soviets have continued to intrude their submarines into Swedish territory, mainly for espionage but also for training. Britain and the USA tend not to make much fuss about such operations because they indulge in comparable activities themselves.

The British Navy's clandestine use of submarines in peacetime is, rightly, held tightly secret, but one example came to light following the Falklands War of 1982. Five years earlier, in 1977, intelligence was received indicating that the Argentines were flexing their muscles and might be making preparations to invade the Falklands, a gesture they had made in the past. As a precaution it was decided to send out a hunter-killer submarine together with a small auxiliary supply force to keep watch and signal any developments. The selected submarine, believed to be the *Conqueror*, was in Gibraltar, and two frigates and a supply ship, elsewhere at sea, were summoned to take part. One of the frigates was in harbour at Kingston, Jamaica, where the captain was holding a large cocktail party. On receiving the signal to sail he ended the party abruptly and put the visitors ashore – a move which could have betrayed the highly secret operation but fortunately did not. The submarine, armed with its torpedoes and ready for action, remained on station in striking distance of any Argentinian assault force until the danger had clearly passed.

My inquiries about this episode at the highest level demonstrated once again the uncertainties besetting deception operations even among those involved in them. I wanted to know if the presence of the submarine had been deliberately leaked to the Argentinians to deter them from attacking. One admiral who had been concerned with the operation assured me that it had, but another, more senior, insisted that it could not have been. He recalled how it had been decided that, in the interests of secrecy, the submarine crew would have to go without their Christmas mail. He over-rode that decision and had the mail dropped by air, but was sure that the action had not been spotted by the Argentinians.

David Owen who, as Foreign Secretary, was concerned, had a different recollection. He was sure that the intention was to keep the operation entirely secret unless the Argentinians moved, which they did not. However he suspected that the MI6 chief, Sir Maurice Oldfield, might have leaked it for his own devious purposes by spreading the information through gossip in South American embassies and bars. Later Owen went so far as to arrange a search of Oldfield's old notes, still held at Century House, the MI6 headquarters, but they revealed nothing.

With so much deception the participants seemed to have ended up deceiving each other. James Callaghan, the Prime Minister at the time, was so sure that the Argentinians had been deliberately warned by surreptitious means that he mentioned the episode when criticizing Mrs Thatcher for her handling of the crisis when the Argentinians did invade the Falklands in April 1982. I informed Mrs Thatcher of the incident as I remembered it, having got wind of it at the time and being asked to suppress the information. She replied that she was not permitted to consult the papers of the previous Labour Government. This is a standing convention which may have other purposes, but also means that no Government can check on records of the activities of its predecessor, including any dirty tricks it may have perpetrated.

The issue had been raised in connection with the sinking of the Argentinians' only cruiser, the *General Belgrano*, which the Labour Party was describing as a dirty trick by Mrs Thatcher in a vain attempt to gain some political advantage from the war. They were arguing that she had ordered the sinking to prevent any possibility of a negotiated peace.

In national, as well as international, politics disinformation, is probably employed more regularly and more cavalierly than in any other sphere.

22

Defectors Extraordinary

While no nation had needed to devote so much ingenuity and effort on projecting disinformation as the Soviet Union, the Western intelligence agencies make use of it when it suits their purposes. As with the Soviet Union, though more selectively, the domestic population is sometimes the target, as happened on 26 February 1990. On that evening, with the possibly un-witting assistance of the BBC, MI6 foisted a fabricated story on the British public when Oleg Gordievsky, a former KGB officer who had defected to Britain in the summer of 1985, appeared for the first time in public on the *Panorama* programme.

Heavily disguised, because he still faces the death penalty as a traitor should he ever return to the Soviet Union, where he was born and owed allegiance, Gordievsky explained how, after serving MI6 as a spy inside the KGB for several years, the last two as the designated acting head of the London Mission, he had fallen under deep suspicion. He said that, having been lured back to Moscow by the KGB, he was intensively inter-rogated over several days in a tucked-away cottage but was allowed to sleep at night in his eighth-floor flat in a big building in Moscow. He claimed that, though obviously under close surveillance by the KGB, who would be waiting for him to try to escape, he went jogging in a park, made his way to a railway station and escaped by train to Finland.

The real escape was very different and far more exciting. MI6 field officers operating in Moscow knew of Gordievsky's plight and realized that extreme methods would have to be used to try to rescue him. A large cocktail party was being given at the British Embassy and one of the guests, who was unlikely to be suspected, was induced to hide Gordievsky in his diplomatic car and smuggle him past the Soviet guards into the Embassy compound. Next day he was taken out of the Embassy in a false compartment in a diplomatic van used for transporting non-urgent documents and, under the Vienna Convention of 1815, immune to being searched or interfered with in any way. The van was bound for the British Embassy in Helsinki and crossed the Finnish border without incident. Gordievsky's wife and two children were out of Moscow and had to be left behind. Gorbachev has declined to allow them to leave.

The puerile story which, for sensible security reasons, MI6 required Gordievsky to tell on *Panorama* did not fool the Soviet authorities. They knew the truth and, most unusually, confirmed it in a statement issued by their London Embassy in 1990, conceding that he had been 'smuggled out of the USSR illegally'. It took the opportunity to complain about the misuse of diplomatic privilege, though they have abused it hundreds of time to smuggle out prohibited goods. So what was MI6's purpose in propagating the lie, which was clearly done with the blessing of the Foreign Office? It was more than a routine deception to hide the truth about an illegal operation. The Government wanted the opportunity to undermine the credibility of the renegade MI5 officer Peter Wright, who had caused so much trouble, and in particular to rebut his allegation that the former MI5 chief, Sir Roger Hollis, had been a Soviet agent. On the programme Gordievsky was able to claim that, while serving in Moscow in the British section of the KGB in 1980, he had access to files and had never seen anything about Hollis.

Another purpose, dear to MI6, was to pre-empt a TV programme due to be screened in Britain eulogizing the infamous MI6 defector to the KGB Kim Philby, who had been given a hero's funeral a few months previously in Moscow. The programme, which contained interviews with several KGB officers, made MI6 look hopelessly inefficient, as Philby had spied within it for eleven years and then successfully defected. Gordievsky was an almost exact counterpart of Philby and his *Panorama* programme was slanted to make the KGB look so stupid that its suspect, who had spied for nearly thirteen years inside it, escaped from its clutches while jogging and under active surveillance.

True to form, the Soviet Government responded with a press conference at its London Embassy to claim that Gordievsky was a small fish trying to make himself look a big one –

common enough with defectors, whose livelihood depends on their information. They accused him of talking nonsense on the *Panorama* programme, saying that he had never been senior enough to have access to the kind of information he was claiming to know. According to rumour, probably emanating from MI6, Gordievsky had been heading the KGB mission in London, but in fact a full colonel was still in charge there.

As a rule, when defectors are permitted to appear in public the controlling intelligence authority, whether it be MI6, MI5, the KGB or the CIA, has to manage the output to prevent the release of still-secret information and may introduce some tailored disinformation to confuse the other side. The Philby television programme had been packed with obvious official disinformation and was typical of the dirty tricks which such competing agencies never tire of playing on each other.

However, I suspect that another more subtle motive lay behind MI6's willingness to promote Gordievsky as a great catch on television. This related to another more senior KGB officer, Vitaly Yurchenko, who had caused an even bigger sensation in Moscow when he had defected to the CIA, shortly before Gordievsky, on 1 August 1985, while on a visit to Rome, as I have already described.

Yurchenko betrayed not only Ronald Pelton, the American spy who had sold the Ivy Bells secrets to the KGB, but another traitor, Edward Lee Howard, who had worked in the CIA. After being fired for drug offences Howard had solved his financial problems by selling secrets which enabled the KGB to eradicate Russians who had been spying for the Americans.

According to American sources Yurchenko also immediately warned his CIA interrogators that, if they were running Oleg Gordievsky, who was still in Moscow, they should waste no time in trying to get him out because he was under grave suspicion. Yurchenko, who had been away from Moscow for only a few days, clearly thought that Gordievsky was still there.

The exact date on which MI6 spirited Gordievsky out has not been officially revealed but my informants say that it was 2 August. If that is correct then his panic removal at such diplomatic risk could have been the result of Yurchenko's warning, which would have been rushed to MI6 by the CIA.

MI6 may already have been aware of Gordievsky's plight, but I have been told by an in-the-know authority that there was a majo. element of luck in his successful extraction. The chance tip from Yurchenko may have been that element and would account for the extreme haste with which Gordievsky was withdrawn. The Foreign Office did not announce his defection until 12 September.

Yurchenko would certainly have known about Gordievsky's position. They had served together in the KGB's First Chief Directorate, in which Yurchenko was responsible for the investigation of suspected espionage incidents involving KGB staff until March 1985, while in the succeeding months he been mainly concerned with espionage work against the USA.

All Yurchenko's tips were so valuable that there seemed to be no doubt whatever that he was a genuine defector, though Howard and Pelton were no longer of much use to the KGB because they had ceased to have any access to secrets and had told all they knew. If Yurchenko was a false defector he might have been instructed to play the well-established dirty trick of 'burning' those two to establish his good faith with the CIA. His tip about Gordievsky, however, seemed to be absolute proof that he was genuine because all the signs indicated that his former KGB chiefs were furious when Gordievsky was rescued by MI6.

Regrettably, on the evening of 2 November 1985 Yurchenko eluded his CIA minder in Washington and redefected to the Soviet Embassy, having probably made some prior arrangement by telephone call while in a shop, allegedly to buy a hat. At a press conference called after his redefection he claimed he had not defected in Rome but had been kidnapped and drugged there and seemed to have no fear whatever of returning to Russia.

Yurchenko's redefection occurred just before the summit meeting between Reagan and Gorbachev in Geneva. It had been widely publicized that Reagan intended to tackle the Russian leader about the Soviet failure to implement human rights as it had promised to do under the so-called Helsinki Accord, which had been a deception operation in itself so far as the Kremlin was concerned. Yurchenko's claims about his rough treatment by the CIA, which he later repeated at a press conference in Moscow, offered Gorbachev a robust response to any charges Reagan might make about the Kremlin's treatment of its citizens.

If Yurchenko's original defection had been genuine it was generally expected that he would be tried and severely punished on his return, and the Washington lie machinery was soon putting out stories that he had been executed. In fact he was back working for the KGB, though at what level and capacity has not been established. He was even put on show for journalists to see that he was alive and well, though the CIA lie machinery indicated that it had information showing that he had been beaten up and tortured. He then gave a brief interview to West German TV in Moscow and, later still, claimed to be back in his old post. He was quoted again in *Izvestia* in September 1987.

The question that has seriously worried some intelligence officials ever since is this – as the KGB knows that Yurchenko tipped off the CIA about the need for Gordievsky to be rescued, why has he been so easily forgiven for such a monstrous and apparently damaging betrayal? Even if Gordievsky had already been spirited out, Yurchenko's tip about him was an unforgiveable act of treachery.

Yurchenko's shopping of two American spies, Howard and Pelton, led to enormous injury to the reputations of both the CIA and the NSA. So it is possible that the KGB wanted the former spies 'burned' for that purpose. Did the KGB also want Gordievsky rescued as part of some highly sophisticated dirty trick, and did they turn a blind eye to it? If so, what was their objective? It is a question which demands an answer, because in the secrets world anything is possible.

I am not suggesting in any way that Gordievsky is a false defector like Yurchenko may have been and like others in the past certainly were. One of them, a KGB officer with the codename Fedora, bamboozled the legendary FBI chief J. Edgar Hoover for many years with information cleverly larded with false material which went straight to the White House and affected presidential policy. Gordievsky is undoubtedly a genuine defector whose main motive appears to have been total disillusionment with the Soviet system. What is possible, though, is that the KGB had discovered his treachery long before he defected and controlled him by feeding him false information which he then unwittingly passed on to MI6. Such devious action is a well-established dirty trick in the counter-intelligence world to limit the damage cause by a traitor and to secure some advantage. If Gordievsky lasted nearly thirteen years as a defector-in-place before raising suspicion, as MI6 claims, he is unique in KGB annals, especially as several senior officers in Danish Intelligence were also fully in the know about him, increasing the overall risk of leakage.

There is some evidence to support the contention that he may have been, unwittingly, under a certain degree of control, which has been the basis for effective KGB deceptions with past defectors. When Gordievsky was fully debriefed by MI6 after his defection, to an extent which had not been possible before, he was asked for the names of any British subjects who were assisting the KGB as agents. He was unable to name any of consequence. Instead he assured MI6 that the London Mission had been so ineffective in recent years that it had been unable to recruit any Briton able to penetrate anywhere with important access to information. On the *Panorama* programme he claimed to have run only one agent, who appeared to be an MP, likely to be functioning as an agent of influence rather than as a spy with access to secrets.

Proof that the KGB was interested in recruiting Britons at the time came from Sam McCluskie, general secretary of the National Union of Seamen and treasurer of the Labour Party, who publicly claimed that it had tried to recruit him on a visit to Moscow in 1983. So while the 1980s was the Decade of the Spies in America, with many extremely damaging traitors recruited by the KGB for money, and scores recruited in West Germany, the London Mission, which also had unlimited re-sources for that purpose, had recruited none.

Most intelligence officers with experience of the KGB's efficiency and ruthlessness find this hard to believe, especially as Gordievsky had confirmed the names of so many other Soviet intelligence officers working in and around London that twenty-five of them were expelled, causing a diplomatic rift between Mrs Thatcher and Gorbachev. These names were already known to MI5 and the defection was made the excuse for their expulsion, as had happened in 1971 when the defection of the KGB officer Oleg Lyalin triggered off the expulsion of 105 Soviet officials.

Gordievsky was also asked to produce a list of the Britons whom the London KGB Mission regarded as important agents of influence – people in influential positions who did whatever they could to further the Kremlin's interest. I have been assured by more than one source that his list did not contain any names other than those I could have compiled myself.

What is certain is that, contrary to some predictions, no British agents have been prosecuted or sacked from positions of trust following Gordievsky's disclosures and none seem to have fled. What more convincing way could the KGB devise for protecting its British agents than to deprive the second-in-command of its London Mission of the true information about them, and then force him to defect and assure his new masters that there were none?

The KGB has made great sacrifices to protect crucial sources in the past. For example, when the British and Americans had tunnelled under the Berlin Wall and tapped into Russian military cables, the KGB, which had been tipped off about it, occasionally transmitted information about agents operating in West Germany knowing that they would be identified and arrested. This confirmed the Allies' belief that the Russians knew nothing about the taps and enabled Soviet Intelligence to continue sending damaging disinformation through the cables, which the British and Americans swallowed, confident that it must be true. The false defector Fedora was permitted to 'burn' a British KGB spy, Frank Bossard, to strengthen Hoover's faith in him. All Fedora had to do was to supply a photostat of the first page of a report which could only have come from a small department in the Aviation Ministry where Bossard operated. The ploy worked.

When Gordievsky was posted to London in 1982 MI6 considered it a marvellous fluke, but it could conceivably have been by KGB design.

How and when did the KGB first get wind of Gordievsky's double-dealing? The accepted belief is that the KGB Centre in Moscow slowly became aware that because there had been so many leaks there must be a mole in the ranks, and in the middle of May 1985 Gordievsky was recalled home for questioning as one of several suspects. He has told MI6 that, when he had been in Moscow only four months previously, his masters had been so pleased with him that they had promised to promote him to head of the London Mission, though on the television programme he indicated that he had been questioned then about leaks and had bluffed his way through. His recall in May was camouflaged as the need for further talks about that promotion.

It is extremely rare for any spy to be unmasked as a result of such detective work by the opposing side. In almost all instances where the facts are known, spies have been betrayed by a defector or by the interception of a revealing message. So the truth may be that the KGB *knew* that Gordievsky was a traitor because of an inadvertent but specific leak about his activities. This is certainly the belief of some officers in the CIA, who claim that the security gaffe occurred in London and had ministerial repercussions. The need for Gordievsky to defect was, of course, a disaster for MI6, which wanted him to remain 'in place' so that he could continue to supply information.

If the KGB knew, or even had only strong suspicions, that he was the culprit, why did they not arrest him and interrogate him toughly in close confinement, which has always been their practice? The decision to allow him the degree of freedom which led to his escape was entirely out of character and suggests that there might have been a motive for it.

In 1983, when Gordievsky was based in the London KGB Mission before his defection, he did alert MI6 to the fact that a young MI5 officer, who turned out to be called Michael Bettaney, was trying to contact the mission to offer secrets. That event might have firmed up the KGB Centre's suspicions, but they may have entertained them sooner.

Bettaney was later sent to jail, but he was never a loss to the KGB because Gordievsky's chief in London had wanted nothing to do with him, being convinced that he was just part of an MI5 dirty trick, a 'provocation' to cause trouble – a deception to which the KGB is particularly allergic. There had been many instances in the past in which British counter-intelligence officers had tried to incriminate KGB men by telephoning them and leaving messages which they knew would be overheard and reported to the men's superiors. A message such as, 'Whatever you do don't keep that appointment on Friday', with the telephone slammed down, would sometimes be enough to raise deep suspicion about the man concerned.

In fact the Bettaney case provoked massive trouble for MI5. It revealed that the organization was still wide open to penetration and led to another public scandal, especially about the extent of excessive drinking in MI5's ranks, and a slump in its morale. As a result a major overhaul was ordered by the Prime Minister under a new Director General.

Some of the information provided to MI6 by Gordievsky has defied the belief of many defence experts. For example, he reported that in November 1981 the Kremlin was so worried that the British and Americans were about to launch a surprise nuclear strike against the Soviet Union that the London KGB Mission was required to spy on Whitehall to see if lights were burning at night, indicating a frenzy of activity, and whether Mrs Thatcher was making extra visits to Buckingham Palace. This makes no sense, because the signs of NATO mobilization on the East-West frontier or the readying of nuclear weapons elsewhere could not have been hidden from the Kremlin's spy-in-the-sky satellites or its ground agents and, apart from routine exercises of which the Soviets were informed, there were none whatever. Although the Kremlin has recently ridiculed Gordievsky's nuclear panic story, it may have had some reason for provoking it at the time as part of an on-going deceptive operation. Its unusual course of denying that Gordievsky ever had access to high-level political information could have been part of the regular process of 'muddying the waters'.

There is also serious doubt about Gordievsky's claim to have had wide access to the KGB's archives, including the identities of secret foreign agents who are its life-blood. No intelligence agency as professional as the KGB is likely to give such access to any officer who is to be sent abroad, as Gordievsky was, and who might then defect, as Gordievsky did.

After his defection, Gordievsky was used to brief both Mrs Thatcher and President Reagan before meetings with Mikhail Gorbachev, but that would seem to have been to Gorbachev's advantage from the way the relationships subsequently developed. Gordievsky appears to be a supporter of Gorbachev.

Recently he has published a book claiming to reveal secrets which he learned while browsing through KGB archives. His naming of John Cairncross as the Fifth Man of the Cambridge Spy Ring contributed nothing because it had been publicly known for ten years. The paucity of his information raised serious doubts about his credibility as a source of KGB history. His naming of a British spy with the code-name 'Elli' as the self-confessed traitor Leo Long made no sense. Long had been recruited by the KGB while 'Elli' was a GRU spy. 'Elli' was known to have had access to files which Long never saw and to have had 'something Russian in his background' which Long did not.

As many senior intelligence officers have told me, it is a golden rule of the dirty tricks world that no defector, who is automatically a traitor to his own country, can be entirely trusted, even if his defection was quite genuine, because he might have been the subject of a major deception operation himself. Nevertheless, whatever MI6 may discover in the future about Gordievsky it will never permit this triumph to be sullied if it can avoid it. Too many reputations hang on the conviction that his recruitment was a major coup – every bit as damaging to the KGB as Philby's operations were to MI6.

The trouble with any dirty trick is that the perpetuating agency can rarely be sure of its success. Such are the confusions and doubts in the wilderness of mirrors that it never really knows whether its adversary is licking its wounds or laughing its head off.

23

The Truth about Star Wars

Of all the dirty tricks in the intelligence repertoire there is none which brings more satisfaction to deception operators than what they call 'a really good dangle'. A dangle is the presentation of a tempting opportunity to an adversary intelligence service in such a way that it will be accepted, to the adversary's detriment, and without its being aware that the offer is deliberate.

An example, not uncommonly practised in this age of technology, is the creation of an opportunity for a Soviet techno-bandit to acquire a particularly attractive item of banned equipment such as an advanced computer designed for defence communications. Unknown to the recipient, who believes he has been clever at acquiring it, the computer software has been loaded with a 'virus' guaranteed to wreck any Soviet defence system with which it connects.

Another, called the blind alley dangle, is being regularly used and needs only to be occasionally successful to prove costly to the recipient. When any high-tech objective, such as a new guidance system for a missile or torpedo, is being sought in the secret defence field, different lines may be pursued by separate teams of research scientists and engineers to find the best solution. Inevitably some lines prove to be blind alleys and have to be abandoned, though often not before large sums have been expended on them. If suitable for a dangle, the data of a blind alley are handed over to scientific disinformation experts who write up false research reports, stamped Top Secret and indicating that the progress has been highly promising. Ingenious steps are then taken to ensure that the reports fall into the hands of spies in such a way that they will be led to believe they have secured a rich prize to be handed to their masters without delay for use in their own research. It is widely suspected that such false information about the Anglo-French Concorde supersonic airliner was fed to Soviet spies and contributed to the ultimate abandonment of the Soviet version, the so-called Konkordski. This kind of dangle is certainly being employed in high-tech commercial fields to send competitors up blind alleys, the intermediaries usually being industrial spies.

A technological dirty trick, which was jointly organized by MI6 and GCHQ, involved the Enigma code-producing machines captured from the Germans after World War II and which worked effectively until 1974. The British intelligence triumph, known as Ultra, had cracked the seemingly unbreakable codes generated by the Enigma machines which were used by the German forces; this made a crucial contribution to the Allied victory. It rendered the machines obsolete but, as the British secret was well kept, hundreds of Enigmas recovered in Germany were reconditioned and sold to other Governments, mainly in the Third World, as a completely safe way of communicating. Unwittingly, West German and Swiss firms also manufactured new ones for general sale. This enabled GCHQ and the American NSA to listen in to the secret diplomatic and military messages of many countries, some friendly, some not, until 1974 when the late Fred Winterbotham exposed the Ultra secret, which the authorities reluctantly agreed had reached the limit of its usefulness.

Dangles are almost a daily occurrence, but there is one which stands out above all and will always be truly historic, continuing to affect all nations into the foreseeable future. This is centred on the American defence project commonly called Star Wars, officially the Strategic Defence Initiative, which has turned out to be a profoundly prophetic name. Considered by most people as a science fiction attempt to achieve the impossible – the shooting down of showers of incoming nuclear warheads while still in flight – it has been essentially much more political than military. That is why the American, British and other Governments involved in the ploy have continued with it in spite of repeated warnings by scientists, who were not in the know, that it was a waste of money because it could never work. In fact it has turned out to be one of the most productive scientific investments in history.

The concept was conceived towards the end of 1982 when President Reagan and his advisers had realized that, with the restraints of Congress and for other political reasons, the Soviet Union's lead in long-range nuclear missiles, which had been achieved largely by deception, could not be matched. The awful extent of this lead had been fully exposed during the intelligence assessments of the damage inflicted by Geoffrey Prime and other Soviet agents operating in the USA.

In addition the Soviets had secured a major advantage which the Americans could not contest for social reasons. They had successfully mounted new missiles on rail-cars and lorries so that they could be continually moved to different parts of the country. Never knowing where they were, the Americans could not knock them out, so the Soviets could be certain of always having enough missiles to destroy New York, Washington and other cities in any nuclear exchange. The Pentagon could have followed suit, but the public of a free society would never accept the continual random movement of nuclear missiles on roads and railroads, as the Soviet people were forced to do.

The idea of building a system of computer-controlled weapons, some based in space, others on the ground, that could defend the USA and its allies by destroying most of the Soviet warheads which might be fired at them, was already under serious discussion by scientists and strategists. Then, intelligence reports of the Soviet reaction to this Star Wars possibility forced the realization in Washington and London that it carried a particular advantage which had not previously been appreciated. Including information from at least one deeply hidden Soviet source recruited by the CIA, the reports showed that the Soviets were so backward in the areas of technology, on which Star Wars would depend, that they could not possibly compete.

The Soviet source, one of the most valuable ever secured by the West, was Adolf Tolkachev, an electronics scientist working at the Moscow Aeronautical Institute. Over several years he handed over to CIA field officers in Moscow photostats of secret documents about aircraft, radar, electronic warfare and weapons systems, enabling analysts to judge not only Soviet capabilities but weaknesses, especially in the Star Wars area. Large teams of Soviet scientists had been experimenting with beam weapons and lasers to destroy satellites and incoming missiles, but Tolkachev's information showed that they were severely handicapped by backwardness in super-computer technology, micro-electronics and total lack of the most advance silicon micro-chips available to the US researchers.

Further, the Soviet economy was in such straits that it could not bear the costs of such a protective system, which would be colossal, while the American economy could. So it was seen that if the Soviet leadership could be convinced that Star Wars had a reasonable chance of working, it would have to come to terms with it somehow. It would be essential for the Soviets to maintain a viable military machine if they could, because that was the only thing that gave them superpower status.

Of course, Star Wars could not be just a facade, a totally fictitious operation like some of the non-existent 'phantom' divisions created during World War II to fool the Nazis. To make it credible vast sums would really have to be spent on projects which might come to little, involving substantial parts of American industry, along with continuing publicity to convince Moscow that the US Government meant business. With admirable political courage, Reagan gave the concept his whole-hearted support with major personal involvement in the publicity campaign. He began with an address to the nation in March 1983 in which he called on American scientists to turn their talents to the cause of eliminating the threat posed by nuclear missiles. By the autumn three studies, ordered by the President, declared the project sufficiently feasible for 26 billion dollars to be earmarked for basic research alone.

Reagan had not alerted Britain or any other ally about this extraordinary venture before announcing it. As a strong supporter of the nuclear deterrent based on the East-West threat of mutual destruction by long-range missiles, Mrs Thatcher, by training a scientist, was both incredulous and astonished because she did not believe Star Wars could possibly work. Not knowing its ulterior purpose, she stated her doubts about it publicly.

In December 1984, when Mikhail Gorbachev met Mrs Thatcher in London, prior to becoming leader, he worked hard to convince her that there could be no effective degree of disarmament unless the Americans dropped Star Wars. He said that, instead, the Soviets would have to escalate the arms race by building so many more nuclear missiles that some would get through any space shield that could be devised; but he already knew that the state of the Soviet economy made such a massive escalation impossible. He was aware that Mrs Thatcher, who appeared to agree with him, was to visit Reagan within the next few days and hoped that she would argue the case on behalf of both of them. It was no coincidence that, while Gorbachev and Mrs Thatcher were talking, the US Government announced big Star Wars contracts for several major defence contractors, who were encouraged to give them maximum publicity.

Mrs Thatcher duly arrived in the USA and after talks with Reagan, mainly at Camp David, his country retreat, she was indoctrinated into the political purpose of Star Wars and agreed to support the project. In return, Reagan agreed to a joint statement stressing that Star Wars would enhance rather than reduce the nuclear deterrence which had kept the peace for almost forty years. Also, while Star Wars research would continue at full blast, the actual production and deployment of any systems could be a matter for negotiation in arms talks. This Camp David Accord, which was something of a deception in itself, enabled Mrs Thatcher to explain her turn-about and claim a diplomatic success from her visit. In fact, from then on she was an important part of the operation, solidly supporting the concept and opposing its critics. In a later visit to Washington, in February 1985, she went out of her way to assure Congress of her firm support for the President's Strategic Defence Initiative.

Meanwhile, immediately after the Camp David visit, the White House published a long document explaining the meaning and objective of Star Wars. It had the double purpose of informing the American public and assuring the Kremlin that the USA meant business. It also disinformed by envisaging a parallel deployment of a Star Wars defence system by the Kremlin which the White House knew it could never afford. The Pentagon rubbed in the reality of the effort by inviting eighteen allied Governments to participate in the programme.

By the time Gorbachev came to full power in 1985, the Kremlin's scientists and economic advisers had agreed that there was no way that the Soviet Union could compete. While the Americans could afford the research, which was progressing steadily, the Soviets could not. The deliberate publicity and debate about the project, together with the actual implementation of American and Allied research involving huge sums was, in essence, a multi-billion-dollar dangle and the Soviets swallowed it.

Additionally, in June 1985 Tolkachev was caught by the KGB contacting his CIA control officer for another hand-over of secrets in a Moscow street. Like many before him he was the victim of the dirty trick which all traitors fear – that they will be betrayed by the agency they are assisting. A young CIA officer, Edward Lee Howard, who had been briefed about Tolkachev because he was going to Moscow to handle him, was summarily fired after admitting a drugs and drinks problem during a polygraph test. In revenge, and for money, Howard visited Vienna and talked to the KGB, later escaping to Moscow from the USA when about to be arrested.

The loss of Tolkachev was a major disaster for the CIA and for Britain, which had benefitted from his information, but his confessions to the KGB, lasting four months before he was executed, made the Soviet leaders realize the extent to which the USA was aware of their technological weaknesses. Only two moves remained open to the Soviet leadership as possible solutions to the countrys difficulties, short of a pre-emptive nuclear war, which had already been abandoned as an option by the military chiefs. First, they could mount a worldwide dirty tricks drive to have the Star Wars project stopped by discrediting it as useless and a major threat to world peace. A previous campaign to prevent production of the battlefield neturon bomb had been remarkably successul. If that failed, there would be no alternative but to begin genuinely constructive talks with the USA, with the aim of disarming to an extent which would make Star Wars unnecessary and still leave the Soviet Union with a big enough military machine to maintain superpower status. It was decided to concentrate on the propaganda ploy first and Gorbachev entered into it wholeheartedly, with the KGB, the GRU and every other agency mustered into the assault.

Almost immediately after Reagan's first announcement in March 1983, the Soviet propaganda machine had reacted instinctively by inducing more than two hundred Soviet scientists to sign a letter to the *New York Times* denouncing the new initiative. Two years later Gorbachev emulated Reagan and took command of the campaign. He immediately demanded the scrapping of Star Wars as being essential to any arms talks, the project being branded as an American plot to threaten people with nuclear weapons in space. Agents of influence everywhere, some of them scientists who were 'willies', unaware that they were being used, were pressed into the service of damaging Star Wars as a dangerous, destabilizing threat to world peace. It was widely ridiculed as a waste of American taxpayers' money, as many in Congress already believed it was. The 'peace' movement was mobilized, with petitions from Communist front organizations. The Governments of allied countries taking part in the research were targeted. Left-wing media throughout the world branded Reagan as a mad warmonger misled by even madder scientists. There were dark threats of retaliation. Soviet officials staged walk-outs from arms control talks.

At the summit meeting in Iceland's capital, Reykjavik, in October 1986, Gorbachev played his last propaganda card against Star Wars by insisting that Reagan must ban all further development of the system before any progress could be made. When Reagan adamantly refused the talks seemed to have collapsed, but the President was confident that Gorbachev would have no option but to retract that requirement. He invited the Soviet leader to Washington for further talks.

Meanwhile, the Soviet army of spies operating in the USA, Britain, West Germany, Japan and even Israel, which were all taking part in Star Wars research, confirmed the continuing spending, with real advances in knowledge giving the project an increasing degree of feasibility. Gorbachev claimed that the Soviet Union was making as much progress with Star Wars research as the USA but, thoroughly briefed on the Soviets' true position, Reagan and his advisers held fast and the propaganda campaign failed and finally collapsed. Gorbachev and his colleagues were forced into meaningful negotiations with results leading to the unstoppable political changes which have already changed the face of Europe and ended the cc'd war. The Soviet leader seized the opportunity provided by the relaxation of the military tension to advance his need for Western economic and technological assistance in support of his concept of *perestroika* – the restructuring of the Soviet economy. Reagan and later Bush, who as Vice-President had been privy to the whole operation, did all they could to encourage the new Soviet stance and support Gorbachev against those of his colleagues who believed he was going too far and too fast.

As the Kremlin's intentions increasingly appear to be genuine, and probably irreversible, the USA has been able to reduce the spending on Star Wars and scale down its goals; however the work continues, with major advances being achieved in flight trials involving laser beams, particle beams and a new concept of small, light-weight interceptors codenamed Brilliant Pebbles. Having served its main purpose, Star Wars will be kept going at least until Soviet nuclear disarmament is truly significant and the possibility of a military takeover in the now-chaotic Soviet Union has diminished. The investment is still being made and the Soviet leadership is in no doubt about it because a team of Soviet experts has visited some of the Star Wars laboratories.

According to President Bush, 'In the 1990s, strategic defence makes more sense than ever before', but the multi-billion-dollar dangle has already achieved its main political purpose, which historians will credit to Reagan and his associates.

24

Abuse of the Media

The Soviets made skilful use of the foreign media, in its propaganda drive against Star Wars, as it always has with previous campaigns, which were more successful. The 'active measures' – dirty tricks – operations were not restricted to the KGB. Other departments of the Soviet state, especially the International Department, which has hundreds of officers stationed abroad in various guises, helped to orchestrate the manipulation of foreign newspapers, radio and television.

The Soviet citizens themselves were targeted for the same deception through the state-controlled media, as they have been on an unprecedented scale on every other issue for seventy years. Until the very recent introduction of *glasnost* – openness – deceptive propaganda has been a mass industry inside the Soviet Union, affecting every aspect of life from infant education onwards. As can now be seen from the plight of its peoples, the Communist system has been one monstrous dirty trick played on those whom it suppressed as well as on the rest of the world. The official history, the *Great Soviet Encyclopaedia*, published by the 'State Scientific Agency', is a gross falsification of world events, boosting Communist 'achievements' and denigrating those of the democracies; presumably it will now have to be rewritten. To the anger of the Soviet hard-liners, official admissions of massive deceptions about the true conditions in the country are being made daily, though these are being conveniently blamed on Stalin rather than on the Communist system, which has really been responsible.

The extent to which a clever and ingenious disinformation campaign can bamboozle the world, as well as the indigenous

259

population of the country concerned, has been exposed more completely and in finer focus by the situation which prevailed in the much smaller country of Romania under Nicolae Ceausescu. Through an elaborate campaign of disinformation and deception, codenamed Horizon, he deluded Western governments into believing that Romania was a different and caring kind of Communist country which they should support because it was independent of Moscow. Ceausescu's former intelligence chief, Ion Pacepa, who defected to the USA, has described how propaganda, agents of influence, disinformation, forgery, bribery and sex were all pressed into service to secure huge Western credits and other trade favours for a regime that was the most corrupt and repressive Communist dictatorship on record. The British Government was sufficiently duped for the Ceausescus to be invited to stay with the Queen at Buckingham Palace in 1978 and for the dictator to be given an honorary knighthood.

In theory, the *glasnost* innovation in the Soviet Union should have resulted in a diminution of disinformation for foreign consumption and, at the Washington summit in December 1987, Gorbachev promised that there would be 'No more lying. No more disinformation.' Nevertheless active measures aimed at undermining the West continue, with little significant change.

The biggest, most vicious and most sustained of recent attempts to smear the image of the West, and the USA in particular, is the totally false allegation that the Pentagon created the AIDS virus in genetic engineering experiments aimed at producing new germ weapons and then accidentally released it. The originator of the lie was Professor Jacob Segal of East Berlin, who claimed that the virus had been engineered at the Pentagon's microbiology laboratory at Fort Detrick in Maryland. Although leading Soviet virologists rejected Segal's theory, being convinced that the virus had arisen by the normal process of natural mutation, the story was taken up by the KGB and planted in a pro-Soviet Indian newspaper in 1983. As the spread of AIDS progressed, the KGB secured the Politburo's permission to mount a full campaign to reinforce Soviet propaganda claims about American germ warfare preparations. These have continued since Gorbachev became leader and, with greater force, since his Washington promise. The Soviet media have promoted fabricated extensions of the story, such as rumours that Zaire and Pakistan had been chosen by the CIA for experiments on the virus's 'depopulating effect'. Abroad, this myth was buttressed by bogus scientific papers and other documents, including forged press releases, and appeared in many newspapers in eastern and western Europe, Britain and the Third World. A major objective of this type of dirty tricks campaign is to speed the departure of American forces from Europe by generating hostility towards them. This has been Soviet policy since Stalin's day and it has not changed, save in the way it is projected.

Early in 1987, for example, the Soviets began circulating the incredible story that South American babies were being kidnapped to be butchered to provide spare parts for transplanting into rich Americans. It was successfully planted in various newspapers in Brazil, Guatemala and elsewhere – being, of course, reprinted in *Pravda* from which it travelled to the media of more than twenty countries, eventually reaching Britain.

At the same time the Soviet propaganda machine began to spread disinformation claiming that the women encamped outside the cruise missile air base at Greenham Common were being 'zapped' with dangerous rays. In 1988 Radio Moscow transmitted a story that the USA and its allies, including Britain, were manufacturing an 'ethnic weapon' which would kill only non-whites.

The Soviet deception machines have been particularly adept at using the foreign media for political character assassination of people considered dangerous to the Politburo's interests. The best-attested of these, and the most successful, was the long campaign against the West German politician Franz Josef Strauss, which was fully disclosed in 1984 in the evidence amassed by Sir James Goldsmith for a libel action in London, which was eventually settled out of court. I have recorded this in detail in a previous book, *The Secret Offensive*, and all that needs to be said here is that Strauss and his party, the Christian Democrats, were effectively discredited through smears planted in both the East and West German media. The campaign led to his resignation and his removal as a candidate for Chancellor, as Moscow had desired.

Until recently Mrs Thatcher was a candidate for similar treatment. Foreign journalists were paid to publish scurrilous articles and pamphlets and induced to print KGB forgeries in the hope that they would be reprinted elsewhere.

The threat of publication of damaging information in the media has always been a powerful blackmail weapon and the KGB has never hesitated to make use of it. In addition it has shown great expertise at creating the required information, usually exploiting sexual weakness for the purpose by staging what have become known as 'honey-traps'. One of the most infamous of these was resurrected in April 1990 in the obituary notices of Sir Geoffrey Harrison, the former Ambassador to Moscow, following his death at the age of eighty-one.

After arriving in Moscow with his wife in 1965, Harrison developed a reputation for being highly professional, lecturing his staff frequently on the need for good security and secrecy. Regrettably, he was as prone as many other men to the opportunity for casual sex, which cuts clean across intellect and judgement, and had fallen victim to the charms of Galya, a Russian chambermaid in his residence.

As he should have suspected, Galya, described as 'blonde, ample and looking a bit of a tart', was under the control of the KGB, which took the opportunity to record His Excellency's illicit activities on camera. Galya was one of a long list of sexually attractive women selected and trained by the KGB for seduction purposes, some being pressed into service, others simply being hired. Those chosen for a particular task are trained for it, as Galya would have been instructed to give satisfaction in her domestic duties as well as in her KGB function.

The KGB did not apply pressure on the Ambassador until the Czech crisis of 1968, when he was informed of his plight and told that, unless he influenced the Foreign Office to take a less hostile view of the Soviet attitude to the crushing of the Prague Spring, he could be publicly disgraced by leaks of the photographs to the media. Then aged sixty, Harrison was due to retire after thirty-six years of untarnished service in the diplomatic service. Wisely, he informed the Foreign Office of his situation and was immediately ordered to London, the media's preoccupation with the invasion of Czechoslovakia covering his recall.

The consternation among the few Foreign Office men in the know also seized the counter-espionage branch of MI5 when

Harrison claimed that there had been only one lapse – in the laundry of the residence. The possibility that KGB photographers could have penetrated the residence raised appalling prospects but, when inquiries in Moscow showed that this could not have happened, Harrison told a different story. He then admitted having a regular affair with Galya, and that on one occasion he had visited a flat in Leningrad with her. The flat had been set up by the KGB for tape-recording and surreptitious photography. In spite of the predicament in which Galya had landed him, he had written to her from London in infatuated terms and was shown the letter, which had been intercepted by MI5.

Having lost its prey, the KGB took no further action and the Foreign Office managed to keep the scandal secret, but Peter Wright told me the full story in 1980. When confronted by the media, he did not attempt to justify his behaviour but simply said that 'his defences were down'.

In obituary notices it was stated that, having fallen for such an old KGB dirty trick, Harrison was retired without the usual honours. On the contrary, shortly after his disgrace, which was kept secret, the Queen, who was among those deceived, invested him with the Grand Cross of St Michael and St George, the GCMG, said in Whitehall to stand for 'God Calls Me God'.

This would have compounded the scandal had the KGB still carried out its threat, and the Foreign Office had damage limitation statements ready for issue. The fear there had been justified, because three years earlier the KGB had issued surreptitious photographs to ruin the career and private life of Commander Anthony Courtney. A former Naval Intelligence officer fluent in Russian, he had been deputy chief of the British Naval Mission in Moscow during the war and had become an able Conservative MP. In his private business he was involved in promoting East-West trade, which required frequent visits to Moscow. The friends he made there included an attractive woman called Zina Volkova. While in Moscow for an industrial exhibition in 1961, and while he was between marriages, she accompanied him to his bedroom in the National Hotel, which, like many of the rooms let to visitors, was bugged and set up for concealed photography.

Courageously, because it was not in his business interests,

Courtney pointed out repeatedly in Parliament that the Foreign Office permitted itself to be intimidated by the Kremlin in the way it allowed Soviet diplomats concessiions which the KGB habitually abused. The KGB did not like these statements, and during visits to the Soviet Embassy he was warned that his speeches were being 'badly received' in the Kremlin. Still, he did not abate his campaign to introduce a Bill limiting the extent of the diplomatic immunities granted to the Soviet Bloc.

The London Mission of the KGB responded, in August 1965, by sending out a montage of embarrassing photographs taken in the Moscow hotel, four years previously. MI5 discovered that Zina Volkova was on its list of known KGB seducers. The pictures were received by most newspapers and various ministers and MPs. Courtney's political career was destroyed and the repercussions shattered his new marriage.

Just how rewarding the honey-trap, with the threat of media exposure, continues to be was shown by the behaviour of Marine guards in the US Embassy in Moscow as disclosed during a trial in August 1987. The chief offender, Marine Sergeant Clayton J. Lonetree, had been unable to resist an affair with a young Russian woman employed at the Embassy and the inevitably meetings with a KGB officer, posing as her uncle, followed. He had permitted Soviet agents to enter the Embassy late at night where they are believed to have planted bugs in sensitive areas. The size of his sentence – thirty years – indicated the extent of the damage he had inflicted.

British intelligence agencies are not supposed to make use of sexual blackmail in their activities, but the rule is bent occasionally when the behaviour of a potentially valuable target indicates that he might think his world well lost for lust. Several Soviet Bloc defectors have been recruited that way, and more than one Middle East diplomat has been surreptitiously photographed in compromising circumstances.

While ruthlessly prepared to use almost any means of securing foreign assistants in its 'active measures' operations, the KGB has always preferred willing auxiliaries and none more so than agents of influence – the 'Trojan horses' who can use their positions, power, influence and credibility to promote the Soviet Union's objectives in ways which seem totally sincere and spontaneous. They are hidden persuaders in such fields as politics, the trade unions, the Churches, Government departments and especially the media. Newspaper and broadcasting journalists who are either Communists or pro-Soviet supporters can be of immense propaganda and disinformation value in connection with specific deception operations or in the long-term process of attrition of truly democratic ideals. Britain has been and continues to be a highly productive field for such Soviet attention. While some media people would honestly deny being pro-Communist, they are prepared to promote the propaganda if it helps to undermine a Government to which they are opposed.

At a conference held in Stockholm in January 1990, two Soviet representatives responded to a paper on Soviet dirty tricks which had been presented by a Western delegate. They spoke with great pride about the KGB's disinformation achievements, especially the many successes scored during the Brezhnev era, maintaining that the propaganda war was essential so long as the world was divided into capitalist and Leninist camps, as it still is. One of the representatives, Aleksey Izumov, an economist, praised the KGB as 'one of the few things in the USSR that works'. These two intelligent Russians must have been aware of the horrific extent to which the KGB has been used as a weapon against the Soviet people, but they seemed to be subject to the Communist delusion that, however unjust it might have been, it was still 'correct', because Lenin would have approved of it.

While the openness of truly democratic societies does not stop lying and deception it severely limits their use, especially on the domestic front. Ministers are allergic to lies by their departments which might rebound on them in Parliament, especially since the advent of civil service 'whistle-blowers' who commit the previously unheard-of sin of sending confidential documents to Opposition MPs and to the media. In recent years there has been a Whitehall rule that any deception operation which has 'political content' must be approved by the Minister concerned. Such MI6 and GCHQ projects, for example, have to be approved in person by the Foreign Secretary. Much therefore depends on the courage of Ministers, and some have been notoriously over-cautious. During the early stages of the Falklands War, for instance, serious thought was given to inducing various former service chiefs, who pontificated on TV and radio, to give deliberately false predictions of where landings might be made; but this was not politically acceptable. As a result, the experts sometimes made the right predictions, which could not have been unhelpful to the Argentinians.

The British media cannot be ordered to print disinformation but this does not stop some Government departments, which have their deception machinery, from trying to foist it on to them either in the form of 'managed' briefings or through hand-outs or tip-offs. Several senior Ambassadors have admitted to me that their Embassies are frequently required to issue disinformation and that they may have to back it up personally. As one of the more cynical put it, 'All's fair in love, war and diplomacy.' When separate diplomatic negotiations are being conducted with two nations at the same time, the one that is less preferred may have to be strung along with a few untruths. The most infamous historical example is the pact which Stalin concluded with Hitler while still negotiating with Britain, but there have been many others since, if on a smaller scale.

For many years the Foreign Office had a whole department concerned with the production and dissemination of disinformation, among other functions. Cosily called the Information Research Department (IRD), it was set up by the Labour Government in 1947 and lasted for thirty years, kept secret from the public and most of Parliament. It was essentially the psychological warfare branch of the Foreign Officer to counter Soviet Bloc propaganda, undermine Communism in Britain and expose Communist front organizations. For that purpose it was well supplied with information from MI6, MI5, GCHQ and the diplomatic service. Its best-known head, Sir John Rennie, eventually became the Chief of MI6.

Selected officers from MI5 and MI6, some retired, played an occasional role in planting IRD disinformation on journalists. Some MI5 men were cleared to frequent the Fleet Street pubs, though I never encountered any because I did not go there. One of those from MI6, Sir Maurice Oldfield, whom I met over lunch or dinner, sometimes tried to plant disinformation on me; and as I have confessed, he occasionally succeeded.

Housed in an office block in Millbank, IRD had a full-time staff of several hundred, many of them emigrés from Communist countries; they produced anti-Communist literature, including what would now be called 'smear campaigns' against some foreign leaders, especially agitators in the Commonwealth and Colonies. It also employed Fleet Street journalists part-time on a payments basis, especially those who could command space in their newspapers or wrote regular columns. I was approached through a Defence Ministry contact as a possible recruit but declined, as I wished to remain entirely free.

Its products were pushed out to selected journalists on a strictly secret, non-attributable basis. Then, once a story was published under an established journalist's name, the IRD would ensure that it reached agencies worldwide. It also financed publishing companies to sponsor angled books which would otherwise not be commercially viable.

The IRD was severely pruned during Edward's Heath's premiership and its final demise in 1977 at the hands of the Labour Foreign Secretary, David Owen, was not unconnected with the Watergate scandal. A smaller and more open Overseas Information Department replaced it until 1981, when it was absorbed into the general Foreign and Commonwealth Office Information Department.

British journalists are occasionally requested to print what they know to be disinformation, but usually only when the purpose is an issue of serious national interest. In 1987 a book called *Christmas Island Cracker*, by Air Vice Marshal Wilfrid Oulton, provided the first official confirmation of such a service which I rendered. I feel justified in including it here because it is the best example I know of the principle of economy with the truth being used for a strategic intelligence purpose.

In 1957 the Government was determined that Britain should remain a nuclear power for political as well as defence reasons. This could continue only if British scientists were able to test the H-bomb which it had developed without American help. Because of costs and lack of facilities an underground test was impossible; and an international ban on tests in the atmosphere, which the Government would be unable to avoid joining, was imminent. It was therefore essential that the tests planned round a base created on Christmas Island, in the Pacific, should go ahead and succeed.

There were no technical problems but political pressure against the tests was swelling, based on the worldwide hazard of the long-term radioactive fall-out which the explosions would create. This could be ignored, but there was an immediate danger from Japan. The anti-nuclear movement there, which had immense support because of the Hiroshima experience, was threatening to prevent the tests physically by sailing a thousand small ships into the Christmas Island area. Intelligence reports indicated that the threat was real and that some Australians were preparing to join in. If the tests had to be abandoned, Britain's entire defence policy was in the discard and hundreds of millions of pounds already spent would have been wasted. The Government therefore decided that a dirty tricks operation to deceive any interferers was essential.

The plan was to convince them that the tests, scheduled for mid-May, had been postponed because of technical problems which would take weeks to resolve. The Government was not prepared to lie, but permitted the Defence Ministry deception planners to be economical with the truth. It had been correctly announced earlier that Sir William Penney (now Lord), Britain's chief nuclear weapons expert, would not be attending the tests. A June flight intended to look like the first leg of his journey to Christmas Island was therefore booked with an airline by the Defence Ministry. As several other seats were reserved at the same time it seemed that he would be taking a team out there after all. I was asked – by the Chief Scientist of the Defence Ministry, not by MI5 – to leak this in the *Daily Express*, along with the suggestion that it could imply that the tests had run into technical trouble and been postponed.

With the editor's agreement I ran the story as a front-page splash on 29 April, and other newspapers and radio programmes in Britain and abroad repeated it. When the first H-bomb exploded on time and I arrived on Christmas Island for the second it was the view of Air Vice Marshal Oulton, the task force commander, that the deception had probably done the trick.

The deception operation was, to some extent, a dirty trick on our readers, though it told no actual lies, but I have no regrets and would gladly do the same again. For I am in no doubt that Britain's strategic nuclear deterrent helped to keep the peace in Europe for forty-five years and that, without it, the current relations with the Soviet Union would not be as promising as they seem. Those who argue that Britain's deterrent was never of any consequence do not know the facts. For many years the

RAF had the responsibility of providing 80 per cent of the first retaliatory bomber strike against a Soviet nuclear attack, being much nearer the targets, and the Russians knew it. The Kremlin has always had deep respect for the British deterrent because it has been targeted on cities and the Soviet leaders credited British Governments with the resolve to use it. Further, the recent visual exposure of what life under Communism is really like – hell rather than the paradise claimed by the creed's supporters – justifies any contribution I might have made through newspaper articles or books to prevent its spread.

Books written by defectors, or former spies who have been released from prison, are a major medium for disinformation, usually intended to blacken the adversary, and must always be suspect in that regard. The same applies to television and newspaper interviews given by them or on their behalf. MI5 was probably first in the field in the 'book ploy' with *Handbook for Spies*, published in 1949 under the name of the British Communist traitor Alexander Foote, but really written by an MI5 officer. Another important 'sponsored' book was *The Penkovsky Papers*, which had been written with material supplied by the CIA. Books over which the KGB had control include Philby's memoirs, *My Silent War*, *Guy Burgess* by Tom Driberg and *Spy* by Gordon Lonsdale, the Russian agent who ran the Portland spy ring in Britain and was released from prison in exchange for the captured British agent Greville Wynne in 1964. In his book Lonsdale was required to maintain the fiction that he was a Canadian, born of a Red Indian mother. The truth, which I heard in detail only recently from Charles Bates, the FBI officer who discovered it, is a splendid example of the value of ordinary detective work in counter-espionage and of a dirty trick widely used by the Soviets and much copied in both fiction and fact.

Lonsdale, who had a passport and a birth certificate showing that he had been born in Canada, was such a professional that he refused to be of any assistance to MI5 after he had been arrested, behaving as a loyal intelligence officer should. MI5 was inclined to accept the Canadian documents, which had proved to be genuine, but Charles Bates, then serving as head of the FBI station in San Francisco, was certain that, somewhere in the spy ring which Lonsdale had run, there had to be a professional Soviet agent. He suspected that Lonsdale was it.

As part of the legend which Lonsdale had built up about his past he claimed to have been at a kindergarten in San Francisco, known as the A to Z School, and to prove it he had a photograph showing himself with other children there. There could be no doubt that the child was Lonsdale because his face had changed very little.

Bates' men tracked down the old headmistress of the school, who remembered the names of almost all the boys she had taught. Without hesitation she recognized Lonsdale as Konon Molody, a young Russian boy who had been placed in the school by an aunt, who was a ballet dancer. The FBI traced the aunt to Paris, where she was teaching ballet, and she confirmed that she had looked after Konon, having brought him out of Russia as her own child during the famine when her sister was starving. She recalled that when Konon was fifteen he was offered the chance of staying in the USA as an American citizen or going back to Russia, and had chosen the latter.

When Lonsdale denied being Molody, MI5 asked the Royal Canadian Mounted Police to make inquiries about the real father of the Gordon Lonsdale named on the birth certificate. He turned out to be a half-breed Indian who said that his wife had deserted him and taken their baby with her to Finland, where he believed they had both died. In fact the child had died there, and somehow the KGB had secured his birth certificate for possible future use.

The father recalled a frightening incident in the backwoods of Canada when the child had suffered a dreadful haemorrhage while being circumcised by a local doctor. A check with the prison where Lonsdale was held showed that he had not been circumcised, so he was confronted with the proof that he was really a Soviet citizen called Konon Molody. He still denied it.

MI5 was so sure there were other members of his spy ring that, to persuade him to talk, they threatened to leak to the KGB the information that he had broken down and admitted his identity. They pointed out that the KGB would remember that once he was released. Lonsdale's bland answer was to say that he had lived on a knife-edge for years, had always coped with that and had no doubt that he could do so again. Both MI5 and the FBI then devised ways of leaking to the KGB that he had confessed to his identity, which he never did – a dirty trick by any standard.

A spate of tainted books is now in prospect, following the armistice in the Cold War and the release of various convicted spies from prison. They are all likely to be under the control of various intelligence agencies which will be unable to resist making use of them.

While much disinformation by both sides has been directed at character assassination, there has been one extraordinary case of its use to build up the character of an intelligence officer, a man whom many believe to have played a major role in Britain's history – the late Sir William Stephenson, better known as the 'Man called Intrepid'. Stephenson was a Canadian businessman who headed the British intelligence and security effort in America, called British Security Co-ordination, during World War II. He claimed that he had been appointed personally by Churchill, with whom he said he had been on close terms. In fact there is no evidence that he ever met Churchill or had any direct dealings with him. The truth is that he had been appointed by MI6 in 1940, probably at his own suggestion, and later took on MI5's responsibilities in New York for a couple of years. He used the immodest code-name Intrepid, claiming that Churchill had suggested it to him, when it was really a telegraphic name he invented himself and registered in New York, the location for his wartime head-quarters.

In a book, for which he supplied the material, he claimed to be the greatest spymaster of the war, responsible for all manner of daring deeds with which he was never associated. These included being instrumental in obtaining the German Enigma coding machine, running a huge network of spies and subversive agents in Europe and involving Hollywood stars. He claimed to have been present on daring raids and to have hastened America's entry into the war by an ingenious forgery. He also claimed to be the other person in a famous wartime photograph showing Churchill in the bombed out ruins of the House of Commons when, in fact, the companion was the politician, Brendan Bracken.

His extraordinary catalogue of achievements included being amateur lightweight boxing champion of the world, which he never was, and being a member of the French Legion of

Honour, though the French authorities have no record of such an award. He even faked his *Who's Who* entry.

The book about him has been shown by numerous reviewers to be a mass of myths, but Stephenson nevertheless received honours from the USA and Canada. When he died in 1989 most newspapers lauded him as the great heroic spymaster, reiterating many of his phoney claims as though they were true. Such is the power of the legend and the newspaper cuttings.

I was in frequent touch with Stephenson, who lived in Bermuda, and know that he did an efficient wartime job in New York, for which he was knighted. So why did he have to blow up his reputation so grotesquely? Not for money. He was rich enough. I suspect that he was mentally deluded, because otherwise it would have been obvious to him that his claims were so absurd that he would be bound to be exposed. His wartime years in the secrets world may have been a cause. On leaving it he suffered from withdrawal symptoms and compensated for the loss of excitement and importance by fantasy. 'No memory of having starred atones for later disregard.'

25

Pipe-dreams

The Defence Ministry has a department devoted to the concoction of tactical deception operations and other dirty tricks. Many of them remain contingency plans because the reason for them disappears or some other Government department, usually the Foreign Office but sometimes the Cabinet Defence Committee, over-rules them. The Staff Chiefs have the courage and determination to carry them through. It is usually political will that is lacking. This is understandable when an operation would involve the infringement of another country's territory, with severe political penalities if it was exposed, but there are occasions when the Staff Chiefs feel that they are frustrated by faint-heartedness.

In the early 1970s the security forces in Northern Ireland were finding substantial caches of arms, which often included Sten guns and their ammunition. The Defence Intelligence Staff put forward the view to the Joint Intelligence Committee that the ammunition should be doctored so that the Sten guns would blow up in the faces of the terrorists using them and kill or injure them. Several Sten guns were blown up so effectively in experiments that the Army was keen to put this dirty trick into immediate operation. Not only might more terrorists have been killed by 'own goals', which always raise the Army's spirits, but there would have been such doubt about all the Sten gun ammunition that the IRA might have been unable to use the weapon for months. The project was quashed before it could be tried because, to use a Defence Intelligence officer's description, 'yellow-bellied civil servants' heard about it and it was too dirty for their refined tastes – a further example of how the Army has consistently been required to fight the IRA murderers with its hands tied.

To recover some advantage from all the effort the Defence Intelligence Staff then suggested that photographs of shattered Sten guns should be inserted in newspapers to suggest that parts of the IRA armoury were so old that they were dangerous to handle, but even that was vetoed.

Such doctored ammunition had in fact been used effectively by the Army in guerilla actions during the Malayan Emergency, in the 1950s and I have been given details of one of them. A small communist force led by a particularly clever guerilla leader in south-east Johore was inflicting casualties on patrols and outposts and proving impossible to track down. In great secrecy it was decided to leave a bandolier of doctored .303 ammunition for the force to find in the hope that it would blow up their rifles and Bren guns. A British patrol scouted in the jungle until they found a recent encampment of the guerilla group in a clearing. Having occupied it for a couple of weeks, the commander arranged for supplies to be dropped from the air knowing that the guerillas would hear the aircraft and eventually come to investigate. As the patrol left the camp, the bandolier was left in a place where it looked as though it had been forgotten. The Communists found it and used it, destroying several weapons and those firing them.

In the 1970s the Foreign Office applied a last-minute veto to another operation which could have saved many lives. Defence Ministry Intelligence, with the assistance of MI6, planned to kill or topple Idi Amin, the dictator of Uganda, and establish democratic government there. An airborne force to be led by the late Air Marshal Sir Neil Cameron was to make a surprise landing on the runway at Entebbe, much as the Israelis were to do later. Instead Amin was left to continue his bloodthirsty reign, disposing of anyone he disliked or distrusted. In a later attempt, which had MI6's approval but not its active support, a grenade was thrown at Amin but bounced off, killing someone else.

It is perhaps not surprising that some of the most ingenious dirty tricks are those which are vetoed. From a substantial collection, dating back over many years, I cannot resist recalling two which give some insight into the mind of the professional dirty trickster. The first was concocted by MI6 during the war, before the Japanese attack on Pearl Harbor. At that time many of the sanitary towels used by American women were imported from Japan, so a lively MI6 officer devised the idea of loading a huge consignment of them with itching powder and infiltrating them into the USA, all boldly marked 'Made in Japan'. The second was hatched by a friend of mine in the Defence Ministry during the Kenyan Mau Mau insurgency in the 1950s. Botanists at Kew Gardens were asked if they could devise a way of making large baobab trees, which are sacred to some Kenyan tribes, wilt within an hour. They found a method and provided the Defence Ministry planners with a powerful liquid and syringes with which to inject it. Plans were then laid to inform the tribesmen that their ancestors, whom they believed to be associated with baobab trees, were angry that people were being forced into taking the Mau Mau oath against the white rulers. A Dakota aircraft was to be despatched to stage a display of fireworks over Mount Kenya and, while those tribesmen within view of it were wondering what it could be, the neighbouring baobab trees would begin to wilt. Sadly, though not for the baobab trees, the operation was cancelled.

Another MI6 stroke of genius was actually used in World War II after an informant from the perfume industry suggested that, just as chemists could make Eau de Cologne they could make Eau de Shit, which would smell so strongly of human faeces when streaked on to German uniforms in the occupied countries that the men wearing them would be hopelessly embarrassed. Convinced that if done on a big scale it could have an impact on morale, MI6 authorized the production of Eau de Shit and in various occupied countries small boys and others were employed to apply it to the enemy in cinemas and on the street. It was even used in neutral countries. To burnish their image with the Swedes, the Germans mounted an exhibition of Holbein paintings in Stockholm; MI6 agents streaked them with the foul-smelling scent, with a catastrophic effect on attendances.

More recently the KGB mounted an even more despicable deception in view of the consequences. It knew that several spies and defectors had managed to escape across the Finnish border, presenting themselves at a certain Finnish border post where they established their identities and then passed on to safety. The Soviets built a complete replica of the border post several miles inside their own territory, manned it with border guards in Finnish uniforms and captured several would-be escapers, who condemned themselves out of their own mouths before realizing their plight.

One of the most extraordinary deception operations ever practised by the British Defence Ministry was aimed at one of its own major components, the Royal Navy, and it was done at the express requirement of the Prime Minister, then Harold Wilson. By 1967 experiments had convinced the Ministry's nuclear planners that the Navy's Polaris missiles would soon cease to be a credible deterrent. Intelligence had shown that in the event of nuclear war the Soviets intended to explode huge H-bomb charges high in that part of space through which the warheads of British and American missiles would have to pass. Tests had shown that the shock of the intense nuclear radiation produced by such blasts would knock out most of the warheads. It was not such a problem for the Americans, who could send over so many hundreds of warheads in an attack that some would be bound to get through, as the Russians knew. For Britain, however, with only one Polaris submarine ever on patrol at one time, it spelled the end of credible independent deterrence.

Harold Wilson and the few trusted Ministers on his Defence Committee were informed and faced a highly charged political decision. Here was a genuine opportunity to scrap the British nuclear deterrent, as they had promised before the 1964 election but had failed to do because they had found it gave them political clout in international relations. The alternative was to set in motion a long research programme to improve the warheads so that they would be able to withstand the radiation shock if ever they came to be fired. They chose the latter course, which had the code-name Chevaline, although it was clearly going to be so expensive that it ended up costing £1000 million.

It was a courageous decision because if certain left-wing Ministers and Labour backbenchers, who were nuclear disarmers, found out about it they could cause deep trouble for Wilson. Absolute secrecy was therefore so essential that Wilson insisted that the Navy should be kept in total ignorance of the project, even though it was being done to upgrade Polaris, which was a naval weapon. His reason was that if the Navy learned about it the admirals would insist on running it, and then too many people would know and the secret would leak.

For at least two years many millions of pounds were spent at the atomic weapons establishments at Aldermaston and at Farnborough, and nobody there outside the relatively small staffs involved knew anything about Chevaline. Even Navy personnel working inside Aldermaston were kept in ignorance through the judicious use of disinformation and strict application of the principle that only those who needed to know could be told anything.

Eventually the Navy was informed in 1970 by the incoming Tory Government and took the project over. In spite of Wilson's fears the 'silent service' remained that way, and the Labour left-wingers and nuclear disarmers still got no wind of what was happening.

By the time Labour returned to power in 1974 Chevaline was entering its big spending phase, but Wilson and his new Defence Secretary, Roy Mason, decided to keep the project going. Michael Foot, a passionate nuclear disarmer, was then in the Cabinet, so steps were taken to keep any news of the project and its costs away from him and the other left-wingers.

As Chevaline progressed, it became necessary to carry out many nuclear tests. Wilson gave permission for them only so long as they could be kept secret. The tests, which had continued during the previous Heath Government, were carried out in Nevada, using the American underground facilities there, and for each one a team of about fifty people had to fly out to Las Vegas, the nearest airport. Various deception operations were considered to cover their presence as visiting gamblers, but were never needed. Each warhead itself was a technological deception because, although quite small, the scientists had managed to pack several decoys into it to dupe Soviet anti-missile defences.

Shortly after Wilson's return in June 1974, I discovered what was happening for a quite extraordinary reason. While on a salmon fishing trip to Scotland I dreamed that a British nuclear test had taken place in secret and made a note to ask the Defence Ministry, on my return to London, whether such an event had occurred. The answer was that the Ministry could neither confirm nor deny that there had been one or that there might be one in the offing. The publicity chief, John Groves, indicated that there might be something in the wind by asking me not to publish a story at that time because any outcry from the Labour Left might make any test impossible. I telephoned him a few days later and he tried, even harder, to persuade me not to print anything. I was so convinced that a test was imminent that I published a report, which was quickly followed up by the TV, radio and the Sunday papers. As a result of further inquiries, I was advised that a test might have already taken place and wrote a report to that effect.

Wilson was questioned in Parliament and had to admit that my report was correct. His answer caused a row in both Parliament and the left-wing press, with Labour's Tribune group tabling a strong motion against the Government. The Japanese lodged an objection, and when Wilson went to Brussels to attend a NATO conference he was castigated by the French Prime Minister for hypocrisy because Labour Ministers had been objecting to French tests. Even *Nature*, the staid scientific journal, had a long leader headed: 'And now nuclear hypocrisy in Britain'. The much-feared objections within the Labour Government did not materialize, however, and Michael Foot did not resign even when a further successful test meant that the production of at least a hundred Chevaline warheads capable of piercing the defences round Russia's main cities could be commenced.

The Defence Intelligence Services of the technologically advanced nations have no monopoly on technological deception operations, as was dramatically demonstrated in 1990 by the extraordinary affair of the Iraqi supergun. It proved to be a deception operation comprising the whole gamut of intelligence dirty tricks, including an assassination worthy of a spy novel.

The story had begun for me with the news that an old defence acquaintance, Dr Gerry Bull, a Canadian arms dealer, had been shot dead outside his flat in Brussels on 22 March 1990, apparently by a professional hit-man. Though saddened, I was not too surprised, as there is so much ruthless rivalry in the arms-dealing world that many who live by selling the gun perish by it.

In the public mind the first indication of the comprehensive deception which the supergun turned out to be was the seizure by customs at Teesport of eight high-pressure steel tubes, each five metres long and one metre in calibre, destined for Iraq. The firm which made them claimed that they were sections of a 156-

metre pipe intended for the Iraqi oil industry, and I was inclined to believe that until I learned that Gerry Bull's Brussels-based firm, the Space Research Corporation, had been behind the operation.

Years before, I had visited one of Bull's gun-testing sites in Barbados where he was experimenting with what seemed to be an attractively simple idea for putting small communication satellites into orbit without the enormous costs which rocket launches entail. He had bolted two old naval guns together to produce one very long barrel which could be erected vertically and had been able to fire shells to heights of more than 100 miles. I had been involved with research on guns and explosives during the war and found his arguments impressive. He had convinced his American and Canadian backers that an even bigger gun could put shells into orbit. He also believed that it would be possible to pack a satellite into a shell without damaging its electronic contents during its discharge from the gun. This would mean that Third World countries could buy the means of putting up satellites cheaply or pay his company to do it for them.

Bull then concentrated his skills on improving field-gun shells to give them greater range and accuracy, selling his knowledge to Israel and South Africa. The USA had no objection to his efforts for Israel, but when his South African deals were exposed he was jailed for six months for contravening US arms export laws.

I met Bull for a talk in London in 1980, shortly before he returned to the USA to face trial, and understood from him that the satellite project, called HARP (High Altitude Research Project), had failed for lack of support. His backers doubted that satellites would withstand the enormous forces generated inside a gun barrel – a problem not experienced with rockets, which accelerate slowly. He was convinced that they were wrong, remained enthusiastic and was clearly looking for other backers. Although I did not know it then, he had written papers envisaging a huge smooth-bore gun made from high-pressure sections which could be bolted together. What misled me into doubting that the seized piping could be part of a gun was the huge calibre of one metre and the length of more than 500 feet, though it now seems that the total order may have been for several superguns, each, perhaps, 140 feet long.

A joint intelligence operation involving several countries has now established that Bull had convinced the Iraqis that he could build such superguns, not only to put satellites in orbit, but with the range and accuracy to threaten Tel Aviv and other targets in Israel. The huge shells could be filled with poison gas, high explosive or eventually, perhaps, nuclear charges.

This would not have been strategically feasible in the past because the Israelis would have found means of destroying any installations by air attack before they were completed, as they did with an Iraqi nuclear plant in 1981. Nine years later that was no longer a serious threat, because Iraq had amassed a formidable strike air force and would be grateful for an excuse to use it.

In great secrecy Bull designed the guns, and then set about ordering the parts from British and European firms in ingenious ways designed to fool the manufacturers and the Governments which had to issue export licences. The manufacturers believed that the pipes were for a petrochemical plant, though the accuracy required was unusual; through them, the Department of Trade and Industry, which cleared the order for export, was also misled, licences not being needed.

Orders were split up between different countries. When seventeen crates of equipment were impounded at Frankfurt airport in April they fitted other parts seized in Britain. They had been made in Belgium and Switzerland and are believed to be hydraulic equipment intended to be part of the supergun's recoil mechanism. Other parts forged in Italy as petrochemical machinery and seized there appeared to be parts of the breech. Further confusion was established by using several different routes for the deliveries to Iraq, some by sea, others by road.

Eventually two intelligence services – the Israeli and the Belgian, probably working together – got wind of the operation. The Israelis have agents on the ground in Iraq as well as electronic surveillance, and the Belgians had been tapping Bull's telephones. They let it run for a year, as the Israeli General Rabin and the Belgian authorities have admitted. The Israelis then decided that there was only one solution to their very dangerous problem – to get rid of the brains behind it through a hit-man and then expose the whole operation to the world. Nearly all customs seizures are the result of tip-offs, and

I am in no doubt that the information which led to the Teesport seizure originated from the Israelis, who may have used the Belgians to impart it. It came just in time, because the pipes had already been loaded on to a ship bound for Iraq. Bull must have been astute enough to realize he was at risk, but may have felt that the Israelis would not kill him because of his assistance to them in the past. He should have known that, in emergencies, intelligence services do not operate on such principles.

After rather belated information from British intelligence analysts, Nicholas Ridley, the Trade and Industry Secretary, was able to state on 18 April 1990 that the pipes had definitely been intended for the world's largest gun. It seemed possible that Bull had borrowed a German idea for a supergun, partially built near Calais to bomb London during World War II but never used. It was fitted with a series of side chambers to provide successive explosions which would boost a projectile to great speed as it progressed along the barrel, and permitting a very rapid rate of fire.

Mutual friends have told me that Bull was extremely bitter when he came out of prison, maintaining that the CIA had known about his arms deals with South Africa and had condoned them. He was determined to sell weapons to anyone except the Americans, and at one stage during the war between Iraq and Iran was trying to sell to both sides.

There is still concern that enough parts of the supergun reached Iraq for a prototype to have been test-fired, but the main threat has almost certainly been stifled. The Space Research Corporation was wound up by Bull's two sons in April 1990; but the supergun was just one facet of the illicit smuggling of arms and defence equipment, which is a world-wide industry, providing such profits that it is a major arena for ingenious deception operations.

One question remains. If the supergun was unlikely to work effectively, as some ballistics experts believe, was it a dirty trick by Bull on the Iraqis – inducing them to invest heavily over several years in a useless piece of equipment? If so, it is unlikely that he would have survived long anyway.

Bull was by no means the first of my acquaintances to perish by the ultimate dirty trick of assassination. At least six others have gone that way, and several more have survived attempts on their lives. Three of those who died did so as a result of a particularly villainous deception carried out, simply but devastatingly, by a minor Third World player, Idi Amin. One of the victims, Bruce McKenzie, was probably the most remarkable man I have met – a high-level politician, ambassador extraordinary, intelligence agent involved with MI6 and the Israeli intelligence agency, agricultural expert and authority on big game, highly successful businessman, military adviser with close links with Britain's SAS, and outstanding pilot who had won the DSO and DFC flying with the RAF in the war. He had also been awarded the Operation Jonathan medal by the Israelis for his part in the Entebbe Raid – the only non-Israeli to receive it.

A big, fun-loving man of great physical strength and courage, he seemed to know everybody of importance in a score of countries. Having decided to farm in Kenya after the war, McKenzie had realized that black rule was inevitable and decided to give the government of Jomo Kenyatta all the support he could, standing for Parliament and becoming Minister of Agriculture. Because McKenzie was white, Kenyatta, who was intensely suspicious of any black who might replace him, trusted him and he became his chief aide, financial adviser and emissary to foreign rulers. When Kenyatta needed to send an envoy to the British Prime Minister, the German Chancellor, the French President, the Israeli Prime Minister or the Shah of Iran, he usually sent McKenzie.

Relations between Kenya and Uganda had been disrupted by Kenya's complicity in the Israeli raid to release 110 Jewish hostages held by Palestinian terrorists at Entebbe airport in July 1976. Because of his close links with Mossad, the Israeli intelligence service, which had helped the Kenyans to thwart terrorist attacks on their territory, McKenzie had been responsible for securing secret permission for the Israeli transport planes to refuel at Nairobi after the assault on Entebbe and hospitalize any wounded. Amin never forgave him and was intent on revenge. In spite of that, McKenzie, then fifty-eight, was trying to repair political and economic relations between the two countries and do personal business in the electronics and vehicles fields in the process.

When I was lunching with him in April 1978 at his Surrey home he revealed that he had already been to Kampala to see Amin. I warned him to be careful but he dismissed my fears, saying that I did not understand the African mind. Overborne by his enthusiasn, I stupidly agreed to go with him on a future trip for an interview with Amin which he would arrange. On 24 May he flew to Entebbe with two friends, whom I knew and who were also keen to promote trade with Uganda.

The talks were held at Entebbe airport, and as they were preparing to leave McKenzie was asked to deliver a package containing an antelope skin to an address in Nairobi. They were waved away by Amin himself. While they were flying over the Ngong Hills in Kenya, on the way to Nairobi, the small Piper plane exploded, killing the three passengers and the pilot.

Because of McKenzie's importance to MI6 and to the Foreign Office, the forensic examination of parts of the wreckage was undertaken by Scotland Yard. It left no doubt that the package had contained a bomb which had been put together by an expert and detonated by a military time-fuse. Inquiries also established that a renegade CIA agent called Frank Terpil, whom I had met in London, had been present at Entebbe airport. In 1980 he was indicted by a New York Grand Jury of conspiring to transport arms to Uganda, but jumped bail during his trial and disappeared. He eventually surfaced in Lebanon, where he is rumoured to have died. There was no doubt that a trap had been carefully planned and set, and McKenzie had walked right into it.

The level at which McKenzie had operated in Britain and the services he had rendered were indicated when Harold Wilson volunteered to write his obituary notice for *The Times*. The former Prime Minister was so vitriolic about Amin, who was still Uganda's head of state, that the paper declined to print it.

Britain had lost a valuable friend and superb source of information, as indicated by the MI6 representation at his funeral. It fell to me to telephone the news of McKenzie's death to the MI6 chief, Sir Maurice Oldfield, who had been a close friend. He was deeply upset but his reaction was typical for a long-serving spook: 'Did he leave any papers?'

There were serious plans for revenge by the Israeli secret service, but Amin avoided it by fleeing to Saudi Arabia where he was offered asylum because he was a Muslim. Recently, at a dinner party, I sat next to an Arab who ran a chain of dental clinics in Saudi Arabia and told me that one of his regular patients was the former dictator. I envied him his opportunity.

26

Freelance Operators

Deception operations and other dirty tricks are not confined to Government and state organizations. Private individuals can perpetrate them for various reasons – usually, though not always, concerned with commerce. Perhaps the most impressive freelance deception of recent time was Operation Sandstorm, masterminded by Alan Bristow, then the chief executive of Bristow Helicopters.

During the reign of the Shah, Bristow Helicopters had secured valuable contracts with the Iranian oil industry, as it had in many other parts of the world. With the Shah's unexpected fall and the installation of the violently anti-West regime under Khomeini early in 1979, Bristow suddenly found himself with twenty-one Bell helicopters, representing a huge investment, beleaguered in various oil depots and likely to be impounded. There were also the crews and more than three hundred other people, including dependents, mainly housed in Tehran and clearly under serious threat from mobs there.

With a few colleagues Bristow set about planning a complicated rescue operation which had to be effected quickly under the noses of the new Iranian authorities. Their first decision was to stage the rescues simultaneously on a Friday, the Muslim holy day, when the population would be engrossed in its religious duties, especially in view of the fanatical revival of the faith being imposed by the Ayatollah.

Ingenious codes were devised so that key employees in Iran could be contacted without raising suspicion. Various excuses, such as tests, were invented to get the helicopters airborne. There was some deployment of electronic deception, as well as false radio messages to fool the Iranians. The helicopters then escaped in various directions over the desert to Kuwait, Bahrein, Sharjah and Dubai, some coming out through Turkey. Not one was lost, and all the families and other personnel were retrieved.

Incidentally, though the toppling of the Shah, which had great impact on Britain, was very much an affair of state involving convoluted politics, much responsibility for it could be allotted to one individual operating for personal motives. President Jimmy Carter wanted the Shah replaced because he regarded him as a dictator kept in power by a particularly nasty secret police force; so CIA support was withdrawn. The subsequent regime, however, has proved to be far more dictatorial, repressive and bloodthirsty. A further cause was the disinformation about the situation in his own country which was fed to the Shah by his few intimates. Most of the people, and their religious leaders in particular, did not want to be dragged into the twentieth century, with all its technology, which was the Shah's determined ambition. I was in touch with intimates of the Shah, and neither they nor His Imperial Majesty seemed over-concerned about Khomeini, showing how out of touch they were.

The British and Americans were equally out of touch with the realities because neither MI6 nor the CIA had been permitted by their Foreign Offices to carry out any electronic surveillance on the Shah and his entourage. The KGB had been much better informed, as a senior KGB defector to Britain from Tehran, Vladimir Kuzichkin, later testified.

Freelance deceptions are usually on a less heroic scale than Bristow's brilliant enterprise, but are sometimes as dangerous to those involved. This applies in particular to businessmen who, for patriotic reasons, though sometimes for reward, agree to carry out clandestine intelligence tasks when visiting foreign countries. They may do no more than serve as a 'bagman', smuggling in a message, money or a piece of equipment for an agent, or as a courier, bringing out his findings; but in former Iron Curtain countries this could result in trial and imprisonment, because such people have no diplomatic immunity. The same applies to visiting businessmen, journalists and even tourists who are asked by secret services to keep their eyes and ears open on their travels for anything of intelligence interest and, engrossed by the excitement of it, become over-zealous. This may have been the cause of the tragic fate of Farzad Bazoft, the *Observer* journalist who was executed as a spy by the Iraqis in March 1990. He had visited a military base south of Baghdad, where many people were said to have died as a result of an explosion. In view of more recent events, however, it seems more likely that he was simply an insufficiently cautious journalist. The 1990 invasion of Kuwait, when British authorities were convinced that the massing of Iraqi forces was a bluff, showed that British Intelligence had not maintained enough interest in the area to have any effective agents on the ground.

The golden rule for freelances is never to commit anything to paper. However in former Soviet Bloc countries this has not saved some alleged suspects from arrest – because the KGB has planted papers on them.

Intelligence services of all nations occasionally stoop to involving totally innocent travellers as 'willies', inducing them to do dangerous services without their knowledge. They might, for example, be asked by a close friend who is secretly connected with intelligence to smuggle in a letter or small parcel, believing the act to be no more than a sure way of delivering something of little importance. On one occasion, to my knowledge, this method was used to deliver a suicide pill to a captured British agent facing torture.

Western intelligence agencies have smuggled electronic bugs into Communist countries this way and the CIA, in particular, has used travellers to plant 'sneakies' – small electronic transmitting devices which form part of a surveillance network. They are usually disguised as stones, pieces of wood or other natural objects, and simply have to be placed near some area where the intelligence services wish to overhear anything that is happening or need a secret method of communicating with a local agent. Larger devices, such as transponders communicating directly with satellites, are sometimes covered with glass fibre painted to look like the branch of a tree for insertion into a real tree growing near a defence base. They usually have to be entrusted to professional intruders.

The Soviet Bloc has always retaliated in kind and on a greater scale than anything which could be attempted by Britain, which facilitates its opponents' task by being such an open society. Since the Czech revolution the new government has formally admitted that many of their travelling businessmen were trained as intelligence agents. Moscow has not done so, but many Soviet officials have been expelled from Britain and other Western countries after being caught in the act of espionage or preparation for sabotage.

In the early 1980s an important clutch of phoney Russian businessmen was exposed in an admirable counter-intelligence deception coup devised by MI6 and put into operation by Bill Graham, a former security officer who was running a double-glazing business in North London. He secured a contract to double-glaze the large Soviet Trade Delegation in Highgate and, apart from identifying staff who were really spies, he planted bugs which transmitted to MI6 vans and secured a surprising amount of other information which led to several important expulsions. It was a brave undertaking by a genuine businessman, because the Delegation is Soviet territory and there was little that MI6 could have done to help him had he been caught. He was even warned that the Russians were ruthless enough to push him out of one of the high windows on which he might be working if they got wind of his activities.

The extent to which the Soviets have used visiting seamen to carry out reconnaissance of British roads is only now being fully realized with the help of defectors. Once ashore, the seamen have been free to go where they wish and have hired cars to reconnoitre routes to key defence establishments which would be targets for attacks by Spetsnaz forces prior to an invasion. Some of them were genuine seamen, trained for the operation, but others were Spetsnaz officers in disguise, some quite senior. Several of the athletes sent to international competitions by the Soviet Union are known to have been Spetsnaz soldiers who would be expected to make what use they could of their travels for intelligence purposes.

The recruitment of freelance saboteurs to assist such intruders in time of war has already been described. In most Western countries there always seems to be a sufficiency of freelances for operations against their own Governments. In 1986, for instance, Peter Jordan, a retired schoolmaster and a Communist, was jailed for fourteen years for plotting to blow up a former SAS officer. So great was his hatred of the 'ruling classes' that he had become a voluntary intelligence officer for the Irish National Liberation Army. I have seen some of the letters which Jordan wrote while on remand. They reveal his obsession with discovering the names of secret service chiefs and others who might make targets.

The death in 1990 of the British businessman Greville Wynne resurrected the mystery of whether he was just an exceptionally courageous freelange volunteer, who had become enmeshed in an extremely dangerous operation, or an MI6 professional working under cover. What is certain is that he served as the MI6 courier for the Soviet traitor Colonel Oleg Penkovsky, whom many regard as the most important source of secrets ever obtained by the West. Both were arrested by the KGB in 1962 and Wynne was brutally imprisoned while Penkovsky was condemned to death.

Wynne always claimed to have been a career MI6 staff man but that is officially disputed by MI6, which sticks to the story that he was a businessman with Soviet connections through which he met Penkovsky, who was anxious to betray missile secrets because he hated the Communist regime. Whatever the truth, MI6 compensated him financially when the Russians exchanged him for a Soviet spy held in Britain in 1964. It also remained in close touch and continued to use him when it could. On one occasion he was induced to persuade another man to be patriotic for his country at considerable personal risk, but the task proved to be far more dangerous than either had been led to believe. The man lost his life, to Wynne's profound anger and regret.

It would seem to be significant that MI6 chose to be quietly represented at Wynne's memorial service, but the riddle is never likely to be officially resolved because the documents of MI6, MI5 and GCHQ are immune to the Thirty Years Rule under which other secret papers are usually released for public scrutiny. When the Thirty Years Rule was introduced, the secret services secured immunity mainly on the grounds that they needed to be able to offer a perpetual promise to all their sources that their identities would never be revealed. The immunity comes up for review in 1992 but is almost certain to be renewed, whichever political party is in office.

Political parties practise their own lines in dirty tricks, like one attempted on me and other journalists on the evening before polling day of the October 1974 election, which Edward Heath lost to Labour. At about 6 p.m. I was telephoned in my office at the *Daily Express* by a Tory official known to me. He told that, on that very afternoon, Sir Claus Moser, then the Government's chief statistician, had assured a private audience of postgraduate economists at Southampton University that while Denis Healey, then Chancellor, was claiming that inflation was down to $8\frac{1}{2}$ per cent it was in fact much higher and would soon be up to 25 per cent.

The informant, who said he was sure of his facts and was definitely in the Conservative Central Office because I rang him back there, suggested that this information would make a superlative lead story for the newspaper on election eve. He would have been right had it been true; but I managed, only by minutes, to contact Sir Claus's office, which assured me that he had been in Geneva for the past three days and had given no lecture in Southampton – facts which I was able to confirm later from Sir Claus himself. I also learned that the Tory official had telephoned other newspapers with the same hoax story.

Heath could not have known that this was being attempted on his behalf because he was busy in his constituency, but this and similar incidents showed that he was unwise to make complaints about the activities against him by what he called 'the dirty tricks department' of the Tory machine, as he did late in 1981. In fact, my caller proved to be correct about the massaging of Labour's inflation figures and, having received what was accurate information from some source or other, was looking, desperately, for some way of getting it into print fast enough to have some impact, all being regarded as fair in love, war and elections.

The criminal community lives by deception and other dirty tricks, and occasionally they spill over into the worlds of politics and intelligence. I have already described the case of the Littlejohn Brothers who raided banks in Ireland. A more recent instance came to its climax in July 1990 with the conviction in Florida of Howard Marks, a forty-four-year-old Oxford graduate who had been smuggling cannabis for more than twenty years. Nine years previously he had been acquitted on drugs charges at the Old Bailey after persuading a jury that he was an MI6 agent, the drugs racket being really a cover for his activities which allegedly involved penetrating the IRA. MI6 had been briefly interested in Marks but quickly dropped him. Nevertheless he managed to exploit the tenuous connection for many years and planned to make similar claims about the CIA until his associates informed against him.

Another case, of greater interest to most people, arose out of the private sexual proclivities of a Minister of the Crown, Lord Lambton, who was then responsible for the RAF. Lambton was in the habit of patronizing call-girls and one them, Norma Levy, was married to a man with a criminal record. In 1973 Lambton had been trusting enough to pay the girl with cheques bearing his name. Sensing an opportunity to make some money, her husband arranged a KGB-type deception operation to take surreptitious photographs of the two on a bed together and on one occasion with an additional women, who was coloured.

Knowing that her husband proposed to sell the photographs to a newspaper, Norma Levy took advice from a woman who ran a nightclub where she sometimes worked. The woman was concerned for the Government's position and, in turn, took advice from a customer who happened to be a close friend of mine. He saw the dangers even more clearly and contacted James Prior, whom he knew well. Prior told the Prime Minister, Edward Heath; Lambton was called in, admitted the truth and resigned.

Recent allegations that MI5 had been involved in the exposure of Lambton are untrue. I was closely involved with this case, being in touch with Lambton both before and immediately after his resignation. He was exposed by a fluke of circumstance. MI5 was involved only later, in inquiries to ensure that the KGB had not known or tried to take advantage of the circumstances, as proved to be the case.

Criminals are occasionally used by some unscrupulous firms to discover information about competitors and to perpetrate other dirty tricks, such as bribery, in their commercial interests. More usually, firms make use of the freelance investigation agencies which have mushroomed in recent years. Most of these operate strictly within the law but some are prepared to trangress into the realm of dirty tricks, particularly with respect to the planting of bugging and surveillance devices in surreptitious operations.

In a thoroughly legitimate way major commercial organizations are tending to employ professional freelance intelligence advisers who can be of crucial assistance in making decisions about big capital investments in foreign countries. So many banks have suffered grievously from lack of accurate intelligence when lending money in the Third World that directors of companies now require much more reliable forecasts of the political and financial future of countries targeted for investment. These involve intelligence of the quality usually available only to professional organizations like MI6 or the CIA. So it is no surprise that retired members of both organizations are being hired to provide such advice.

These people use their own investigative techniques and expertise to supply 'corporate intelligence', but it would be surprising if they were not also able to utilize their former contacts for assistance. MI6 has always had an economic information section working on behalf of the Treasury and the Bank of England, and it would be in the national interest for it to assist British companies. This would seem to be especially applicable in the case of heavy investments in eastern Europe and the Soviet Union. It would be unwise, for example, for an oil company to spend huge sums on introducing high-technology drilling methods into the Soviet Union if intelligence indicated that a Red Army coup there was still a reasonable possibility. Firms can secure some intelligence advice, originating in MI6 and GCHQ, from the Foreign Office, but the British authorities do not appear to be as open-handed as the CIA and State Department are to American businesses, perhaps being more concerned about danger to their sources.

Like all intelligence operations, those of commercial firms are conducted in secrecy, but one intriguing aspect of them was brought to my notice in the mid-1970s when I was asked to visit Tiny Rowlands at the headquarters of his company, Lonrho, in Cheapside. Rowlands had been connected with Angus Ogilvy (now Sir), who had severed his relationship with Lonrho at a time of adverse criticism of the company by a Government department. He had then taken grave offence at some statement made by Ogilvy and decided to counter-attack. In the course of a meal with Jocelyn Stevens, then managing director of Beaverbrook Newspapers, Rowlands explained his intention of going public by calling in a newspaper without delay. Though Stevens was a close friend of Ogilvy, he felt that if publicity was inevitable then the *Daily Express* should have the scoop. He would also be in a position to enable Ogilvy to respond if he wished. Because of the extreme confidentiality of the material which Rowlands wished to impart, I was asked to interview him, a task I did not relish because Ogilvy was a shooting acquaintance of mine.

I was given a nicely bound blue book containing lengthy correspondence between Rowland and Ogilvy which could have made a quite sensational story. With the *Express* lawyer's assistance I managed to tone the story down as much as possible and took it to Rowlands, late in the evening, explaining that, in the lawyer's view, there were limitations imposed by the risk of libel. He was extremely disappointed, claiming that the account 'lacked punch', which it did. The project was deferred until the following day; happily by that time Tiny's anger had subsided and it was abandoned, though it had been a close-run thing.

He told me that I could keep the blue book, as he had plenty of copies, and that, concerning other people and events, he had a red book, a yellow book and, more menacingly, a black book. I was left in no doubt that his private intelligence network was widespread and highly efficient, as he has shown more recently by the detailed material he has circulated in his battle over Harrods, another saga of deception – and not on Rowland's part.

The commercial world is no stranger to the use of disinformation. Sometimes this may be open and obvious yet still be successful, the classic example being the attempted character assassination of the Anglo-French Concorde airliner by American interests. Every kind of false statement, backed by scientists who were either mistaken or misguided, was issued by various individuals and bodies claiming that the machine would create unbearable pollution, noise and damage to the atmosphere. The motive was to remove a unique competitor, the first supersonic airliner, which was not American. Though the plane survived to disprove the critics, the campaign greatly damaged its deployment in many parts of the world.

The danger which private firms and individuals now face from freelance computer hackers has been well exposed through criminal prosecutions in several countries. The main risk is from industrial spies intent on filching trade secrets and confidential financial information; but the purely mischievous hacker, who achieves satisfaction through the destruction of software, can cause catastrophic damage. Hacking has become known through the activities of freelance operators, but it has long been secretly employed in the professional intelligence war in ways which would make the most sophisticated amateur blink in wonder.

Firms involved with defence contracts have to be perpetually on guard against the employee who might have been recruited by a foreign intelligence agency. With a sophisticated organization like the KGB behind him, a technician can easily slip a carefully camouflaged mini-bug or some other subversive device into electronic equipment such as a computer destined for a place like GCHQ, which has been driven by unpleasant experiences to keep careful watch for such dangerous dirty tricks.

Security agencies offering services to counter such activities in the private sector are flourishing and amount to highly sophisticated intelligence services in themselves, capable of most kinds of undercover operation. Several senior businessmen whom I know regularly have their offices 'swept' electronically to reduce the espionage risk and employ specialist security firms to protect their equipment. There is little they can do, however, against the commercial 'mole', the illicit informer on the staff, who is by no means uncommon.

A new type of freelance 'mole' in Government departments, who informs not for money but for political or 'conscience' motives, is now all too common for the peace of mind of the reigning administration. Until recently it was considered unthinkable that civil servants would betray their trust by abstracting official documents and sending them to politicians or newspapers, but it is now a regular occurrence.

Commonly known as 'whistle-blowers', the type specimen will always be Clive Ponting, a senior civil servant in the Defence Ministry who, while hailed as a hero by civil libertarians, is regarded as a dirty trickster by the 'authorities'. Ponting leaked a document about the sinking of the Argentinian cruiser *General Belgrano* to the Labour MP Tam Dalyell, anonymously in the hope that he would not be detected. He was tried and acquitted in 1985 after successfully pleading public duty, claiming that his loyalty to the state and Parliament took precedence over loyalty to the Government.

Sarah Tisdall, a twenty-three-year-old junior clerk in the

office of Sir Geoffrey Howe, the Foreign Secretary, was not so fortunate. In the previous year she gave the *Guardian* a copy of a memorandum from Michael Heseltine, the Defence Secretary, about the imminent arrival of cruise missiles at Greenham Common. When security officials recovered it after a court order against the newspaper they were able to trace it to Miss Tisdall, who was subsequently jailed for six months under Section 2 of the Official Secrets Act. She had also sent another document dealing with contingency security arrangements which the *Guardian* editor did not use.

Since then a flood of embarrassing documents from many other Ministries has been leaked to Labour MPs or to the media, the real heart of the problem being the photocopying machine, which makes the surreptitious production of extra copies for illicit distribution so easy. There are moves to prevent this practice, one of them being the production of all permitted copies of a document on a special type of paper which will change colour if put into a photocopying machine. The offending official would then have to explain why the copy officially in his possession had gone red or green.

From the Government's viewpoint the most dangerous kind of freelance whistle-blower is the dissident official in a secret service department who decides to go public for reasons of conscience. Discounting Peter Wright, who had other motives, this had not occurred until 1985 when two independent TV producers interviewed two former MI5 employees, the more important of whom was Cathy Massiter, aged thirty-seven, a former intelligence officer then working as a gardener. Her complaint was that MI5 officers were regularly required to break their own rules by tapping the telephones of trade union leaders, peace movement enthusiasts, civil libertarians, journalists and others who, in her judgement, did not merit such intrusions.

She had run MI5's inquiries into CND and the movement for nuclear disarmament in general, and revealed that MI5 had infiltrated an experienced agent into CND's headquarters and tapped the telephones of officials. She also confirmed that Special Branch and MI5 agents and informers infiltrate certain trade unions controlled or heavily influenced by Communists, which had been common knowledge for years. In particular, she claimed that the home of Ken Gill, then the Communist general secretary, was searched during merger talks with another union.

When the TV programme was screened on 8 March 1985 the political Left, including some MPs, accused MI5 of threatening civil liberties. However a Gallup Poll showed support for the monitoring of possible subversive organizations like CND, which the Defence Ministry regarded as falling in that category because it supported actions such as interfering with convoys of nuclear weapons which were part of the nation's strategic deterrent to surprise nuclear attacks by the Soviets. The National Council for Civil Liberties could legitimately be regarded as a threat because, in the past, it had been under the influence of Communist sympathizers.

Ms Massiter's claim that MI5 was breaching its 'charter' through its surveillance of such operations was denied by the Home Secretary after an inquiry,. Her allegations about the improper interception of telephone conversations were investigated by Lord Bridge, of the Security Commission, and he reported that, during her time in MI5, no warrants for tapping had been issued in contravention of the proper criteria.

No legal action was taken against Ms Massiter, presumably because the authorities did not relish having her in the witness box and could not be sure of a conviction, especially after the Ponting acquittal. With the tougher new Official Secrets Act they might well take a different view of such a whistle-blower today.

The identity of one of the most intriguing freelance whistle-blowers of all time, a mystery which has confounded many investigators, has been finally established by the ace of all wartime deceivers, Professor R. V. Jones, author of the classic *Most Secret War*, who published his findings in 1989. The mystery arose when a small parcel was dumped on Jones's desk one evening in November 1939 after being forwarded by the naval attaché serving in the British Legation in Oslo. It followed an anonymous message which had dropped through the attaché's letter-box, saying that if the British would like to know about various German scientific and technical developments the BBC should alter its preamble to its German news broadcasts to 'Hullo, *hier ist London*'. This had been done, and the package had been put through the naval attaché's letter-box. It contained seven pages of typewritten text in German and a sealed box.

The box contained an electronic triggering device for an anti-aircraft proximity fuse. The notes contained a wide range of information about remote-controlled rocket-driven gliders, rocket-projectiles, the use of aircraft as dive-bombers, new torpedoes and other weapons. The report also mentioned Peenemünde, the first time the British had heard of this Baltic research station, which was to be so important as the research base for the V2 rockets which would bombard London.

Jones could not find anyone, apart from himself, prepared to take the report seriously, though it was a stupendous leak. The general view was that it must be a plant – a dirty trick by German Intelligence to mislead British scientists and waste their time. The argument was that the Nazi dirty tricksters had overdone it because no one person could know so many different secrets. It was a dirty trick all right, but against the Nazis.

When it had proved to be only too accurate, Jones remained curious to discover the identity of the person, obviously a highly technical individual, who had sent it. Eventually he did so, but when he learned that the man was still alive he withheld the name until 1989, some years after he had died, because he feared that his relatives could suffer reprisals from Germans who might still regard him as a traitor to his country.

His name was Hans Ferdinand Mayer, and he was a senior electronics expert working for the Siemens company. Aged forty-four when he had sent the report, he was an anti-Nazi, rightly convinced that Hitler would lead his country to disaster, and happened to be visiting Oslo when he decided to write the report on a borrowed typewriter. After falling under suspicion, though not for sending the Oslo Report, he spent several years in Nazi concentration camps but managed to survive.

The intriguing story of how Professor Jones finally tracked him down is told in his latest book, *Reflections on Intelligence*. Mayer played a dirty trick on the Nazis and on his country, but whether he was a traitor or a patriot for freedom is a matter for argument, the dirt, once more, being in the eye of the beholder.

While ordinary people who have no access to secrets cannot function as whistle-blowers, they can be party to deceptions through delusions. The extent to which MI5 is falsely blamed by people who are convinced that their telephones are being tapped is surprising. So is the number who are sure some Government department is subjecting them to bombardment by rays. Perhaps as a result of the many charges against MI5 and the impact of spy cases and spy novels, many people seem prepared to believe anything about the secret services. The concept of conspiracy is catching and can be dangerous.

Journalists, in particular, need to be on guard against self-deluded individuals who claim to have been intelligence agents with distinguished records and turn out to be spies who never were.

Delusion seems to have been the real basis of a tragedy which engaged the attention of the media and some suspicious MPs in June 1983, when Dennis Skinner, the fifty-four-year-old British representative of the Midland Bank in Moscow, fell to his death from the window of his twelfth-floor flat on Leninsky Prospekt. It was alleged that Skinner had sought out John Burnett, the MI5 security officer at the British Embassy in Moscow, and told him that he knew of a spy whom he had identified inside MI5 and that he feared arrest by the KGB. Burnett interviewed Skinner and it seems that what he really said was that there was a spy in the Embassy.

On the afternoon of 15 June, Skinner handed in a note at the home of a neighbouring British businessman. It reportedly said that he believed he was about to be arrested when he attended a party that evening at the Embassy. He believed that he might not get out alive because there was a spy there.

Skinner's Russian-born wife, who had remained in England, told a London inquest that her husband had been in contact with the KGB for many years, reporting back to British Intelligence. The inquest brought in a verdict of 'unlawful killing', the coroner ruling out suicide or accident, but the view in the intelligence services is that Skinner, who was a hypochondriac suffering from fits of depression, was deluded and that his death was suicide.

Another who lived dangerously as a freelance on the fringes of the secrets world and died mysteriously was David Karr, a Jewish American wheeler-dealer based in Paris and deeply involved in promoting trade with the Soviet Union, with several companies set up for that purpose. He was found dead in his flat in the Avenue Foch on 7 July 1979, shortly after he had returned from Moscow, where he had ready access to senior officials of Government departments including, it was rumoured, the KGB. There were signs of a struggle, and papers appeared to have been removed.

I knew Karr, because for a while he was a business consultant to Beaverbrook Newspapers and he was certainly a man of many connections. Officially it was stated that he had died of a heart attack, but his wife suspected that he had been murdered and that the French had covered up the circumstances to avoid friction with the Kremlin at a time of apparent détente.

On occasion ordinary people with no official connections may deliberately involve themselves in deceptions of considerable moment. The most recent exposure of this nature concerns Michael Randall, a teacher, and Pat Pottle, an antique dealer, who have confessed, in a book published in 1990, to assisting the Soviet spy George Blake to escape to Moscow after he had been sprung from prison by an Irishman. In 1961 Blake, an MI6 officer, was sentenced to forty-two years' imprisonment after confessing to having betrayed to the Russians every secret which had come his way.

Randall was in touch with me recently to query a statement I made at the time that Blake's sentence represented one year for every agent he had betrayed, either to death or imprisonment. The extent of Blake's treachery in that respect had been leaked to me by George Brown, the Labour Party deputy leader, who had been given the information by the Prime Minister, Harold Macmillan, relying on the trust implicit in Brown's oath of secrecy as a Privy Councillor. In what Macmillan came to regard as an unforgivable dirty trick, Brown gave me the details, arguing that loyalty to his party, which stood to gain by discrediting the Macmillan administration, over-rode the loyalty required by his oath.

There was no doubt about the truth of his information. In 1989 Alistair Horne, who had access to Macmillan's papers on the case, recorded: 'Vast numbers of agents working for Britain and America had been betrayed by Blake and executed and the enormity of his treason was reflected in the unprecedented sentence of forty-two years imposed on him.' Nevertheless, Randall and Pottle organized the traitor's escape by spiriting him out through Dover to East Germany, hidden in a Dormobile, simply because they felt that his sentence was too savage.

Some members of the public who have interested themselves in the old case of Commander Crabb, the freelance frogman who disappeared while attempting a clandestine examination of the hull of the visiting Soviet cruiser *Ordzhonikidze* in 1956, have recently resuscitated a theory that he was transported to Russia and became a Soviet agent. In May 1990 these efforts drove Rear Admiral Nicholas Poland, a former Director of Undersea Warfare, to beg the Government to issue a statement to end the speculation about Crabb and to clear his name of any suggestion that he had been a traitor. This plea followed a newspaper report based on the recollections of Sydney Knowles, Crabb's former partner on surreptitious dives. Knowles, who lives in Spain, claimed that the missing frogman was a Soviet spy who had used the cruiser incident to defect. He alleged that Crabb had been recruited by Sir Roger Hollis and Sir Anthony Blunt and that he was present at wild parties where they all met. The alleged location where the defection plot was hatched was a flat in Tite Street, Chelsea, with Hollis and others there. Knowles said that he was present, because initially he was to accompany Crabb on the dive and defect with him. The KGB has used the Crabb affair to make anti-British mileage over the years, but the latest version seems to have derived from Knowles himself.

While a body, judged by an inquest to be that of the gallant commander, was washed ashore in 1957, a Soviet defector, Anatoly Golitsin, claimed that Soviet Intelligence knew in advance about his mission and that frogmen were probably waiting for him in an underwater chamber with which the cruiser was fitted. The pro-Soviet Labour MP, Bernard Floud, is reported to have had a friend in MI6 who told him that two naval officers from HMS *Vernon* had seen Crabb intercepted and captured by Russian divers and that GCHQ had intercepted Soviet messages to that effect.

Rear Admiral Poland's plea for enlightenment went unanswered and Nicholas Elliott, the former MI6 officer who was nominally in charge of the Crabb dive, has not been allowed to discuss the case in his memoirs. Though Elliott insists that Crabb died accidentally, the case remains something of a mystery following publication of the official biography of Sir Anthony Eden (later Lord Avon) in 1986. His papers show that he believed that Crabb had been killed by Russians who had been protecting the ship, which had brought the Soviet leaders Khruschchev and Bulganin on a goodwill mission. Eden, who had forbidden any such enterprise, had demanded a full investigation and should have been in possession of the facts.

The Russians regarded the Crabb episode as such a dirty trick – though frogmen examined every British warship that visited Leningrad – that Eden avoided any further mention of it while he was alive. It is most probably because of this political embarrassment that the security authorities continue their silence about the blunder. All cover-ups tend to breed fantasies.

The Crabb case, which will remain of perennial interest as a rare glimpse of what goes on in the secret world, is not the only instance of an officially authorized dirty trick being brought to public prominence by a freelance enthusiast in recent times. Among the most celebrated court cases of 1989 was one which centred on the exposure by Nikolai Tolstoy of one of the most appalling deceptions ever carried out by the British Army. While the case was concerned with claims and counter-claims about the ultimate responsibility for the act, there was no argument about the fact that it had occurred.

Nigel Nicolson, a witness to the events, which took place in Austria in May 1945, put his vivid recollection on public record. Immediately after the end of hostilities in Europe, the British troops there were ordered to hand over to their enemies nearly sixty thousand people, including women and children, who had surrendered to the British and trusted them. As the Army authorities knew their likely fate, they lied to them about their destination in a deliberate deception operation when they loaded them on trains, assuring them that they were bound for the safety of Italy. In fact twenty-six thousand of them, who were Yugoslav Chetniks, the Royalist guerilla troops who had fought against the Germans, were diverted across the Yugoslav border where Tito's Communist death squads were waiting for them. The others, mainly Cossacks and White Russians who had fought against the Soviets, were handed over to the Red Army. Almost all were massacred or sent to prison camps.

Nicolson described the horror as the people, locked in cattle-truck trains, realized in which direction they were going. It has never been doubted that most of them were killed in horrific circumstances. 'These were three weeks that should live in infamy,' wrote Nicolson 'For a momentary advantage and a desire to placate Stalin and Tito, a major betrayal was deliberately organised.'

The surrender of the Cossacks to Stalin was the result of political deals made at Yalta. The cold-blooded handover of the Chetniks to Tito was the result of a long series of dirty tricks dating back to the character assassination of the Chetnik leader, Mihailovitch, by the British Soviet agent James Klugmann and his many pro-Communist friends.

27

Gorbasm

In 1989 I published a novel centred on the question of how President Bush would react if the CIA discovered the details of an impending coup to oust President Gorbachev. I assumed that Bush might well direct the CIA to do what it could by clandestine means to undermine the coup and keep the beleagured Soviet leader in office. Subsequent events have not changed my view that Bush's captivation with Gorbachev is so complete that such that a decision could well be taken in Washington and put into effect.

The almost ecstatic impact of the charismatic Mikhail Gorbachev on the West – what has been called 'Gorbasm' – is, in some ways, even more incredible than his impact on the Soviet Union and its Empire. Both are so astonishing to historians and intelligence officers that many have been driven to wonder how much of what appears to be happening is deliberate deception. Some have gone so far as to suggest that the accession of Gorbachev and what has happened since are all carefully planned chapters of the most elaborate deception operation ever foisted on the West. Its alleged purpose is to induce the West to finance the Soviet Union out of the economic disaster created by Communism but without destroying that ideological system. Then, with the military machine still intact and the West lulled into disarmament, the Soviet Union can return to its task of achieving its allotted destiny – control of a Communist world.

With whatever purpose Gorbachev and his supporters may have started out on their mission, such a scenario, which would constitute the most elaborate dirty trick of all time, makes little sense now. If it was a deception, parts of it have gone badly wrong, but the facts support the thesis that

Gorbachev never intended that events in the Soviet orbit should proceed as they have. His recent actions look much more like parts of a frantic damage limitation operation which has been forced upon him.

When appointed to the leadership in March 1985, at the early age of fifty-four, he was no stop-gap but the man carefully selected for the long task of putting Soviet affairs in order with least damage to the system. Though possessed of a charm which no previous Soviet leader had been able to manifest, he was nevertheless seen as tough, as expressed by the old hard-liner, Gromyko, who remarked that 'He has a nice smile but teeth of steel.' He was soon to reveal the streak of ruthlessness, common to all who reach eminence in Communist regimes, by adroitly ridding himself of those who might stand in his way, including Gromyko. Within four years he was to make himself official master of the Soviet Empire, being not only General Secretary of the Party and Commander of the forces, but President, with supreme powers never available to any previous holder of that particular office. In 1990 he effectively got rid of the Politburo and the hard-liners still in it, limiting its powers to party affairs. Real power in government matters was transferred to a Presidential Council, over which he holds almost absolute control while still maintaining, at least for a while, the leadership of the Communist Party.

It is essential to keep in mind that Gorbachev was an orthodox product of the Communist system, accepting the tenets of Marxism-Leninism almost as holy writ, and totally committed to the oppressive Soviet regime which had been founded on them. Indeed, from the time he became a Communist Youth League official in 1955 he has been a conscientious part of it. His wife, Raisa, is an authority on Marxism-Leninism and there is no evidence that he has become anything else but a dedicated Leninist. He insists that 'disrespect for Lenin is unacceptable' and argues that responsibility for the faults in the system lie with previous leaders, like Stalin and Brezhnev, who have misinterpreted Lenin's teaching.

In 1987 he stated: 'In October 1917 we departed the old world and irreversibly rejected it. We are travelling to a new world, the world of Communism. We shall never deviate from this path.' At the time of the Soviet Communist Party Congress in July 1990 he said, publicly, that he has no intention of divorcing the Red Army and the other Soviet forces from politics, which is a prerequisite for truly democratic rule. The same applies to the KGB, which remains highly politicized. Gorbachev's public struggle at the last Party Congress was to preserve the party and its Leninist basis, while curtailing its power in government. His apparent hope, which seemed to be a contradiction in terms, was the creation of an effective market economy, to boost production of consumer goods, within a Communist system where the minority who have enjoyed privileges at the enormous social expense of the majority would continue to do so. The hard-line delegates, who are part of that minority, seemed to appreciate the impossibility of such a compromise and called for a swift return to the orthodox Communist ways, which have been responsible for all the country's problems.

Until forced out of Afghanistan by casualties and cost, Gorbachev followed the party line that the invasion there was 'assistance against subversion by the West'. He went through all the old motions of trying to drive wedges between NATO and the USA. He even accused the West of having colluded with Hitler against the USSR. More recently he has reiterated the lie that the Baltic states voluntarily joined the Soviet Union, when they were forcibly annexed as part of Stalin's pact with Hitler.

On achieving the leadership, Gorbachev and his supporters were faced with two urgent realities. First was the undeniable fact that the nuclear stalemate and the horrific costs of maintaining it had ruled out any hope of achieving Communism's global or European aims by a military solution. This was a bitter realization for those who had built up the world's biggest military machine for an offensive role at the price of great sacrifice in living standards for the ordinary people. While the impracticability of all-out nuclear war may have seemed obvious to others for several years, Soviet strategy had continued to be based on the belief that Russia could fight and win a nuclear conflict, even involving the loss of major cities and millions of civilians. Only advances in missile technology and the Star Wars gambit finally convinced the Soviet leadership otherwise. The fact had then to be faced that both the hot and cold war strategies had failed.

The second reality was the state of the Soviet economy. The long practice of falsifying the figures could no longer conceal that it was so desperate in so many ways that the people were not even being properly fed. For nearly seventy years the secret police and the Red Army had been able to prevent any organized objections to the miserable standards of the masses and the dreadful damage inflicted on their environment by the juggernaut drive to achieve heavy industrial targets. The myth that they were living in a workers' paradise had been sustained by the all-pervading propaganda machine which grossly falsified conditions in the West. The leadership realized that, with the technical revolution in communications, the truth that Communism had failed on so many counts, compared with capitalism, could no longer be suppressed; it knew there would be ominous effects on the long-simmering resentment of 270 million people queuing for little better than scraps.

There was only one sensible reaction to both realities if the situation was to be resolved before the patience of the people ran out – to approach the capitalist West for quick financial and technological assistance, with a positive offer of arms reductions and an end to the Cold War in return. For this to have any chance of success, the Soviet system would have to be given a more acceptable face.

In the circumstances, Lenin would have approved of such a move because he always counselled zig-zags and subterfuges, however humiliating superficially, so long as the ultimate objective of world Communism remained fixedly in mind. Indeed, the prospect of Soviet Communists being able to parasitize Western capitalists would have appealed to him. Lenin, whose picture and statues still dominate the Soviet political scene, would have insisted, however, than any changes to the face of Communism should be cosmetic rather than surgical, so that they could be easily reversed.

In urgent pursuit of Western aid, the ending of the Cold War and the hand of friendship were proffered in the form of meaningful arms negotiations, though always with the Soviet demands pitched at the highest level so that any climb-down would not be too catastrophic. The propaganda friendship drive to give Communism a kinder face was cleverly centred on the personality of Gorbachev, with stunning impact on a Western world weary for real peace and relief from the threat of nuclear war.

He promulgated the old idea of a common European home

from the Atlantic to the Urals – one enormous common market with more than 800 million people. As easily the most populous single member, the USSR would dominate it.

At home, Gorbachev developed the concept of *perestroika*, which most people have accepted as meaning a remodelling of the Communist system to release the energies of the people by offering incentives. In fact it really means reconstitution, rejigging of the system without too much damage to it, and Gorbachev has named Lenin as its ideological source. Cynics suspect that the real word should be *peredyshka* – breathing space, while the West comes to the rescue – because Kremlin advisers estimate that *perestroika* will take at least twenty more years to produce really significant results. Apart from peptalks, *perestroika* has produced nothing worthwile in the first few years and the impatience of the people was demonstrated at the 1990 May Day parade, where Gorbachev was subjected to catcalls and jeering, culminating in unprecedented humiliation as he and the podium party trooped off prematurely. Those jeering were ordinary citizens of all ages, some even being former soldiers in uniform.

To cope with the increasing general awareness of the true situation in the West Gorbachev introduced *glasnost*, the concept of openness with the people; it offered more scope for critical comment and, he hoped, would reduce the head of resentful steam. At first the media were kept under a considerable measure of control, and some which criticized the Communist Party found themselves deprived of paper and other means of production; but inevitably criticism of the system and those controlling it snowballed, with ever-increasing liberties being taken by courageous editors. Lenin himself is now being indicated as the originator of the rottenness of Soviet life, and in some rebellious provinces his statues are being removed.

Nevertheless the Soviet Union remains a police state, though less obviously than in the past, with no apparent reductions in the size of the KGB. In July 1990 when a retired KGB general, Oleg Kalugin, demanded that the KGB should cease to be an instrument of the Communist Party, he was publicly rebuked and stripped of his military rank and awards.

In the satellite countries Poland was already chafing for its freedom through its trade union movement, backed by the

Roman Catholic church. When the Politburo decided that a military solution to that problem was no longer viable, though it was carefully considered, dissident movements in the neighbouring countries gathered strength – with revolutionary results which, I believe, staggered Gorbachev as much as they did the rest of the world. He wanted more liberal changes there, like those he was introducing at home, but not the demise of Communism and the disintegration of the Soviet Bloc.

Once the revolutions in the satellite Empire became inevitable, Gorbachev did his best to limit the damage by securing an interest in the hope that at least a Soviet Commonwealth of new-style Communist states would survive; but I do not believe that he set out with the intention of completely releasing those nations from Soviet bondage. The consequences of *glasnost* ran away from him. He has since done his best to live with them, claiming what credit he can for offloading bankrupt economies like Poland's on to the West, but is now being openly blamed for the strategic losses by Red Army generals and other hard-liners, as well as for the lack of civil discipline which has led to riots in various parts of the Soviet Union.

Under increasing hostility from the hard-liners, concerned for their quasi-religious ideological beliefs as well as for their privileges, Gorbachev found himself in an intriguingly hazardous position where the West could almost be blackmailed into providing him with aid. Should Gorbachev be unseated by his hard-line opponents through failure to secure sufficient aid in time, the proffered prospect was a return to the Cold War and hard-line Communism. As his Foreign Secretary, Eduard Shevardnadze, put it at the last Party Congress, 'If *perestroika* fails, dictatorship is possible.'

With so many Western leaders pinning political and economic hopes on massive reductions in defence spending, return to the Cold War was unacceptable if it could possibly be avoided. The West had even been made to feel responsible for the fate of the Soviet masses. If Gorbachev failed and was forced out of office, they could be subjected to suppression again and lose the few freedoms *glasnost* had given them.

At the time of writing the West seems to be responding to the threat, which has been openly stated by more than one Soviet commentator, by planning a vast package of aid. Before the

NATO meeting in July 1990, which formally wound up the Cold War, Gorbachev wrote what could be construed as a begging letter to Mrs Thatcher hoping that the rich countries which were about to hold a conference in Houston, Texas, would come to the aid of his country. Fortunately it was realized by Mrs Thatcher, President Bush and others that, while Communism remains, the Soviet Union is an infinite sink for Western money and goods, with $12\frac{1}{2}$ per cent of the GNP still going on military spending. Nevertheless Mrs Thatcher speaks as though Gorbachev has assured her that he is working towards true democracy and that she believes him.

Gorbachev's reaction to Iraq's invasion of Kuwait in the summer of 1990 was particularly intriguing. Iraq was the Kremlin's most important client state in the Middle East, being a major export market for Soviet arms, yet the Soviet Union joined the rest of the world in condemning the invasion and enforcing economic sanctions on the aggressor. It even provided the opposing American and British forces in Saudi Arabia with technical details of the Soviet long-range missiles and advanced bombers supplied to Iraq. This move may have been a response to Iraq's decision to detain Soviet nationals as hostages, but it must have boosted Gorbachev's chance of securing Western aid.

If the aid materializes, then whether Gorbachev's original ploy was a deliberate deception operation or not will be academic because the result will have been achieved. Under the spell of Gorbasm, the West, which has been vilified, harassed and undermined by every kind of Communist dirty trick for more than seventy years, will have taken positive action to prevent the collapse of Communism!

For the past forty years it has been the duty of Western intelligence services to do what they could by clandestine means to bring about the collapse of the Soviet Union. Professional intelligence officers believe that they should now be giving every support to separatist groups in places like the Ukraine, the Baltic states and Armenia to help to achieve that objective. Instead, the various Foreign Offices see the preservation of Communism in the Soviet Union as preferable to the instability which its quick collapse might cause, with the behaviour of its military chiefs unpredictable.

The 1990 Party Congress showed that the situation in the

Soviet Union is not irreversible, as many in the West had hoped. Indeed, Gorbachev said that the leadership would have to resign if *perestroika* failed to produce effective results within two years.

Meanwhile the Soviet military machine remains intact. While some conventional forces are being reduced and some old nuclear weapons are being scrapped, with much publicity, the strategic forces are still being secretly modernized and military research is being generously funded. For example, two entirely new intercontinental ballistic missile systems based in underground silos were deployed in 1989 and three new types have since been detected at a missile test centre. The Soviets are still expanding their force of SS25 nuclear missiles mounted on road vehicles and SS24 missiles carried on railways. A new anti-ballistic missile defence system built round Moscow at vast cost, mainly to protect the leadership and political structure from sudden annihilation, has become operational. Super-sized submarines carrying large numbers of nuclear missiles have recently been launched, and new ones are under construction. In its 1990 Defence White Paper the British Government pointed out that in the previous year the Soviets turned out 1700 main battle tanks, more than 600 fighter planes and 50 long-range bombers. According to the CIA, Soviet defence spending dropped by 4 per cent in 1989, but in the following year Shevardnadze told the Party Congress that the country was still spending the equivalent of about 900 billion dollars a year on arms.

So, in spite of *glasnost*, Russia remains something of a riddle wrapped in a mystery inside an enigma, with such uncertainty about the future there that Mrs Thatcher is wise in insisting that the West should react to what Gorbachev does rather than what he says. The Soviet leader has been playing a weak hand for high stakes, but has shown consummate skill in convincing Western audiences that the Soviet threat has disappeared. In this he has been supported by a massive campaign of disinformation as to the true nature of the developments within the Soviet Union. So long as he can remain in office, his deception machinery will continue to deceive the West about the real prospects for *perestroika* in order to secure Western economic assistance and reduce his defence spending by encouraging the Western allies to reduce theirs.

Events so far would seem to indicate that the reform of Leninist Communism is impossible because it is based on assumptions which have proved false to an extent now visible to the whole world. Because it took no account of individual aspirations it always contained the seeds of its own destruction, and its eventual collapse seems inevitable whatever the West may do to try to prevent it from fear of the temporary instability which its passing would create. Lenin's legacy is simply too horrific, too heartless, too dishonest, too corrupt and too dreary to admit of rejig or repair. Whatever the outcome, it will be far removed from the Commonwealth of new-style communist states which Gorbachev envisaged when he took charge with such energy in 1985.

28

The Future for Dirty Tricks

Euphoria about recent events behind the former Iron Curtain has led many people to believe that the future holds little scope for espionage, disinformation and the other East-West dirty tricks which have characterized the last seventy years. As I stated in the introduction, that is not likely to be the case and, though there have been further extraordinary political developments since I started writing this book, I see no reason whatever to change my view.

The simplest and most effective way to foresee the future is to present the current positions and attitudes of the various agencies which were mainly responsible for dirty tricks in the past. Let us begin with those of the Soviet Bloc, which on the surface appear to have undergone the greatest changes.

The KGB is so large and so interwoven into the tapestry of Soviet life that its demise is unthinkable. Like the poor, it will always be with us. Deception is a fundamental facet of Leninism. So is espionage, because in a closed society, deprived of the access to other countries which free peoples take for granted, it is the major way of securing information. Until the last few months, and maybe still, all Soviet officials resident or travelling abroad, whether requested to or not, were expected to spy and report back anything of interest to the KGB as a matter of duty. So as long as Leninism survives, as it is likely to into the foreseeable future, then the chief exponent of deception and espionage, the KGB, will also survive.

Under Gorbachev it has done better than survive. It has steadily increased its authority and power. Gorbachev was never in the KGB, as commonly believed, but he was a political protégé of Yuri Andropov, the KGB chief who became leader of the Soviet Union, and he is suspected of having been a high-level KGB informer. The organization, which remains as large as ever, has backed Gorbachev so far and he remains dependent on its support. He now has complete control of it because the KGB chairman has been removed from the Communist Party's Politburo but remains a member of the Presidential Council.

With its network of informers at every level and in every area, the KGB has been best placed to see in advance what was happening in the Soviet Empire and in the various republics of the Soviet Union itself. Understandably it has done all it can to ensure its own continued existence, adjusting its various roles to suit the new conditions. The syllabus of its prestigious 'Higher College' for advanced espionage, deceptions and other clandestine activities has been modified accordingly.

So far as overseas spies are concerned, it will be business as before. The Soviet nation's need for technological secrets remains as great as ever, so the army of techno-bandits will be maintained – if not expanded. The West may loosen its ban on the export of advanced technological equipment, but so long as the Soviet military machine remains in being, export restrictions on equipment which could be used to improve it will surely remain. Military spies on the grounds will therefore continue to be used not only to secure defence information but to check on military intentions. As recently as April 1987, for instance, a Soviet spy ring concentrating on penetrating the secrets of the Ariane space-satellite launcher was exposed by the DST, France's MI5. It was a military GRU operation run by one of the air attachés at the Soviet Embassy in Paris.

'Hacking' into Western computer networks from which industrial secrets can be extracted has become something of an industry in itself. The KGB runs specialist courses on it for its agents.

Gorbachev and his close colleagues also have urgent need of reliable political and diplomatic intelligence for appreciation of what Western Governments are really thinking about them, what aid they are likely to give and on what terms. In the past the KGB has usually been highly efficient in supplying supposedly secret information which has strengthened the Kremlin's bargaining power, and will strive to maintain that reputation.

It is unrealistic to expect that seventy years of deep distrust can be extinguished on either side in a few months or even years. The military and intelligence chiefs will always counsel continuing activity, especially in a time of uncertainty. Armies have always worked on the principle that there might be war one day, and therefore they need to be ready for it, good intelligence being an essential insurance policy.

There is abundant evidence to show that espionage has continued without respite under Gorbachev and has not all been directed at securing industrial information. In 1989 a Soviet Bloc spy who called himself Erwin Van Haarlem, posing as an art dealer, was caught receiving a coded message from Prague in his flat in North London. Detectives found the usual spying paraphernalia, and his special interest seems to have been Star Wars research. When jailed for ten years he refused to give any information about his true identity or about other agents with whom he had been in touch.

Earlier in the same year Sir Geoffrey Howe, the Foreign Secretary, gave the Soviets a public warning that once again Soviet 'active measures' had reached an intolerable limit. There had been another build-up of Soviet Bloc intelligence agents in Britain following Gorbachev's accession to power in 1985, and MI5's watcher service had become saturated. The warning was ignored, so the Foreign Office was driven to expel eleven Soviet intelligence agents who had been targeting military as well as technology objectives. To save face, Gorbachev retaliated by expelling British journalists, among others.

Various Americans, including military and air force officers and warrant officers, are still being convicted of spying for the Soviets, money being the main motive. GCHQ and the NSA continue to pick up the signals of the KGB contacting its deep-cover agents throughout the world.

In 1986 the Russians were ordered to reduce their UN staff in New York by 100 because so many so-called diplomats were spies and active measures agents, who joked that the UN building was their tallest 'observation tower'. No doubt there will be more expulsions of Soviet agents but, if possible, quietly and without publicity, to avoid rocking the diplomatic boat while Gorbachev's position remains precarious.

No Soviet leader ever stood in greater need of foreign agents of influence than Gorbachev to convince Western countries targeted for aid that he is totally sincere and moving towards democracy. The KGB is largely responsible for recruiting them, both directly and through its propaganda. The 'Help Gorbachev' movement, which it has skilfully fostered, has been immensely successful – even the US President and British Prime Minister speak up repeatedly on his behalf, while the West German Chancellor seems captivated.

On the home front the KGB is capitalizing on *glasnost* to give the impression that its excesses belong to the past; from now on it wants to be regarded as the friendly shield protecting the citizens' new rights, and no longer feared as an instrument of public control and suppression. It is also cleaning its image abroad as part of the drive to secure aid from the West, expressing regret for excesses in the past such as its admission that about 20 million Soviet citizens had been arrested, many of them spending time in its infamous Lubianka prison. In July 1990 the KGB announced that it was mounting searches for the mass graves of people slaughtered as enemies of the state in Stalin's purges by its forerunner, the NKVD, with the humanitarian hope of 'rehabilitating' them. It had previously admitted that the NKVD had murdered at least a million Soviet citizens – a considerable understatement.

In May 1989 Colonel-General Vladimir Kryuchkov, the KGB chairman, called in the media and announced that the KGB would be embracing *glasnost*. He promised to keep the public better informed about the KGB's work and assured them that it would henceforth work within Soviet law, an admission that it had previously been a law unto itself. The KGB has announced the forthcoming publication of top-secret material which will reveal its triumphs in protecting the nation from foreign spies. It has even opened a public relations centre.

Kryuchkov has proclaimed the abolition of the Fifth Directorate, which was responsible for preventing 'ideological sabotage' – meaning any behaviour disapproved of by the 'authorities'. While claiming to be motivated now by 'humane goals', the KGB remains a secret police force with powers of arrest and maintains its army of informers. Emigration and the movement of citizens within the Soviet Union are still tightly controlled.

As to the possibility, which has been floated, that the KGB might open its files to the West, that is the stuff of fairy tales. All it has done, or is likely to do, is to put various old agents up for interview to impart disinformation and flaunt KGB triumphs. This was done in the most blatant manner through the television programme *Comrade Philby*, screened in Britain in May 1990. It was full of mis-statements and even harked back to the flight of the Nazi, Hess, to Scotland in May 1941 as an example of Britain's perfidy. It claimed that MI6 lured Hess into making his flight after being in touch with him for several months, the purpose being to hatch a plot against the Soviet Union. The programme attributed the KGB's knowledge of the flight's purpose to its great spy, Philby, who was not even in MI6 at the time and had no access. Philby was also erroneously credited with supplying information from Ultra breaks which enabled the Red Army to defeat the Germans in a crucial tank battle; in fact it was supplied by another Cambridge Ring agent, John Cairncross.

In spite of a description of Britain as its 'ex-adversary', the programme's reference to some mysterious Fifth Man of the Cambridge Ring, alleged to be still alive, was almost certainly intended to induce the British security authorities to waste their time trying to identify him. It was also aimed at making the public believe they were stupid for having failed to do so in the past. In June 1990 the Soviet intelligence authorities even dug out Eugene Ivanov, the naval attaché at the centre of the Profumo scandal, to regenerate that embarrassment and to claim that he had been a key figure in the Portland spy ring, helping to smuggle out submarine warfare secrets which sabotaged NATO for a decade.

It is significant that, so far, when any British defector, such as Philby or George Blake, both formerly from MI6, has been produced for questioning by the Western media every opportunity has been taken to make MI6 and MI5 look ridiculously amateurish. When the KGB recently permitted the BBC to interview Blake, its chief living defector, he claimed to have betrayed six hundred British agents and that none of them had been executed. According to MI6 sources both statements were lies. The KGB's main objective in such arrangements would seem to be to further the Kremlin's continuing policy of driving a wedge between Britain and the USA by regenerating doubts about the wisdom of sharing intelligence secrets.

Like the intelligence services of the West, the KGB is worried about its ability to continue to attract high-level talent into its ranks in the current circumstances, though there is no evidence of any shortage as yet. Under the influence of Andropov, who recruited heavily from the universities, requiring candidates to be fluent in least one foreign language and offering extra pay and privileges, the KGB rid itself of its thug image and became an élite force with membership carrying prestige in the community. In spite of this outward change of attitude, however, it remains capable of perpetrating dirty tricks on Soviet citizens when required to do so by its political masters. For example, since the Lithuanian bid for independence, the Lithuanian newspaper *Respublika* received, anonymously, an alleged photocopy of the KGB file on Lithuania's Prime Minister, Kazimiera Prunskiene. It implied that she had served as a KGB informer, which she has denied.

As an essential arm of the Red forces the GRU will obviously continue in being, though possibly with some reduction in its financial resources. With the waning of the likelihood of major war there could be a reduction of its Spetsnaz troops, but as they are so highly and specially trained it will probably be by natural wastage and will take time. The GRU is so little known either in the Soviet Union or abroad that there is little if any need to improve its image or dwell on its past excesses.

It is clear from feelings publicly expressed by Soviet military officers that some of them regret that force was not used to crush the uprisings in the satellite countries. When Gorbachev and his close colleagues realized that force was politically impracticable if they were to get economic aid from the West, they decided that the KGB should do all it could to control the revolutions in the best way to suit Moscow. The bloodless revolution in Czechoslovakia which overthrew the hard-line Communist regime, appearing to be so spontaneous, has recently been exposed as a forceful deception operation planned and executed by the KGB in collaboration with its Czech counterpart, the STB. In defence of Gorbachev's more liberal posture, the Czech hard-liners had been determined to maintain their tough, uncompromising position and were cracking down so severely on street demonstrations in Prague that few people, apart from young students, dared to take part in them. The present Czech Government has established that the KGB's objective was to replace the hard-liners with a Gorbachev-style leader, who would maintain the Communist Party and system but with the kind of relaxations which were happening in the Soviet Union. That way, Czechoslovakia would remain loyal to Moscow.

The chief planners, the Deputy Chairman of the KGB and the Head of the STB, saw that the only way to achieve their objective was to get huge crowds of all ages on to the streets. This would probably happen if a large demonstration of students in Prague was beaten up, and especially if one was killed on the anniversary of the death of a former Czech student 'martyr' murdered by the Nazis. The scenario was accomplished by a young STB officer who had infiltrated the student movement under a false name. Not only did he lead the student march into a trap, where they could be viciously assaulted by the secret police – with more than five hundred injured – but he then pretended to have been killed, his body being carried away by the STB. News of his 'murder' was then spread round the city by STB agents. In response huge crowds, including factory workers, took to the streets in such numbers – half a million at one time – that the STB police could not control them. In any event they had orders from their chief not to do so.

In an attempt to save themselves from the wrath of the crowd, the Communist Government voted the chief hard-liners out of office and were eventually forced to resign themselves. A Gorbachev-style Communist, who had been in exile in Austria, was recalled in the hope that he would form a new, less repressive Communist Government. He declined, even after flying to Moscow to see Gorbachev, who was a former friend.

Then to Moscow's dismay the Czech people saw their opportunity to escape completely from Communism, which had chained them in subjection through fear for fifty years. A non-Communist group, the Civic Forum, assumed power and the dissident writer Vaclav Havel was elected president.

The Czech security service, now called the Office for the Protection of the Constitution, is said to be forging links with Western intelligence agencies to root out Communist spies. In July 1990, as part of an agreement between Britain and Czechoslovakia, arrangements were made for the exchange of certain kinds of information with MI5 and MI6. This may lead to enlightenment about British traitors recruited by the former Czech regime, possibly including some surprising names. The Czech Government is also reported to be in contact with the

Italian and Austrian secret services.

As an independent country, Czechoslovakia must have an intelligence service for its own defence and to provide the Government with the information it needs to make policy decisions and combat terrorism. So the old service responsible for foreign espionage and counter-intelligence has been largely retained within a new Ministry of the Interior. In June 1990 it claimed to have ceased co-operation with the KGB, but so long as Czechoslovakia remains a member of the Warsaw Pact it will have treaty obligations in that respect. These date from a secret agreement signed by members of the Warsaw Pact in Moscow in 1964, which integrated the intelligence services of the member countries with that of the Soviet Union. It stipulated that the main strategic planning should always be done in Moscow, which would also contrive and disseminate operational plans. The KGB would be the organization responsible, save for purely military intelligence which would be controlled by the GRU. The two of them would be the centres to which all information would be funnelled for analysis and action. From that moment the satellite intelligence agencies were little more than arms of the KGB and GRU, serving mainly as collecting agencies and surrogates for terrorism. Moscow would prefer them to continue to carry out their obligations as intelligence collectors, particularly in the field of industrial espionage.

At a recent meeting in Moscow the Warsaw Pact decided to remain in existence as a pact of sovereign states based on democratic principles, with its militaristic image laid to rest. Nothing was said, however, about its intelligence work for the Soviets, and as William Webster, the CIA chief, has said, 'Fundamental changes in intelligence missions are not likely while Warsaw Pact treaty connections are still in place.'

With respect to any continuing relations with the KGB, the former satellites are in an invidious position. They are in desperate need of Western technology, but can they be safely given it if they might pass it on to a still-Communist Moscow? The Bush administration is actively considering the phasing out of export controls to Poland, Hungary and Czechslovakia, while East Germany will qualify following its union with West Germany. So these countries have an added incentive to end their Warsaw Pact obligations, and Hungary has already indicated its determination to leave the Pact in 1991. One thing is certain – if the Eastern democracies are given technological aid denied to the Soviet Union they will soon be crawling with KGB agents in search of it.

The demise of Czech dirty trick activities would be a major bonus for the West because the Czechs have a well-established reputation for efficiency and ruthlessness and Britain, in particular, has suffered from their attentions. The evidence from defectors has shown that the KGB required them to concentrate on securing military and political secrets, using bribery and blackmail.

The new Czech Government has made a few other admissions, such as the fact that many of their 'businessmen' and diplomats operating abroad were really spies. This was no surprise. As recently as 1988, for instance, three Czech diplomats were expelled for attempting to steal aviation secrets at the Farnborough Air Show, while four more Czech 'officials' followed in 1989.

It cannot be reasonably expected, however, that the Czechs or any other previous Soviet satellite, with the exception of the East Germans, will make their records available for Western inspection or necessarily reveal the names of British traitors who have worked for them. Secret services do not behave that way – though it could, conceivably, be made a condition of Western aid.

There have been a few individual informers such as Vladimir Ignatov, a Bulgarian News Agency reporter who has exposed nine agents of the Bulgarian Committee for State Security, virtually a branch of the KGB, operating in Madrid, their main function being to secure NATO secrets. There has also been the expected spate of phoney informers trying to cash in on the situation.

In view of the reunion of East and West Germany, the position of the very large Communist security and intelligence services built up in East Germany over many years is uniquely interesting. Following the revolution, the domestic apparatus of the Stasi for monitoring and controlling the East German people was disbanded. Although mobs looted part of the Stasi headquarters, the 5 million files in the strongrooms were untouched and testify to the incredible extent of the surveillance of the people which, with Red Army assistance, enabled a few nonentities like Honecker to remain in power.

In March 1990 it was announced that East Germany was closing down its foreign intelligence network, recalling its officers and dispensing with its agents, most of whom were not East German citizens. The intelligence staff was to be cut from 4000 to 250 officials. In May the new Government announced the setting up of a new military counter-intelligence service which would liaise with its West German counterpart. It would be manned by former Stasi secret police, who have the necessary experience, and its stated purpose was to prevent espionage and terrorism; it was not supposed to indulge in active espionage. Nevertheless, West Germany feared that the hold of the KGB and GRU was such that many Stasi officers and agents would go on working for the Soviet Union, and the fear was justified.

East German agents with forged passports were arrested in West Germany still trying to recruit others among university graduates likely to find work in industry. The division of the Stasi responsible for espionage continued to transmit coded messages to its agents in the West for several weeks, and some five thousand spies were believed to be hiding there. By June 1990 fewer than two hundred of them had taken advantage of an amnesty promising immunity from prosecution. Defectors have confirmed that extensive telephone tapping and opening of letters continued for several weeks in East Germany, if only because it was such a deep-rooted practice, but more recently a large amount of Stasi surveillance equipment has been put on sale to the general public.

The extent of East German penetration of the West had proved to be even greater than was suspected. Among several people arrested on suspicion of espionage was a woman who had prepared weekly intelligence briefings for Chancellor Kohl! Nevertheless Kohl is anxious to avoid making political capital out of the situation and, while some trials are unavoidable, an amnesty for most of the East German spies seems likely. The alternative would be a spate of trials which could embarrass Western intelligence, especially in cases like that of Hans Joachim Tiedge, the West German counter-espionage officer who defected to the East in 1985 when burdened by debt. The former chief of East Germany's espionage organization, the efficient and much-feared General Markus Wolf, may be put on trial for the very substantial damage he inflicted on West

Germany; but the authorities may settle for his information instead.

East German spies convicted in other countries and released after serving their sentences can no longer expect the heroic welcome and assistance when they return home which was always accorded in the past, sometimes with ceremony. Two such are the husband and wife team, Reinhard and Sonia Schulze, who were jailed for ten years in 1986 for operating a spy ring from a London house.

The whole situation must change with the formal unification of the two Germanies and the formation of a single intelligence service, though the difficulties this presents are formidable. Unification has presented a major problem for Western intelligence because the internal border, near which British, American and West German intelligence installations have been located, has disappeared. There will be pressure to move them close to the new border with Poland and Czechslovakia, which the Soviets are sure to resist.

Meanwhile, to compensate for the loss of its East German agents, the KGB has intensified its own operations. In July 1990 the Bonn government issued a report stating that, while East Germany had stopped spying, the KGB had considerably expanded its operations. It stated that fifty-nine Soviet spies had been arrested in the first six months of 1990 – almost twice as many as in the whole of the previous year. In one case the KGB had offered to provide enough money to prevent a small West German electronics firm from going bankrupt, but only if it supplied all the computers, transistors and various secret defence devices it was developing. There were several cases where the KGB had organized exchanges of university teachers and students to penetrate research departments and steal data. In the week following reunification the Bonn government was driven to urge Gorbachev to end KGB recruitment of former East German agents as spies in the new Germany.

In Romania and Bulgaria the intelligence situation remains confused. The Romanian Securitate was dismantled, with much publicity and some trials, but has been largely reactivated and deceptively called the Romanian Information Service while retaining its role of suppressing opposition by violence. The old apparatus for foreign intelligence operations remains intact. Communism appears to be surviving under the name of

'Socialism' as it does in Bulgaria, where tight internal security control also continues. Bulgaria in particular seems unlikely to admit to any past intelligence dirty tricks, such as its part in the murder of Georgi Markov and the attempted murder of the Pope.

The multitude of uncertainties which beset the disintegrating Soviet Empire has created a critical era for Western intelligence agencies. The situation changes daily and continual, reliable intelligence about what is really going on has never been more essential. A less predictable world is a more dangerous world, and among the least predictable factors in the Soviet equation is the future behaviour of the military chiefs who have built up their machine with such effort and suddenly see it without its stated purpose – world domination. The Red Army is the joker in the Soviet pack and some senior officers, who claim to represent 800,000 committed Communists in the forces, are already stating their profound disagreement with Gorbachev's policies. In this they are supported not only by hard-line Communist ideologues who cannot bring themselves to admit that, for all their lives, they have been following a false star, but by the powerful *nomenklatura*, the millions of bureaucrats and officials who have enjoyed a privileged existence at the expense of the rest.

As GCHQ's intelligence shows daily, there are so many unknowns in the East-West equation that nothing can be taken for granted until there are genuinely free elections in the Soviet Union with parties other than the Communists – and for quite a while, because of the risk of a military counter-coup, not even then. The right policy decisions can be based only on accurate up-to-the minute intelligence, and drawing the wrong ones can be disastrous. If Mrs Thatcher could reveal some of the secret intelligence she receives daily, her reluctance to disarm more rapidly would be more understandable. Democracy has always depended for its survival on secret intelligence, and will continue to do so.

Electronic surveillance will be necessary to monitor arms cuts agreements to ensure that the Soviets are not cheating, as they now admit they have in the past. For years the Kremlin was accused of violating the 1972 arms agreement by building a huge radar installation at a remote place called Krasnoyarsk. Intelligence showed that it was part of an anti-ballistic missile system which was barred under the agreement. The Soviets insisted that it was just an advanced satellite-tracking station until 1989 when it suited Shevardnadze, the Foreign Minister, to admit that it was a fraud. He promised to dismantle it, blaming those who had cheated for the huge costs of the installation's erection and demolition. The fraud had been detected mainly by satellite surveillance, continuing space intelligence – knowledge of what the Soviets are doing into space and its purpose – being an essential part of the whole intelligence picture.

The future of GCHQ and MI6 is obviously secure for many years yet, and they will always have a worldwide function in the gathering of intelligence for the Government's policital purposes. MI6 is also involved in countering terrorism. The same applies to the CIA and the NSA, and the ties which bind Britain and America in the intelligence field look like being indissoluble far into the foreseeable future. GCHQ is making new contributions to this alliance through its research on super-computers to sieve out the few nuggets from the mountains of dross dredged from the skies, and on new cipher machines and codes which it shares with the NSA. It will also continue to indulge in its other counter-intelligence operations, including telephone tapping, the reading of private cables and misleading possible adversaries in various ingenious ways.

In that field it has recently achieved successes which have to remain secret, but they are not dissimilar to the substantial GCHQ coup which led to the arrest in 1974 of the Soviet Bloc's most important agent, Gunther Guillaume, who was a close confidant of Willi Brandt, the then West German Chancellor. Guillaume had been such a successful spy that East German intelligence headquarters sent coded birthday greetings to him and his wife, who was also a spy, and to their son. The messages were intercepted and decoded by GCHQ, which passed them to West German security. From the birth-dates the culprits were easily identified, subjected to surveillance and arrested. Presumably the East Germans learned from their mistakes, because it seems that they infiltrated a comparable spy into Chancellor Kohl's office. If true, GCHQ got no wind of it.

The American NSA and the National Reconnaissance Office, which controls the spy-in-the-sky satellites, are continuing to expand and improve their coverage from space and share their information with the British. The Lacrosse satellite, for example, orbiting at an altitude of 1000 miles, has antennae larger than a football pitch and uses radar to defeat cloud and darkness and transmit immediate pictures as clear as photographs. The truth about the fire which Gaddafi claimed had damaged his poison gas factory is proof of how refined such satellite pictures can be. A satellite had recorded truckloads of tyres being unloaded at the factory shortly before a fire produced a pall of smoke visible for miles. The CIA suspects that Gaddafi's subsequent announcement that the factory had been badly damaged by fire was a deception operation to fool the West and reduce the risk that the USA or the Israelis might bomb the plant.

Satellite surveillance of Iraq's preparations and troop movements in the recent confrontation with Western forces have been of the greatest value in securing essential intelligence when there were few, if any, reliable agents on the ground. The Iraqis even made use of it by openly loading up vehicles with poison gas weapons to deter an assault.

GCHQ is also progressively involved in countering terrorism, the value of intercepting messages between terrorist organizations being obvious. Advances in communications technology are assisting the international effort to counter terrorism as, for example, in the recent mid-air interception of terrorists who had hi-jacked the passenger ship Achille Lauro and believed that they were in their way to freedom.

However sophisticated electronic intelligence may become, there will always be need for MI6 agents on the ground because they are the only sources who can provide information about the intentions of possible adversaries and of secret political moves in dangerous areas like the Middle East. Only human spies can penetrate covered areas and secure documents; their absence in Argentina and, apparently, in Baghdad proved to be costly.

MI6 expects to be unusually busy with a flood of defectors hoping to trade information to the West for a new life there. It looks like being a 'buyer's market' for spies, but special caution is needed against false defectors and con-men. While much of the information which genuine defectors could provide will be of only academic interest if relations with the Soviets continue to improve, MI6 and other Western agencies will welcome it to resolve old cases.

In spite of the common belief that the future for the professional spy is bleak there is no shortage of recruits for MI6, which offers unusually interesting service abroad. The CIA believes that it secures a wider range of talent by openly advertising for it, but at the moment MI6 prefers no publicity of any kind. It is now prepared, however, along with MI5, to permit former officers to publish memoirs, though these are heavily sanitized and will always be suspected of containing disinformation. The same applies to books and statements by KGB and GRU defectors, who are more likely to be put on display now that the risk of assassination has probably receded. MI6 is also now prepared to collaborate in the preparation of obituary notices about deceased employees and to admit that they did work for the service – a secret which in the past was supposed to extend beyond the grave.

The Defence Intelligence Service will not only continue in being but may expand, because when military forces are cut, as they will be, reliable intelligence becomes more essential than ever so that they can be deployed with maximum effect. Similarly, in the Soviet Union the chief of the GRU, Colonel-General Vladlen Mikhailov, recently went on record as saying that 'the diminution of military capabilities will mean that the role of our intelligence will be increasing'. For some time this may require an increase in some types of intrusion operations mounted by both sides, rather than a decline.

In Britain the Defence Intelligence Service has suffered from the fact that its officers served for only short periods before returning to regimental duties, while the GRU has always been an élite force. Recently, however, the service has been strengthened by an improved career structure which allows officers to serve in it for longer periods without loss of promotion.

MI5, officially the Security Service, can rightly claim to be a remodelled agency following its overhaul by Sir Anthony Duff and his successor. Its main aims, as laid down by the Security Service Act of 1989 which made it a statutory body, are 'the protection of national security and, in particular, its protection against threats from espionage, terrorism and sabotage, from the activities of agents of foreign powers and from actions intended to overthrow or undermine parliamentary democracy by political, industrial or violent means'. A further function is 'to safeguard the economic well-being of the UK against threats posed by the actions or intentions of persons outside the British Isles'.

Though the overhaul of MI5 was largely a response to allegations about 'dirty tricks', its remit gives it plenty of scope to continue to perpetrate those necessary for its work. The bugging and surveillance will continue, but under authorization which is, perhaps, stricter than in the past, though no lapses then have been admitted. These activities are now controlled by the Interception of Communications Act of 1985, a framework within which the interception of private messages can be authorized and regulated. The Home Secretary has the power to authorize, by warrant, MI5 actions to obtain information by surreptitious means when it would be of substantial value to its operations and cannot be obtained in other ways. The warrant must be renewed every six months.

The Act is unlikely to interfere with the long-established practice of bugging foreign Embassies, because they all serve as 'safe houses' for intelligence officers running agents under diplomatic cover and as branches of electronic interception agencies. They also offer ways of discovering an adversary's intentions through the coded telegrams sent to Ambassadors, along with their replies.

The extent to which such bugging is universally practised was highlighted by the recent disclosures of the Soviet preparations to eavesdrop on the new American Embassy in Moscow. The Americans permitted the Russian constructors to use Soviet-made prefabricated parts which they riddled with bugging devices including the latest fibre optics, so much so that part or all of the building may have to be torn down. Attempts to bug the British Embassy are no less ruthless. In the past Soviet agents have managed to eavesdrop on the GCHQ cipher machines in the embassy by intruding spies and tunnelling beneath them. Over one period KGB agents regularly entered the room where the cipher machines were housed in between the nocturnal patrols of the guards, which were being carried out at regular two-hourly intervals. The room had a heavy steel door with a lock believed to be unpickable, but the bolts securing it had never been properly fitted. They were only finger-tight and the KGB intruders kept them oiled so that the whole door could be removed within a few minutes. The KGB's intrusive efforts continue, and the resident MI5 security officers who have to counter them are fully extended.

The general value of such electronic surveillance was demonstrated by Britain's blindness during the crucial period before the fall of the Shah of Iran. Because of the closeness of Britain's relationship with the Shah, and to avoid offending him, little attempt had been made to secure any information inside Iran by surreptitious means. This was one of the reasons why his overthrow took Britain by surprise, the CIA being in the same position. It had been assumed that the Shah would act toughly and use his overwhelming military and secret police forces – all intensely loyal – to put down any revolt. The British never thought that he would rather abdicate than fire on his own people, as proved to be the true situation. Its intelligence about the private life of the Shah was so poor that it did not know that he was so ill that his resolve was fatally eroded.

In all countries the bugging of hotels where visitors of intelligence interest are staying has been established practice for many years, and is sure to continue. Regarding MI5 bugging inside Britain, an independent Commissioner, a judge or ex-judge, now keeps the issuing of warrants under review and makes an annual report to the Prime Minister who is required to publish it, subject to security excisions. There is also an independent Tribunal of three senior lawyers to receive and consider complaints from the public about alleged unlawful investigation. In 1988 the Tribunal investigated twenty-nine complaints; none was found to be in contravention of the Act.

What has not been publicized is the fact that the remodelled MI5, like MI6, will continue its old practice of never permitting any of its records to be made available for scrutiny. MI5 will also continue to exert its control over the US Freedom of Information Act. When that Act was introduced, the British Government obtained an on-going assurance from the US government that nothing relating to its intelligence activities would be made public without consultation and agreement, which is rarely given.

Now that MI5 officially exists as a department of state, some interesting questions, only likely to be answered by subsequent events, pose themselves. Will it in future be permitted or wish to defend itself against serious accusations? Or will it continue to take them on the chin to avoid having to make damaging admissions if subjected to questioning? It must have been galling for the MI5 management to have to listen to all the trash about plots to topple Harold Wilson, and remain traditionally silent. The same applies to the obvious campaigns to denigrate the security and intelligence services for political purposes which are mounted by some writers.

Will the new MI5 remain as reluctant as ever to produce witnesses in court cases? Will it defend itself there, or continue to prefer to keep the water muddy? Will MI5 now come to the rescue of former employees like the late Lord Rothschild who are unfairly traduced?

When the Soviet Ambassador is called to the Foreign Office to be told of expulsions of Soviet agents, the Foreign Secretary gives some account of each crime which the individuals have committed or tried to commit. If the Ambassador challenges it he can be given the proof. Now that MI5 officially exists, why cannot the same information be given to Parliament and the public, which would then see how the Government has been driven to take action in the nation's interests? If the hyper-cautious security authorities forbid it, the Prime Minister could over-rule them. That way the public would be behind her instead of being bemused by expulsions when relations with the Kremlin seem so rosy on the surface. Her Labour opponents would also be deprived of the ludicrous gibe that the expulsions have been fabricated for some political purpose.

MI5 will remain busy on the counter-espionage side. Soviet spies, especially of the techno-bandit variety, are still active in Britain, while pro-Soviet agents of influence, working through Parliament and the media, are hard at work urging the Government to disarm massively without further delay because the Soviet threat has disappeared.

MI5 is also responsible for combatting terrorism, and with the problem posed by the IRA alone this is now a major element in its workload. Its battle against terrorism is become increasingly technological, with the horrific threat of mass terrorism – the possible possession by terrorists in the not too distant future of chemical, bacterial or even nuclear devices capable of destroying whole communities. Countries like Libya, Syria and Iraq, which support terrorism, have the capacity to make such weapons now or in the near future.

With the end of colonial rule the opportunities for service abroad available to MI5 officers were greatly reduced and, coupled with the spate of bad publicity, this has exerted an unfortunate effect on recruitment, though it is not as severe as some newspapers have suggested. Following the *Spycatcher* Affair many young people seem to think that the work is 'dirty' and the universities, which had become the main source of graduate recruits, are showing greatly reduced interest, as career officers there testify. The impact of the false belief that intelligence and security will soon be in the discard cannot have helped.

The extreme secrecy involved imposes further drawbacks. Those who join a secret service quit the real world and enter a *demi-monde* which is likely to appeal to odd people and make them odder. An MI5 officer is not supposed to let his children and friends know what he does. Lies, deception and surreptitious action are the basis of his daily work, and this is bound to contaminate and corrode character. The limited social life tends to be incestuous. Officers tend to marry within the service, and if they run off with somebody else's spouse it tends to be that of another officer.

In spite of the new safeguards, MI5 is still no place for anyone strong on conscience, ethics or civil liberties. 'Wanted James Bonds' would attract recruits, but it would be fraudulent because most MI5 work tends to be dull. An officer is always more likely to have a date with a desk than with a blonde, and nobody is licensed to kill in peacetime.

There needs to be much closer examination of recruits to exclude politically unstable people like Michael Bettaney, and character-defectives like Peter Wright, who will always be held up as the classic example of the type who should never have been allowed near the service. To this end, and for other reasons not unconnected with the spate of whistle-blowers in Government departments, more rigorous vetting procedures came into force in the autumn of 1990. Those with access to secret as well as top-secret information will be required to undergo much more intensive checks which will involve interviews with associates. Any whose personalities might make them unreliable will be barred.

In the past, recommendation for posts in the secret services has mainly been by word of mouth from trusted sources and by recruitment from the police, colonial police and the forces. This preserved the need for secrecy and reduced the fear that enemies might gain entry as spies and saboteurs. Then the unmasking of Philby, Maclean, Blunt and others in high positions of trust put paid to the belief that people from good families could never be traitors. MI5 and MI6 nevertheless turned to Oxford and Cambridge and, later, the red-brick universities, for undergraduates who could be recommended by their teachers. It also advertised under surreptitious cover for secretaries and low-level officers.

The obvious solution is a sustained and sophisticated publicity campaign to promote MI5's image, especially by highlighting its secret successes, but I cannot see that happening. It could prejudice secret methods and sources and would make it difficult for the Government to prosecute journalists and authors who expose its failures.

As an occasional author of spy novels I am often asked whether the genre is now dead with the apparent ending of the Cold War and the passing of such old props as the Berlin Wall. It is not. The new situation between East and West is an intriguing and fertile field for ideas in fiction, and even more so in reality.

Bibliography

Castle, Barbara, *The Castle Diaries 1964–70*, Weidenfeld and Nicolson 1984

Crossman, Richard, *The Crossman Diaries* (ed. Anthony Howard), Hamish Hamilton and Jonathan Cape 1979

Cudlipp, Hugh, *Walking on the Water*, Bodley Head 1976

Foot, Paul, *Who Framed Colin Wallace?*, Pan Books 1990

Gormley, Joe, *Battered Cherub*, Hamish Hamilton 1982

Haynes, Joe, *The Politics of Power*, Coronet 1977

Hedley, Peter and Aynsley, Cyril, *The D-Notice Affair*, Michael Joseph 1967

Hennessy, Peter, *Whitehall*, Secker and Warburg 1989

Horne, Alistar, *Macmillan*, Vol. 2, Macmillan 1989

James, Robert Rhodes, *Anthony Eden*, Weidenfeld and Nicolson 1986

James, R.V., *Reflections on Intelligence*, Heinemann 1989

King, Cecil, *Diary 1965–1970*, Jonathan Cape 1972

King, Cecil, *Diary 1970–1974*, Jonathan Cape 1975

Leigh, David, *The Wilson Plot*, Mandarin 1989

Marenches, Count de, *The Evil Empire*, Sidgwick and Jackson 1988

Margach, James, *The Abuse of Power*, W. H. Allen 1978

Pacepa, Ion, *Red Horizons*, Coronet Books 1989

Penrose, Barrie and Courtiour, Roger, *The Pencourt File*, Secker and Warburg 1978

Pincher, Chapman, *Inside Story*, Sidgwick and Jackson 1978

Pincher, Chapman, *Their Trade Is Treachery*, Sidgwick and Jackson 1981

Pincher, Chapman, *Too Secret Too Long*, Sidgwick and Jackson 1984

Pincher, Chapman, *Traitors*, Sidgwick and Jackson 1987

Pincher, Chapman, *A Web of Deception*, Sidgwick and Jackson 1987

Rothschild, Lord, *Meditations of a Broomstick*, Collins 1977

Rothschild, Lord, *Random Variables*, Collins 1984

Turnbull, Malcolm, *The Spycatcher Trial*, Heinemann Mandarin 1989

Turner, Stansfield, *Secrecy and Democracy*, Sidgwick and Jackson 1986

Weinberger, Caspar, *Fighting for Peace: Seven Critical Years at the Pentagon*, Michael Joseph 1990

Wigg, Lord, *George Wigg*, Michael Joseph 1972

Wilson, Harold (Lord), *The Labour Government 1964–70*, Weidenfeld and Nicolson 1971

Wilson, Harold (Lord), *Final Term: The Labour Government 1974–76*, Weidenfeld and Nicolson 1979

Wise, David, *The Spy Who Got Away*, Fontana/Collins 1989

Woodward, Bob, *Veil*, Simon and Schuster 1987

Wright, Peter, *Spycatcher*, Viking, New York 1987

Young, Hugo, *One of Us*, Pan Books 1990.

Index